Jackson, J.
The riot that never was.

PRICE: $29.95

MAY 2010

THE RIOT THAT NEVER WAS

James Jackson

THE RIOT THAT NEVER WAS

The military shooting of three Montrealers
in 1832 and the official cover-up

Baraka
Books

Library and Archives Canada Cataloguing in Publication

Jackson, James, 1947-

The riot that never was: the military shooting of three Montrealers in 1832 and the official cover-up / James Jackson.

Includes bibliographical references.

ISBN 978-0-9812405-0-3

1. Elections-Québec (Province) – Montréal – History – 19th century. 2. Montréal (Québec) –History – 19th century. 3. Montréal (Québec) –English-French relations – History – 19th century. 4. Languedoc, François, d. 1832. 5. Billet, Pierre, d. 1832. 6. Chauvin, Casimir, d. 1832. 7. Québec (Province) – History – 1791-1841. I. Title.

FC2947.4.J32 2009   971.4'2802   C2009-906216-X

Cover based on *Battle of St-Eustache, 1837* by C. W. Jefferys, conserved in Library and Archives Canada

Legal Deposit — 4th quarter 2009
Bibliothèque et Archives nationales du Québec
Library and Archives Canada
ISBN 978-0-9812405-5-8

Cover and book design: Folio infographie
Copy editing: Robin Philpot

Trade Distribution & Returns
LitDistCo
C/o 100 Armstrong Ave.
Georgetown, ON
L7G 5S4
Ph: 1-800-591-6250
Fax: 1-800-591-6251
orders@litdistco.ca

For Denise, this forgotten chapter
of Quebec's history.

Contents

Acknowledgments

My research began when I was still a member of the French department of Trinity College Dublin. I wish to thank the Provost, John Hegarty, for granting me generous sabbatical leave to enable me to complete my research. I also wish to acknowledge the helpful guidance and cooperation I received from the staff of the National Library in Ottawa, the Bibliothèque nationale du Québec in Montréal and the McCord Museum. In the early days of my research I was fortunate to meet two dynamic researchers in the field of nineteenth-century Quebec history, Denise Beaugrand-Champagne and Georges Aubin. Both were extremely helpful whenever I sought guidance. I am grateful to Yvan Lamonde for his advice and encouragement and to Danielle Grenier, André Joli-Cœur and Michel Morin for answering difficult questions about Quebec law. Special thanks go to my editor, Robin Philpot, under whose expert guidance this book was given its final form. Finally, it is a particular pleasure to be able to single out Dr Patrick Vinay, a close friend for over thirty years, who was the first to encourage me to pursue research into nineteenth-century Quebec history.

It goes without saying, however, that without the love and support of my wife, Denise Bombardier, this book would not have been completed.

Introduction

A book entitled *The Riot that Never Was* requires some explanation about riots. For the inhabitants of Montreal, they were once a fact of life and never more so than during the nineteenth century. While the causes of the violence were invariably linked to the social, political or religious tensions of the time, the authorities were often tempted to interpret the breakdown of law and order as potentially seditious, placing the very security of the province in danger. When occasionally British troops used deadly force against rioters, the reading of the Riot Act beforehand granted them immunity from criminal prosecution.

The term "riot" was imprecise under both common law and statute law, a fact that allowed the authorities considerable discretion when deciding whether a riot was in progress. The Riot Act itself came into force in Great Britain in 1715 at a time of civil unrest.[1] According to the terms of the act an offence was committed where more than twelve people were "unlawfully, riotously, and tumultuously assembled together." After a magistrate had read the proclamation, rioters had one hour to disperse or face the consequences of being declared felons and even being killed.[2] English common law offered magistrates almost a free hand: "A riot is where three or more actually do an unlawful act of violence, either with or without a common cause or quarrel: as if they beat a man; or hunt and kill game in another's park ... or do any other unlawful act with force and violence," wrote William Blackstone.[3] W.C.Keele's *The Provincial Justice* added a further refinement to the definition stating that it was not even "necessary that personal violence should have been actually committed."[4]

In theory, therefore, the authorities could declare even minor brawls involving a handful of men a riot. In practice, they resorted to such drastic measures as calling out the military and having a magistrate read the Riot Act only when confronted with major disturbances involving large groups of people. A study of some well documented riots shows that the authorities were not consistent in the way they applied the law.

* * *

When war broke out between Britain and the United States in the summer of 1812, military officials in Lower Canada found it increasingly difficult to draft certain inhabitants, mainly farmers and rural labourers, into the militia. The district of Montreal with its long history of resistance to militia service was particularly defiant. Attempts to arrest those who refused to report for duty proved fruitless and instead provoked a combined resistance movement of all the parishes targeted by the military authorities.

A crowd of some 400 men, half of whom were armed, gathered at Lachine. The authorities in Montreal reacted immediately and sent a magistrate accompanied by a military detachment and two field artillery pieces. When the magistrate failed to persuade the crowd to disperse, he ordered the troops to fire above the heads of the crowd. The crowd responded with small arms fire. Another volley from the troops above the heads of the crowd was no more successful.

The third volley was fired directly into the crowd, killing one man and seriously injuring another.[5]

For the authorities, the collective resistance of the rural farmers was tantamount to a rebellion and there were real fears that the province was on the verge of a civil war. Nevertheless, considerable restraint was shown despite British regulars being faced by a huge crowd prepared to shoot at them. Since it was hoped that *Canadiens* would eventually join the ranks of the militia in large numbers it is understandable that every attempt was made to keep casualties as low as possible. It was not always to be so.

Over thirty years later, Irish immigrants had become a significant proportion of Montreal's work force. Large numbers of them found employment working on the Lachine and Beauharnois canals. But long hours, poor pay and inadequate accommodation led to frequent strikes, many of which turned ugly. In 1843 a general strike was called by those working on the Lachine Canal. Contractors brought in the army from Montreal and the strike eventually petered out.

At the Beauharnois Canal, events took a different turn. Over a thousand men joined the strike which gradually got out of hand. Property was damaged and contractors were threatened. One contractor who was also a magistrate called for military backup. On June 12, British troops confronted a large group of unarmed strikers. A magistrate ordered the labourers to disperse and when they refused, he read the Riot Act. The strikers still did not disperse. The magistrate ordered the army to use force. A volley was fired at the crowd and the cavalry charged with drawn swords. Six men were killed outright while others were driven into the river and drowned. The strike ended with victory for the contractors. Later, a coroner's inquest declared the deaths were justified homicide.[6]

Ten years later, in June 1853, the Irish were once more involved in a bloody confrontation with British troops. The scene was Montreal's Hay Market where Zion Church was to be the venue of a controversial lecture by the Italian national-ist, Alessandro Gavazzi, a former monk and anti-Catholic campaigner. A large crowd of incensed Irish Catholics attempted to disrupt the lecture. Shots were exchanged between the rioters and some of Gavazzi's audience. The police lost control of the proceedings and the mayor immedi-ately called out the military. He then read the Riot Act. Who gave the order for the troops to open fire on the crowd was never fully elucidated but fire they did and up to fifty people were either killed or wounded.[7]

Montreal's most notorious riot occurred in 1849 as a result of the anger felt by the city's loyalist population at the passing of the Rebellion Losses Bill by the legislature of the Province of Canada. The riot lasted two days, involved thousands of people, caused huge damage to property and completely destroyed the Parliament building. No magistrate read the Riot Act and British troops were nowhere to be seen.[8]

* * *

The Montreal "riot" of May 1832, which resulted in the deaths of three French Canadian men at the hands of British regu-lars, does not easily compare with the riots described above. The "rioters" were not organised Irish labourers demanding better working conditions nor were they some outraged group of Catholics attempting to defend themselves against religious slander. They were not resisting militia duty nor were they attempting to foment rebellion. Some were mere bystanders. Others were the supporters of an Irish-born by-election can-didate who appeared to be on the verge of a famous victory over the English party candidate and favourite for the seat. Why those supporters should have rioted and jeopardised that victory is a question that seems not to have occurred to the many distinguished historians who have written about the "riot" over the past hundred years or more.

Readers have in fact been given a very one-sided view of the final days of the by-election. Among English-language historians, there has been a tendency to defend the military intervention. C.D. Clark interpreted the shooting as part of the spirit of rebellion that led up to the events of November 1838. The troops were called out to maintain order, he wrote, the Riot Act was read by a magistrate, and three persons were killed after a clash between the assembled crowds and the troops. He saw no reason to question the good faith of the authorities.[9]

The American historian Helen Taft Manning was one of the first historians to deal extensively with the shooting in her much quoted study of French Canadian nationalism.[10] She left her readers in no doubt where her sympathies lay—and they were not with Daniel Tracey. Claiming that the Irish candidate was known for "the coarse and abusive style of his editorial comments," she also cast doubt on the legality of his eventual electoral victory.[11] Her account of the events of May 21 was based on the written submissions of the returning officer and of the senior magistrate and so exonerated the soldiers who opened fire. As for "some of the conflicting accounts of eyewitnesses" that she had promised her readers and which might have given some balance to her own account, she failed to include any.[12]

A similarly one-sided version of events was produced by Elinor Kyte Senior, a noted authority on the history of British troops in Lower Canada. Relying on the dispatches that Governor Aylmer sent to the colonial office in London concerning the affair, Senior staunchly defended the official British version in her various publications.[13] In her eyes, the military conducted itself in exemplary fashion:

> In this 1832 incident, soldiers of the 15th East Yorkshire Regiment had been properly summoned by a magistrate. Their action followed precise military procedure for the use of troops at riots. They were commanded by commissioned officers, and were in the charge of a magistrate. They fired only after the Riot Act had been read by the magistrate who then ordered the commanding officer to quell the riot. Firing was accomplished with perfect discipline, the soldiers firing man by man, and ceasing to fire instantly upon order.[14]

It is no surprise to learn that she considered Daniel Tracey, in her words, a "boisterous Irish immigrant doctor and editor," partly responsible for the trouble visited on Montreal: "Not only was the editor recently arrived from turbulent Ireland," she wrote, "he was even more recently released from jail in Quebec City." And if the Patriote party was not directly responsible for the riot, it was, she maintained, behind a "policy of calculated agitation" that followed the shootings.[15]

Such was Senior's authority in the area of military history that even Desmond Morton relied on her for the details of the May 21 incident. In a chapter on British garrisons in Lower Canada, Morton allowed himself to sympathize with the lot of the poor British soldier forced to face unruly Irish and French Canadian mobs:

> [An officer] and his men might face furious Orange and Catholic rioters, striking navvies on a canal site or a hired election mob, recruited to overawe timid voters. Whatever happened the troops took the abuse. When blood was spilled in an 1832 election riot in Montreal, British officers were jailed on the charge of murder. *Patriote* orators improved the occasion with sugges-

tions that the bloodthirsty redcoats had deliberately slaughtered innocent *Canadiens*.[16]

It might be thought that French-language historians would provide a more balanced version of events pointing out some of the many errors found in Manning, Senior and Morton— British officers were not jailed on the charge of murder—but most have sided with their English-language counterparts. Gérard Filteau's *Histoire des Patriotes*, originally published in 1938 but still popular made only fleeting references to the killings.[17] Robert Rumilly provided a factual summary of the day's incidents in his *Histoire de Montréal* and *Papineau et son temps* but expressed no surprise that the intervention of British troops should have caused some fatalities among the crowd.[18] Fernand Ouellet recognised the importance of the 1832 West Ward election, describing it as one of the most famous in Canadian history, but made just one brief mention of the three deaths in reference to the physical violence that arose during the contest.[19] His main criticism in fact was reserved for Papineau whom he accused of having orchestrated events from the safety of his nearby home and then of exploiting the deaths for political reasons.[20]

A change in approach occurred in the late 1970s when France Galarneau defended an MA thesis on the political and social analysis of the Montreal West by-election.[121] She was the first to raise doubts about the official version of the shootings when she concluded that the army had been confronted not by a riot but by a brawl ('bagarre'). Unfortunately, for reasons she did not explain, she omitted all reference to her conclusion when she published a shortened version of her thesis.[22]

* * *

In more recent years, the 1832 by-election has attracted little serious attention from historians. Bettina Bradbury has shown some interest in the subject but she confined herself to a very narrow perspective: the sociological aspect of the votes cast by the women voters. The article threw no light at all on the events of May 21.[23] Similar criticism can be made of a small book that at the time of its publication appeared to make a significant contribution to the subject. However, Gilles Boileau's *Le 21 mai 1832 sur la Rue du sang* is disappointing, being made up largely of extracts from the Patriote newspaper, *La Minerve*, with litle or no explanation of the historical context, and is thus of only limited use to the reader who wishes to understand fully what happened on May 21.[24]

* * *

Common to all these historians is their astonishing neglect of a source that should have been the corner stone of their research. Had the source been hidden away in some private archive, jealously guarded and protected from the prying eyes of historians, it would be easy to understand the lack of any reference to it. Instead, it has been in the public domain since 1834 and was published in the *Journals of the House of Assembly of the Province of Lower-Canada*.

Seven months after the killings, the House of Assembly began an extensive enquiry into many aspects of the 1832 by-election, calling before it eyewitnesses of the shootings, people involved in the by-election and some office holders. The House also demanded from Governor Aylmer all documents in his possession pertaining to the military action and to the subsequent defence of the two British officers implicated in the shootings. In addition, the House received copies of statements made by some of the magistrates on duty on the day itself and copies of affidavits sworn by the two British officers, by some of the rank and file soldiers who fired on the crowd and by many of the special constables present during the by-election. Why such a wealth of information should have been ignored by historians for over 175 years remains a complete mystery.

My book is the first examination of the 1832 Montreal West by-election to be based on both the House of Assembly's printed record of its proceedings and on the actual pollbook where the votes were inscribed. The narrative account of the events that led up to the day of the shootings is based mainly on the newspapers of the time. To the possible dismay of certain academic colleagues, I have avoided wider historiographical issues surrounding the events of May 21 such as the nature of civil-military relations at the time, their impact on society and political life, the role of ethnicity in what happened and the use made of public space. Instead, I have concentrated on events rather than on theory, though underlying those events is the relationship between the judiciary, local elites and the exercise of state power. Theory in any case will not explain what happened on a crowded Place d'Armes and in St James St between 2.30 and 5.15 on the afternoon of Monday, May 21, but the testimonies of the very many people who were present might do so, provided they are subjected to close critical scrutiny. In a public enquiry into an event as controversial as the Montreal West by-election, some witnesses may lie to cover up individual responsibilities. It is clear that some of the 1832 witnesses lied during the House enquiry or in their affidavits. It is the task of the historian and of any serious investigator to determine where the truth lies. That is why I wrote this book.

The title indicates where my sympathies lie. I run counter to what has been accepted as the truth by generations of historians. Some historians have accused me of a being biased in favour of the Patriote version of events, though they would not accept that they were biased in favour of the governor and the military. Why have historians been content down the years to act as mere mouthpieces for the version of events propounded by Governor Aylmer and a packed grand jury? My approach from the outset has been to subject all the affidavits and all the answers elicited during the Assembly's inquiry to a strict critical examination. It was not a question of believing reports in the *Vindicator* or *La Minerve* rather than in the *Montreal Gazette*. Where contradictions are evident, I say so, where logic and common sense dictate a response, I say so. In my opinion, all the evidence points to just one conclusion, the one that I give to my book and its title.

The unanimity among historians concerning what happened on May 21, 1832 has meant that the event has been seen as a tragic incident but ultimately as having little or no significance for Canadian history. It would be a pity if such an attitude were to persist. The shooting dead of three innocent bystanders during a by-election that was won by the Patriote party candidate came at a time when the party was going through a crisis of conscience. Taking its lead from Papineau, the party had already embarked on a more reformist path. For some members, the bloody violence of the by-election was the final straw. The killings led to a major split within the ranks of the party and to the further radicalization of those who remained faithful to Papineau. For the younger members of the party, like Louis-Hyppolyte La Fontaine (aged 26) Côme-Séraphin Cherrier (aged 35), Édouard-Étienne Rodier (aged 29) and Chevalier de Lorimier (aged 29), the by-election was an opportunity to cut their political teeth.

More significant however for the subsequent course of events, the reaction in Patriote circles to the killings and the official cover-up was the catalyst for the Ninety-two Resolutions drafted in 1834. The many resolutions passed in assemblies throughout the province strongly condemning the shootings represented in a sense the first draft of that historical document. The final draft was produced during the heightened tension within the House of Assembly as the enquiry revealed the extent of the cover-up. The long-term consequences of the by-election were the tragic events of 1837.

And finally, though the names of François Languedoc, Pierre Billet and Casimir Chauvin have long been forgotten, the true story of their tragic deaths still deserves to be written.

1

The Legislative Council or the "Oppressive Incubus"?

Montreal was the success story of the early nineteenth century in Lower Canada. By the 1830s it had become the economic and cultural metropolis of British North America. The incorporation of the city was finally achieved when its first charter came into effect in 1833, transforming the running of municipal affairs. Its commercial importance also improved when it was made a port of entry in 1831 no longer subject to the supervision of the port of Quebec City. Extensive work on the city's harbour facilities had already begun in 1830 to keep pace with the ever increasing trade with the mother country. The influx of immigrants from the United Kingdom since 1815 had increased the city's growth and reinforced its ethnic divisions. The 1831 census showed that in a province of just over 500,000 inhabitants, Montreal's population stood at 27,000, a considerable increase in just twenty years.[1] The city was also about to become for the first time in its history a predominantly English-speaking city. The margin was narrow but the trend was set for the foreseeable future. The majority of the population lived in the city's six suburbs. The inner city was divided into two wards, home to some 6,000 people, but it was the West Ward where most of the commercial and political life of the city was concentrated.

The limits of the West Ward were to the north, Craig St, to the west, McGill St, Commissioners Square (otherwise known as the Hay Market) and Ste-Radegonde St, to the south, the St Lawrence river and the Petite Rivière, and to the east, St Joseph St (St-Sulpice St) and the Place d'Armes. St Paul St was the longest and widest street in the area and was where the majority of the city's commercial enterprises were situated. Immediately to the north were two elegant residential streets, Notre-Dame and St James.* Notre-Dame was the longer of the two, running for just over three quarters of a mile from McGill St as far as Dalhousie Square and the Queb'ec suburbs on the eastern edge of the city. Great St James St which ran for 433 yards from the Hay Market as far as the Place d'Armes contained the homes of such people as the Molsons, Dr William Robertson, Montreal's senior magistrate and Captain Robert S. Piper of the Royal Engineers, the man responsible for the erection of new wharves in Montreal's harbour. At one end of the street, close to the Place d'Armes, stood the impressive Bank of Montreal building erected in 1818 and next to it the Wesleyan Methodist Chapel built three years later. The opposite end of the street was dominated by the new American Presbyterian Church built to the design of James O'Donnell in 1826 while the Irish-American architect was still working on the new parish church of Notre-Dame in the Place d'Armes.[2]

Early in 1832 the street was chosen to be one of the first in Montreal to have its road surface rebuilt using the very latest

---

* The street names and place names used are those in the official documents of the time (e.g., St James for Saint-Jacques, William Henry for Sorel, St. Peter for Saint-Pierre).

method of laying crushed stone on a firm base of large stones invented by John MacAdam. Residents looked forward to seeing their street transformed from a muddy quagmire into a hard-surfaced and well-drained carriage-way but for the time being they were forced to live with the inconvenience of mounds of stones waiting to be broken into smaller fragments. Across the Place d'Armes, a much narrower street known as Little St James St, continued in an easterly direction.

The Place d'Armes had undergone a major change in appearance in 1830 when the old parish church that had once faced Notre-Dame St in the direction of McGill St was finally demolished. The old church had stood on the site since 1683 but the rise in the population of the city had eventually led the Sulpicians to construct a much larger edifice set back from the Place d'Armes, with St Joseph St on one side and its own seminary and gardens on the other. The new parish church of Notre-Dame had opened its doors in 1829. Anxious to preserve control of the ground on which the old church had stood, the church authorities left part of the church's outer wall standing thus creating an enclosure area between the southern part of the square and the entrance to the new church. Untouched was the old free-standing square-sided bell tower partly blocking the entrance to Notre-Dame St.[3]

The West Ward was also the area where Montreal's five newspapers were published. Four of them were published in English. The political leanings of three of the newspapers, the *Montreal Gazette*, the *Montreal Herald* and the *Canadian Courant*, reflected the importance in the city of the English merchant class and its support for the Constitutional or English Party. The other two papers, *La Minerve* and the *Vindicator*, offered unconditional support to Louis-Joseph Papineau and his Patriote party in the Assembly.

The 1831 petition

As the year 1831 drew to a close there was for the first time in several years some hope that the political impasse that had long soured relations between the governor and the Assembly was on the point of being resolved. Twelve months earlier no such optimism had been possible. The persistent failure of the British government to implement the recommendations of the 1828 parliamentary committee on Canada intended to address the many grievances of the Assembly had been a constant source of frustration within the province. On the initiative of John Neilson, one of the three delegates sent to London in 1828 to represent the Assembly, a major debate on the state of the province had been held in March 1831. As in 1828 it had been an opportunity for many Assembly members once more to attack the constitutional status of the Legislative Council as established under the 1791 Constitutional Act. Few had had a good word for it. Thomas Lee had argued that the defective state of the Council was the fault of the Imperial Government and that the Constitutional Act had been an evil instead of a benefit for the province. Louis Bourdages, the doyen of the Assembly, had been even more dismissive: "the entire abolition of the Legislative Council was what was required," he stated. "We not only can easily do without it, but shall be far better off."[4]

As usual, the major attack on the Council had come from Papineau. The Legislative Council had been a pet hate of the Patriotes for years, dating back to the time when their party was still known as the *parti canadien*. Relations had deteriorated even further in 1822 when an attempt had been made to bring about the union of Upper and Lower Canada. In 1824 François Blanchet, co-founder with Bourdages and others of *Le Canadien*, published a pamphlet entitled *Appel au*

View of the old and new church of Notre-Dame from the Place d'Armes. The old church was demolished in 1830 except for its steeple and a high semi-circular wall in front of the new church. Lt-Col Macintosh sheltered his troops under the new church porch on the afternoon of May 21. (Public Archives Canada — C 12531)

Parlement impérial et aux habitans des colonies angloises, dans l'Amérique du Nord, sur les prétentions exorbitantes du gouvernement exécutif et du Conseil législatif de la province du Bas-Canada. The grievances aired by Blanchet became part of Patriote oratory. In 1827 Papineau had made constant reference to them in his successful campaign to win the Montreal West seat and they had formed the basis for the Assembly's own list of grievances as set down in 1828. When Papineau rose to speak in March 1831, his audience knew exactly what to expect. It was a preposterous idea, he told the Assembly, to imagine that an aristocracy could be created either in Upper or in Lower Canada; and it was even more absurd to compare the Legislative Council to the House of Lords in England. The links between the Council and the Executive could never be independent as long as it was appointed by the Executive. "It is easy for the administration to purchase a servile majority of so small a body as compose the Council which they have themselves appointed—but they cannot do so with eighty-four members chosen by the people." The result, he concluded, was that there was no real government in the province, only despotism.[5]

The petition dispatched to London following the debate had produced, by the standards of the time, a fairly rapid answer. On November 15 the governor opened a new session of the Provincial Parliament and announced that Lord Goderich, Secretary of State for the Colonies, had addressed the complaints of the House in a dispatch dated July 7. The Assembly received a copy of the document a few days later and a debate was held on the subject on November 25. The general consensus among the Patriotes was that Lord Goderich had been sympathetic to their grievances except on two issues of major importance: Crown lands and the status of the Legislative Council. On the latter, Goderich had merely

Louis-Joseph Papineau, leader of the Patriote party and speaker of the
House of Assembly. He played no part in the by-election until after
the killings. He put pressure on Governor Aylmer to turn over all
official documents concerning the military intervention.
(Musée du Québec — G 5258)

promised a separate communication at some later date. Papineau attempted to be conciliatory in his public reaction to the response from Westminster, but for the likes of Bourdages, the province's legitimate grievance against the Legislative Council had once more been ignored.

Defamation and breach of privilege

In the final two weeks of 1831 several Montreal newspapers began reporting the difficulties being experienced by William Lyon Mackenzie in Upper Canada's parliament as a result of his strident editorials in the *Colonial Advocate*. On December 12 the Tory majority in the Upper Canadian Assembly had taken offence at Mackenzie's description of it as a "sycophantic office" and had voted to expel him for what it termed as a breach of privilege and a libel on the House. If this news caused the editors of *La Minerve* and the *Vindicator* any alarm, the first editorials of the New Year gave no indication that they were prepared to tone down their language when it came to criticizing the Legislative Council.

The first issue of *La Minerve* in 1832 appeared on January 2. Since its foundation in 1826 the paper had served as the principal organ of the Patriote Party and now had some 1300 subscribers. Its owner, Ludger Duvernay, was a publisher of considerable experience and a man who had experienced the wrath of a previous governor when in 1828 he and Jocelyn Waller, the Irish editor of the *Canadian Spectator*, were briefly imprisoned on a charge of libel.[6] In its first editorial of 1832, commenting on the major political events of the previous year in Europe and South America, *La Minerve* complained that the 1830 Revolution in France had not produced the expected wider extension of rights and freedoms. Instead, despotic government was still the order of the day in Europe and the

Americas. Its only reference to Lower Canada came in a few critical remarks concerning Colonial Secretary Lord Goderich's July dispatch.[7] The following day, the *Vindicator*'s editor, Daniel Tracey, produced his review of the international scene. Tracey, from Roscrea, Co. Tipperary, had studied medicine in Dublin and practised there before immigrating to Lower Canada in 1825 at the age of thirty.[8] He had rapidly involved himself in the politics of the province and had played a significant role in formulating the 1828 petition to the British government. In September 1828 he had become one of the founding members of the Society of the Friends of Ireland, an organisation that aimed at raising funds for Daniel O'Connell's Catholic Association of Ireland. As a means of publicizing the work of the society, Tracey, president of the Montreal branch, founded the *Irish Vindicator* in October 1828. O'Connell's success in 1829 had led to a fall in subscriptions and only the timely intervention in the May of that year by a group of influential Patriotes that included the Perrault family, Denis-Benjamin Viger, Ludger Duvernay and Édouard-Raymond Fabre, saved the paper from closing. The small but significant change to the paper's title indicated its more deliberate pro-Patriote orientation.[9]

Tracey's main concern in his first editorial of the year was the state of affairs in England and the reports of serious rioting in Bristol. Clearly, Tracey wrote, the rioting was "the consequence of the dissatisfaction resulting from the rejection of the Reform Bill." A second item followed but its smaller typeface suggested that it was of less importance. It announced a forthcoming debate in the Assembly scheduled for January 10 on a motion of Louis Bourdages calling for the reform of the Legislative and Executive Councils. Tracey welcomed the news since he had learned that the Legislative Council had rejected two more bills sent up from the

Assembly. Echoing the sentiments and language that Papineau and others had used the previous March, Tracey added the comment: "It is quite an absurdity to think that about eight or ten men with scarcely common talent, and no better interest in the country than others, can act with all the caprice that this body does." Only the total annihilation of the Council would improve the situation in the province, wrote Tracey, and he ended by expressing his full support for Bourdages's motion: "We hope the House will exert its accustomed energy on this occasion and will not hesitate to enter into such as will obtain relief from the oppressive incubus."[10]

The following week, on the eve of the debate on the Bourdages motion, *La Minerve* published an anonymous correspondent's letter that was extremely critical of the Legislative Council. The author was Charles Mondelet, a lawyer and former journalist from Trois-Rivières who would soon turn on his erstwhile friends. For ten years he had been an active critic of successive administrations in the province and had sided with the Assembly in its opposition to the Legislative Council. In 1828 he had narrowly avoided prosecution for having published an attack on Governor Dalhousie's policies in the *Quebec Gazette* and this had brought his political activism to a temporary halt. The election of his brother and fellow lawyer, Dominique, to a seat in the Assembly in October 1831 once more whetted his appetite for political journalism. The formal opening of a new session of the provincial parliament in November 1831 spurred him into taking up his pen once more. *La Minerve* published four letters from him, all equally critical of the British administration in Lower Canada and all written under the pseudonym of "Pensez-y Bien."[11]

In the final letter, Mondelet denounced the Legislative Council as an undemocratic institution. Accepting as Papineau did that the legislature needed a second chamber, he insisted that it had first to be completely reorganised so as to become in the long term an elected chamber. In the more immediate term, Mondelet proposed the same solution that Tracey had six days earlier and did so with similarly forceful language: "The existing Legislative Council being perhaps the greatest nuisance we have, we should take the means in our power to get rid of it and demand its abolition in a manner to obtain that object."[12]

It is easy to comprehend the frustration of Patriote members of the Assembly at the constant failure of its many bills to pass the hurdle of the Legislative Council. Council appointments were in the gift of the governor and councillors were appointed for life. The majority of the twenty-seven members accepted that their principal allegiance was to the Crown and to its official representative in the province, an attitude that was reflected in their voting record. As Papineau was fond of repeating, though with some slight exaggeration, in a province where French Canadians made up ninety per cent of the population, only eight members of the twenty-seven strong Legislative Council had French Canadian names. This imbalance, however, was only part of the problem for the Assembly. The major grievance related to the small number of councillors who actually turned up for sittings. The Assembly had won an important concession from the British government in having the three judges of the King's Bench, Kerr, Bowen and Taschereau, excluded from sitting as council members, but had failed to prevent Chief Justice Sewell from continuing to sit as speaker of the upper chamber. Given the strong pro-British sentiments of the dozen or so council members who regularly turned up to vote, the Assembly knew it was impossible to pass legislation that ran counter to the wishes of the governor.

On Tuesday, January 10, 1832 the Assembly sat to debate Louis Bourdages's twelve resolutions including one that called

Jonathan Sewell, chief justice of Lower Canada and speaker of the Legislative Council. The son of American loyalists, he favoured the total anglicization of Quebec and pressed for severe restrictions on the liberty of the press. He committed Daniel Tracey and Ludger Duvernay to jail in 1832 for libelling the Legislative Council. (McCord Museum I-23417.1)

for an elected Legislative Council. The debate produced the well rehearsed arguments on both sides of the Chamber for or against the existence of the council. Perhaps emboldened by the action taken against William Lyon Mackenzie by the Upper Canadian Assembly or simply wishing to influence the debate in the Assembly, the council decided to make an example of the two Patriote newspapers. On Thursday, January 12 fourteen councillors and the speaker sat as a committee of the whole house on privileges and reflected on the terms "oppressive incubus" and "greatest nuisance" as applied by the newspapers to the council.

The following day, the council met again to debate whether Tracey and Duvernay should be arrested for defamation and breach of privilege. Opinions were strongly divided. Three councillors, John Hale, Thomas Coffin and Samuel Hatt, were uncertain whether they had the power to arrest individuals and proposed leaving the matter to the ordinary courts of the province. Herman W. Ryland, the most conservative of the councillors, voted against the motions on the grounds that they were too mild. He wanted the council to inform the governor that a revolutionary tendency now existed in the province and that seditious newspapers were being published that called for the overthrow of the monarchy and the setting up of a republic. John Caldwell, William Felton and Mathew Bell argued that the council had never exercised the power of arrest before and that the present occasion did not justify a first resort to a measure that would give undue importance to two "contemptible and insignificant" people. Among the seven councillors voting in favour of arrest were two Montreal magistrates, George Moffatt and Louis Gugy, sheriff of Montreal. On the casting vote of Chief Justice Sewell, the sergeant at arms was ordered to travel to Montreal and arrest Tracey and Duvernay.[13]

Imprisonment

The summons was served on both men in Montreal on the evening of Sunday, January 15. Before leaving for Quebec City, Tracey had just time to write his editorial for the next issue of the *Vindicator*, a defiant appeal to public opinion to judge the injustice of the predicament he found himself in. In an act of deliberate provocation, he reprinted his original editorial of January 3 and a translation of the equally controversial Mondelet letter in *La Minerve*.

The men arrived in Quebec City early on Tuesday afternoon January 17, and were immediately brought, each in turn, before a closed session of the Legislative Council presided over by Chief Justice Sewell. The timing could not have been worse. On the previous day, in a speech lasting one and a half hours, Papineau had accused the council of servility to every governor and of making a mockery of the representative system of government. The council was now looking for revenge. In answer to the charges laid against him, Duvernay replied that he was merely the printer and publisher of *La Minerve* and not the author of the article that had appeared on January 9. Tracey adopted a more robust stance. He stated that he was both publisher and editor of the *Vindicator* and indeed the author of the January 3 editorial. Asked if he had anything to say in his defence, Tracey jumped at the chance to have his say. He stated that what he had written was the simple truth. When he went on to repeat that the council was a perfect nuisance the Speaker immediately intervened saying that he did not think it appropriate to hear any more. After a short deliberation, the council reached its decision. Both men were found guilty as charged and ordered to be imprisoned for the remaining period of the parliamentary session.[14]

The sentence caused consternation in the ranks of the Patriotes. Supporters of the two men immediately began to organise a series of protests. Notices appeared in the local press and hand bills were handed out calling for people to attend a protest meeting at the Ottawa Hotel the following Thursday evening. The event attracted up to 500 people according to the estimates of the *Quebec Gazette*. Prominent among those who spoke at the meeting were William Henderson, a local magistrate, Elzéar Bédard, a lawyer and aspiring politician, Étienne Parent, editor of *Le Canadien* and Dr Edmund Bailey O'Callaghan, Tracey's countryman and the man who would one day succeed him as editor of the *Vindicator*. After the meeting, a sizeable section of the crowd set off for the jail where Tracey and Duvernay were being held, chanting slogans in favour of the freedom of the press and denouncing the action of the Legislative Council. Their spirits high, they then proceeded to the house of Chief Justice Sewell where more insults were chanted and a pane of glass broken. A hastily improvised song was sung to the tune of the *Marseillaise* before the crowd made its way to the Assembly building to express its loud support for Papineau.[15] Local papers described the late night trouble as nothing more than high jinks and some fun, but the *Quebec Mercury* was not amused: "If 'fun' was intended," it wrote, "it was in very bad taste—if mischief or intimidation was designed, the conduct of the leaders and their followers was pusillanimous and contemptible."[16]

Protest meetings continued in Quebec City and the movement quickly spread to Montreal. The numbers of people turning out to protest soon began to alarm the conservative press. In its first comments on the affair, the *Canadian Courant* appeared reluctant to be seen defending a writer whose French pseudonym associated him with "one of the most violent of the writers of the Jacobinical party of the French Revolution" but it decided the imprisonment of Tracey and Duvernay raised the fundamental principle of freedom of the press, one that could not be ignored on partisan grounds.[17] Neilson's *Quebec Gazette* adopted the same moderate approach: "We are not the apologists of licentiousness of the Press," it wrote, "but we think it ought to enjoy a very great liberty; that that liberty *must exist* here in respect of public bodies and of public men in spite of all efforts to repress it."[18] Only the *Montreal Herald* and the *Quebec Mercury* persisted in their unflinching support of the hard line adopted by the authorities.

In Montreal, the numbers of people attending protest meetings matched those in Quebec City. A group calling itself the Friends of the Liberty of the Press called a meeting at P. Lavoy's hotel on Saturday, January 21, and between five and six hundred people turned up according to the *Vindicator*. Dr Robert Nelson, who had held the Montreal West Ward seat with Papineau between 1827 and 1830, was elected chairman. In his opening remarks, he set the tone for the rest of the meeting:

> This violation of Civil Liberty may serve to the legitimates as a precedent, and tomorrow any of us, each of us, or all of us, if they may be strong enough, and the prison large enough, may become companions of these two defenders of Public Right and of Public Liberty. When there is no law to protect us, or when the laws are not administered to that end, it is time for us to look about; and according with the spirit of the age, and the prevalent genius of liberty, of Freedom, and also of public Patriotic virtue, we, as men, are bound to protect ourselves, and not suffer like slaves, the rigour and brutality of antiquity—(Bravos) when milder means fail, we may be driven to the necessity of asserting the Sovereignty of the People, (Yes, Yes).

Next to speak was Charles Mondelet. His identity as the author of the incriminating article in *La Minerve* was not yet public knowledge though certain people at the meeting may have guessed from parts of his speech:

> Duvernay and Tracey were martyrs!!! But in their persons we were all attacked, the liberty of the press had received a serious blow, and as it was the soul of our political existence, we would be fit tools for slavery, were we to allow such dangerous attack to pass unnoticed; the people were therefore bound to express its feelings and to hasten by energy and activity the reform of a body which everyone, except the council itself, admitted was quite different from what it ought to be.[19]

On January 25 another meeting in support of the imprisoned men was held and several resolutions were passed. One that received unanimous backing from the meeting proposed offering Duvernay and Tracey a gold medal each on their release from prison. The presentation would be made, it was announced, following a triumphal return to Montreal that the Patriotes intended to organise. The cost of the medals was to be funded by a public subscription. A committee was appointed to coordinate activity with a similar committee in Quebec City. Among those appointed to it were some of the most important Patriotes in Montreal: Dr Robert Nelson, Dr Guillaume Vallée, Dr Alexis Demers, member for Vaudreuil, Louis-Hippolyte La Fontaine, member for Terrebonne, Joseph Roy, a magistrate, Charles Mondelet and John McDonell, a lawyer and a friend of Duvernay. Édouard-Raymond Fabre, bookseller and newspaper printer, was elected treasurer. At the end of the meeting, a large group of those present, including Édouard-Étienne Rodier, a lawyer and close friend of Duvernay, decided to emulate their counterparts in Quebec City by organising an impromptu noisy march through the streets of Montreal. Singing the *Parisienne* and the *Marseillaise*, the crowd set off first for the house of Sheriff Gugy, the councillor who reportedly had moved the resolution in the Legislative Council to declare the articles in the *Vindicator* and *La Minerve* as libellous. There the crowd indulged in a vociferous demonstration before moving on to George Moffatt's house where it gave a repeat performance. Finally the crowd made its way to the offices of Montreal's two main conservative newspapers. At the first there were shouts of "Down with Armour and his Gazette!" and at the next "Down with Ferguson and his Herald!"[20]

The *Vindicator* and *La Minerve* kept up the pressure in more conventional fashion by publishing editorials and readers' letters that seemed designed to goad the Legislative Council into taking further action against the papers. In Quebec City, Étienne Parent became the leading supporter of Tracey and Duvernay, using his editorials in *Le Canadien* to lambaste the Legislative Council, and in organising visits to the two men in prison, a gesture that each acknowledged in the form of a defiant letter of thanks published in *La Minerve* and the *Vindicator*. Both letters showed that neither prisoner felt in any way cowed by the treatment meted out to him. Commenting on the term an "oppressive incubus" which had landed him in prison, Tracey wrote:

> I have no hesitation to repeat the expression, from an entire conviction of its correctness, and I am ready to submit to the consequences of the promulgation of an opinion, long since formed, from a close observation of the conduct and motives by which this body appeared to me always to have been guided.[21]

On February 8 lawyers for Duvernay and Tracey applied for a writ of *habeas corpus* to the Court of King's Bench. The writ was granted and on the following day, Andrew Stuart, brother of the attorney general, appeared before Justices James Kerr, Edward Bowen and Jean-Thomas Taschereau to question the legality of his clients' imprisonment. He argued that the matter before the court was a constitutional one with implications for the cause of civil liberties. The court had to decide whether the Legislative Council could claim the same rights, powers and privileges as enjoyed by the House of Lords to imprison individuals for breach of privilege in cases of libel. Citing numerous authorities in support of his case, Stuart argued at length that the council had in fact no such power and that the 1791 Act had conferred no such authority on it. If the council really felt the need to be protected from insults or outrages, suggested Stuart in conclusion, then the law of Lower Canada was adequate to the task.[22]

Stuart knew that the odds were stacked heavily against his clients. Chief Justice Sewell as Speaker of the Council had had to disqualify himself from presiding over the court but his recent decision to use his casting vote to prosecute Duvernay and Tracey weighed heavily on the court proceedings. Both Bowen and Taschereau had studied law under Sewell and Bowen in addition was related through marriage to John Caldwell of the Legislative Council. Equally damaging for his clients' case was the ill-will between the judiciary and the Assembly. In the previous session of the parliament, complaints had been made against the attorney general, and there was talk of his possible destitution. James Kerr himself was involved in a similar scandal of his own—just four days earlier he had been accused of "high crimes and partiality" in his administration of justice. The overriding difficulty, however, was that all three judges were still members of the Legislative Council, and had long resisted the ultimately successful attempts to prevent them from attending council meetings. Having listened to Stuart's arguments, the three justices announced that they needed time to consider their decision

Judgment came on the following Monday, February 13. The court, to no one's surprise, unanimously found in favour of the council. Scottish-born James Kerr agreed that the Legislative Council did not have the same extensive privileges as the House of Lords or Commons, but denying it the right to imprison someone would condemn it to sink "into utter contempt and inefficiency," he said. As for relying on the law as a form of protection, Kerr, surprisingly, had little faith in the system: too slow and too uncertain to protect the council from the "effects of contemptuous and defamatory libels." Far better to risk the abuse of such power, he concluded, than to leave it without this means of self-defence.

Edward Bowen, originally from Kinsale in Ireland, concentrated on the theme of self-defence. The council had the same right to defend its moral person and functions as did an individual his own character, personal security and personal liberty. Defamation was a direct assault upon its character and an obstruction of its political duties. The right of the council to imprison Duvernay and Tracey did not depend, therefore, upon the judicial authority vested in it but upon the principle of self defence as exercised by the House of Commons in similar circumstances or by the House of Assembly as far back as 1817. Why being described in a newspaper as an "oppressive incubus" or a "nuisance" should be considered an obstruction of the council's political duties was not addressed.

Justice Taschereau had little else to add. The Legislative Council, he asserted, was the sole judge of contempt against its own body and the guardian of its own privileges and the *habeas corpus* act did not give the Court of King's Bench the right to judge those privileges or revise the council's proceedings.[23]

It was clear that the three judges were unwilling to involve themselves in what was essentially a political confrontation between the pro-Patriote press and the Legislative Council.

As to the constitutional aspect of the affair, this had been the first time that the courts had pronounced on the legality of the privilege exercised by the legislature. As the *Quebec Mercury* pointed out, there was a precedent for the exercise of this ill-defined prerogative in the province. It had found three examples in the previous twenty-six years when the Assembly had attempted to imprison editors or publishers for similar offences but had failed each time to apprehend the offenders. Nevertheless, the paper, which was not in the habit of professing support for the Patriote Party, seemed to accept that the legal authorities cited by counsel for Tracey and Duvernay were sufficient to cast doubt on the legality of the proceedings brought against them. In the present matter, the paper concluded, the Legislative Council had lost sight of the fact that such prosecutions, far from restraining such publications, "tend rather to promote them, by creating candidates for that martyrdom, the honor of which is always assigned by the public to those who are punished for offences of the Press."[24]

The animosity of the Tory press towards Tracey and Duvernay further increased when it became known how supporters of the imprisoned men were planning to celebrate their eventual release. There was to be a triumphal procession all the way from Quebec City to Montreal where Dalhousie Square, so the rumour had it, was to be renamed *Place de la Liberté* and a liberty-pole erected in the middle of the square displaying the tricolour. This was too much for the *Montreal Gazette* which conjured up images of the province being overtaken by anarchy and revolution. In an editorial full of foreboding, the paper warned its readers to prepare for the possibility of a riot or civil commotion, adding for full measure the information that insurance policies in the province did not cover losses caused by the actions of a lawless mob.[25]

The Sicotte letter

In normal times, the Patriotes would have dismissed such warnings as unnecessary scaremongering but they suddenly found themselves in an embarrassing predicament. On Thursday February 16, three days after the Court of King's Bench had published its judgment, *La Minerve* printed a letter signed S**** which offered a highly contentious interpretation of the relations between the English and the French Canadians since the time of the Conquest. The *Montreal Gazette* claimed the views expressed amounted to "revolutionary opinions and treasonable recommendations."[26] The other Tory papers reacted in similar fashion. Within a few days, both the *Montreal Gazette* and the *Montreal Herald* had provided their readers with an English translation of the "seditious" document.

The letter had been written by Louis-Victor Sicotte, the future government minister and judge, but at the time a nineteen-year-old student of law with a passion for politics. His views were no different from those that were frequently heard in Patriote circles, but what was new and particularly alarming for that section of the population still imbued with a "garrison mentality", was his proposed solution for the ills facing the province: revolution. Sicotte had been careful to add that he was using the term to mean the non-violent remodelling of the constitution for French Canadians though he must have known that his opponents were unlikely to accept this distinguo.

As a people, Sicotte wrote, French Canadians had suffered while outsiders had arrived and heaped riches and honours on themselves. French Canadians had proved their loyalty in 1812, yet just ten years later the Union Bill had attempted to deprive them of their institutions, their language and their laws. In short, their future as a British colony was doomed to failure:

> there exist here two partners, of opposite interest and manners—the Canadians and the English. These first, born Frenchmen, have the habits and character as such—they have inherited from their fathers a hatred for the English, who in their turn, seeing in them the children of France, detest them. These two parties can never unite, and will not always remain tranquil: it is a bad amalgamation of interests, of manners, of language, and of religion, which sooner or later must produce a collision.[27]

The only possible solution, Sicotte concluded, was for Lower Canada to declare itself independent of England.

Sicotte's letter was far more radical than anything that had been published before by *La Minerve* or the *Vindicator*, both of which had always laid emphasis on the constant loyalty of French Canadians to the British Crown. Had Duvernay not been in prison it is unlikely that Sicotte's letter would have been published. As was later revealed, Léon Gosselin, a lawyer by profession and the paper's editorial writer since the previous November 17, had been in sole charge of the paper since January 15, the day of Duvernay's arrest.[28] Sicotte took fright at the reaction he had caused and left for New York. Gosselin, fearing he was about to be arrested, went into hiding and Michel Bibaud took temporary charge of *La Minerve*.[29]

With the release of Duvernay and Tracey now only a matter of days away, *La Minerve* did its best to defuse the uproar but its explanation of what had happened merely added to the scandal. In an editorial published on February 20, Gosselin claimed that none of the people working for the paper had actually read the offending letter before it was printed. Now that he was aware of its contents, he was not prepared to accept the interpretation that the paper's Tory opponents had given to the word 'revolution': it meant only a redress of grievances, Gosselin insisted, not a revolt. In a final reassuring word, the paper predicted that if French Canadians were ever to gain independence, it would be by legal and constitutional means only.

Étienne Parent in *Le Canadien* suggested that Sicotte's letter should serve as a warning to the British government whose long-term plans for the province were fraught with possible danger. As colonists, he wrote, Canadians had the right to decide when they were ready to govern themselves, but numbering only 600,000 they were unlikely to maintain their independence and nationality next to a powerful and enterprising nation with which it had so little in common. It was in the best interests, therefore, both of England and of Lower Canada for the specific French identity of Canadians to be preserved and supported until they were in a position to defend themselves from the encroachments of their neighbours. If on the contrary the country were completely anglicised, Canadians would no longer have a specific identity to defend and would naturally, though as a last resort, throw in their lot with their neighbours rather than remain subjects of a nation lying thousands of miles away.[30]

In Montreal, certain elements saw their chance to exploit the uproar surrounding the letter. On 20 February, the day that *La Minerve* had attempted to defuse the situation, Louis Gugy, the sheriff of Montreal and one of the legislative councillors who had voted to imprison Duvernay and Tracey, called an emergency meeting of his fellow magistrates. Gugy told his startled audience that he had in his possession two letters written in English that had been sent to Major Grierson at the Montreal garrison. Though anonymous, they were purportedly written by an Irishman who had attended the various assemblies planning the homecoming of Tracey and Duvernay. One letter revealed that on the "day of triumph" the real plan was to set fire to the Hay Market and other places in order to draw the troops from their barracks which would then be vulnerable to attack. Two other houses would also be targeted including the British American Hotel belonging to John Molson Sr, a fellow magistrate and a recent appointee to the Legislative Council. With the aid of several thousand people from the country who would be in Montreal on that day, the ringleaders would take control of the town. The second letter claimed that a number of French Canadians had already crossed over to Île Sainte-Hélène to assess the number of canon that were serviceable and to plan the capture of the arsenal.

Gugy urged the magistrates to take immediate measures to prevent what he claimed was a planned insurrection. Calmer heads among the magistrates urged caution. Austin Cuvillier, a former Patriote supporter who had broken ranks with the party, nevertheless sided with Joseph Roy in ridiculing the sheriff's panic recommendations. Even Molson, who had more reason than the others to be alarmed by the rumours, laughed off the supposed plot. Cuvillier and Roy wanted the letters to remain in the possession of the magistrates but Gugy claimed that the military authorities had instructed him not to give them away. *La Minerve* reported the meeting three days later. The letters, it said, were full of spelling mistakes and grammatical errors and were obvious forgeries. In the paper's opinion they were probably part of an orchestrated campaign to pass off all French Canadians as potential traitors.[31]

Whatever the origin of the letters, it was clear that certain people in the city were hoping to turn the Patriotes' "day of triumph" into a confrontation between the French Canadians and the authorities, both civil and military.

The involvement of Major Grierson in the matter had ominous overtones. He belonged to the Fifteenth or Yorkshire East Riding Regiment of Foot. It was a regiment that had had first-hand experience of Irish "rebels." Posted to Ireland in October 1822, the regiment had briefly occupied Dublin's Richmond Barracks at a time when Tracey was still establishing himself as a doctor in the city. Over the next four years the regiment was stationed in Waterford, Cork and Templemore. When the regiment next drew attention to itself, in 1826, Tracey had already left for Lower Canada. A detachment of the regiment was stationed in Thurles under Captain Henry Temple. A riot broke out which the captain and the police managed to put down. Several people were killed but Temple won praise from the town's magistrates and principal inhabitants "for his cool and judicious conduct." A year later the regiment left Ireland under the command of Lieutenant Colonel Alexander Macintosh and arrived in Canada at the beginning of July 1827. After four years spent first in Kingston and then in Quebec City, the regiment finally moved to Montreal in May 1831. Twelve months later, the regiment's history would be for ever linked with Montreal.[32]

Triumphal return

Duvernay and Tracey were eventually released from imprisonment on Saturday, February 25, the last day of the parliamentary session. Their incarceration had lasted forty days. The pair immediately left in the company of a large group of supporters for Saint-Augustin where Papineau was waiting to greet them. From there, they travelled as far as Berthier, forty-five miles north-east of Montreal, from where the procession was due to begin on the following Tuesday. In view of the alarmist language that had appeared in the *Herald* and the *Gazette*, the organisers had decided to rid their celebrations of anything that smacked of revolutionary trappings. The journey was planned to extend over two days with more and more carioles and carriages joining the cavalcade as it drew near to Montreal. On the Tuesday night, escorted by some thirty carioles, Tracey and Duvernay reached L'Assomption where the inhabitants had organised a banquet in their honour. The next day, Wednesday, February 29, the number of vehicles increased to between two and three hundred carioles and carriages. In addition, numerous other people had turned up on horseback. At their head marched a band of musicians.

Once the procession reached Montreal, it took a carefully calculated route through the main streets of west Montreal: along Notre-Dame, St Joseph, St James, St Denis, Bonsecours, then St Paul, McGill and Craig. The band played the *Marseillaise* and the *Parisienne* as planned but had clearly been instructed to add *God save the King* to the repertoire. The British flag was also prominently displayed. The procession ended with Tracey and Duvernay being escorted to their respective houses where each expressed his thanks for the support he had received. There had been no sign of trouble all day.[33]

In his first editorial since his return, Tracey singled out for comment the reaction of the authorities to the event. It seemed obvious to him that they had been expecting trouble since they had doubled the guard at the guard room next to the New Market and had issued several rounds of ammunition. As the procession passed, it had been subjected to insults from the officers present. In a comment that was unknowingly prophetic, Tracey wrote: "Perhaps these Gentlemen not having a foreign enemy to fight with, cannot endure the *ennui* of the City of Montreal, and would be happy, for want of better, to exercise their Military prowess on the defenceless Citizens."[34]

Duvernay for his part was content to congratulate his fellow citizens for the peaceful nature of the welcome surrounding his and Tracey's return to the city and to wonder rhetorically what had become of the terrible revolution the threat of which had been used by some to frighten the inhabitants of the province against the idea of constitutional reform.[35]

The show of force by the Legislative Council, if that is what it was supposed to be, had been a failure. Calls for its reform continued unabated and the press sympathetic to the Patriote cause refused to be silenced. The conservative press did its best to downplay the importance of the "day of triumph" and even suggested that Duvernay and Tracey had been snubbed by their most prominent supporters since the likes of Papineau, James Leslie, Jacob De Witt, Jacques Viger and Dr Robert Nelson had not taken part in the procession. The events of the previous two months, and in particular the Sicotte letter, had indeed produced misgivings among the Patriotes about the more radical direction that Papineau was taking and for some 1832 would be the year that they broke ranks with the party. The stand taken by John Neilson in opposing Bourdages's motion in favour of an elected Legislative Council was just one sign of the growing disenchantment within the party. It was for this reason that Tracey was keen to distance himself from the position that Sicotte had advocated. The author, Tracey wrote, "used expressions which a more mature judgment would have discountenanced. The opinions he gave, are by no means the sentiments of the people of Canada, and have been almost universally disclaimed."[36]

In the short-term, however, it was a time for celebration. What political capital the Patriotes might derive from the imprisonment of Tracey and Duvernay would be considered at a later date. On Monday, March 5, a dinner was organized in their honour at Montreal's Nelson Hotel attended by some eighty guests. During the course of the evening, among the numerous toasts proposed were those to Daniel O'Connell and Ireland, William Lyon McKenzie and the freedom of the press in Upper Canada, the memory of Jocelyn Waller and the defenders of the press in 1827 and the memory of those who were imprisoned in 1810 "for the liberty of the country and that of the press." Prominent among the after-dinner speakers who eulogised the courage of Tracey and Duvernay in opposing the Legislative Council was Charles Mondelet. It was to be his final act of public support for the Patriotes.[37]

By-election Candidates on a Collision Course

The East Ward

Towards the end of March, Montreal's newspapers carried announcements of two forthcoming by-elections in the East and West Wards of the city. It was the prelude to two months of political agitation the like of which had not been seen in the city for some considerable time.

The East Ward election was called following the resignation of Hughes Heney whose acceptance of the post of law clerk of the House of Assembly meant relinquishing a seat he had held since 1820. Heney's profession as a lawyer and his less than distinguished performance in the Chamber prompted some of Montreal's newspapers to air their dissatisfaction with the succession of "professional gentlemen" who were regularly being elected to the Assembly. It was time, some editorials suggested, to elect a new type of representative, one who would reflect the changing needs of the city. The *Montreal Gazette*'s wish was "to see some independent mercantile gentlemen come forward, who will support and advance the growing interests of this commercial emporium."[1]

A candidate partly fitting that description soon made known his intention to stand for election. Antoine-Olivier

Berthelet was, like his father before him, a wealthy land speculator and landlord but not someone who had made a major contribution to the commercial prosperity of his native city. His opponent was Clément-Charles Sabrevois de Bleury, a native of William Henry (Sorel) and a lawyer by training, who moved easily in the elegant circles of Montreal society.[2] Heney had generally supported the Patriotes but had begun to distance himself from them in the months leading up to his resignation. Sabrevois de Bleury was the more politically committed of the two candidates and though brought up in a conservative Anglican family he openly supported the more radical wing of the Patriote party. Among his supporters were Édouard-Étienne Rodier and Louis-Hippolyte La Fontaine, two of the Patriotes' leading young lawyers. Surprisingly, he also received the endorsement of Robert Johnson, editor of the fiercely conservative *Montreal Herald*.

Berthelet had the solid backing of the city's business con-fraternity and the enthusiastic support of Robert Armour's *Montreal Gazette*.[3] Much to the annoyance of the Patriote party, the lawyers Dominique and Charles Mondelet allowed their names to be added to the official list of Berthelet supporters. Just six months earlier Dominique had won the Montreal County seat with the help of the Patriotes who saw him as one of their rising stars. Charles's articles in *La Minerve* had reinforced his credentials as a leading Patriote. Their open support for Berthelet so soon after the return home of Tracey and Duvernay signalled in dramatic fashion the dissension in the Patriote ranks even in Montreal.

The election itself attracted little attention. Polling began on April 3 and ended three days later. Over six hundred people turned out to vote in what appeared to be a trouble-free election. To the satisfaction of the conservative press, Berthelet won the seat with a majority of fifty-seven votes.

Among the enthusiastic crowd of supporters waiting to greet him when he returned home from the polling station was Charles Mondelet. There was no longer any doubt about where the Mondelets' new allegiance lay.

Cholera warning

The day before the East Ward election ended the Official *Gazette* published a proclamation from the governor ordering a day of public fasting and humiliation to be observed throughout Lower Canada on Friday, May 4.[4] This was just the latest in a series of measures that the authorities had been taking in the hope of preventing a cholera epidemic from breaking out in the province. For months newspapers had been carrying reports of the rapid progress of the disease across Europe and of the hysteria that outbreaks had caused in some English cities. The British had been the first to describe the disease in 1817 following an outbreak near Calcutta in India. The disease had then spread rapidly and had become endemic in most of Asia. A new pandemic began in 1826 in Bengal and eventually reached Moscow in August 1830, and Berlin a year later. In October 1831, the disease struck England and Wales causing more than 21,500 deaths and Scotland where 9,500 died despite desperate quarantine measures. In March 1832, Ireland in turn saw cholera reach its shores. It was only a matter of time before the disease would reach Lower Canada.

The port of Quebec City was already equipped with a new hospital at Pointe-Lévy designed to care for "fever patients" and administered by Dr François-Xavier Tessier, the port's health officer. It was clear, however, from reports arriving from Europe that cholera was of a very different nature from the more usual maladies that afflicted the thousands of immigrants who would arrive each year in late spring. In October 1831, the Assembly had sent Tessier to New York to see at first hand how a major port organised a health and quarantine service but few practical measures had been taken in the province. Eventually, in February 1832 the governor set up a board of health for the city under the chairmanship of Dr Joseph Morrin who immediately drew up quarantine procedures for inspecting incoming ships. A quarantine station was established at Gaspé and another at Grosse Île, an island thirty-three miles down river from Quebec City. As an added precaution, two infantry companies and a detachment of Royal Artillery were also dispatched to the island. In Montreal, the city's magistrates left it dangerously late before reacting. They waited till March before requesting the governor to set up a board of health. As a result, it took until May for the board to be established in the city.[5]

The West Ward constituency

The second by-election was expected to take place shortly after the first. John Fisher, a merchant and justice of the peace, had announced his retirement from the West Ward seat on health grounds a few days after Heney. The Montreal Gazette and similar papers had good reason to suppose that the election would be a mere formality. The ward's two seats were traditionally occupied by a French-speaking Patriote and an English speaker representing the city's commercial interests. Papineau had held one of the two seats since 1814. Fisher had been elected to the second seat in 1830 and his replacement appeared to be a straightforward affair. Even when it was learned that a "professional gentleman," the lawyer William Walker, had declared himself as a candidate, the Montreal Gazette expressed no alarm since, as it reassured its readers, Walker had "a thorough knowledge of commercial transactions, from having originally been brought up to a mercantile life" and was "justly ranked as our first commercial practitioner."[6]

Within days, other names emerged better suited to the profile proposed by the newspaper: merchants Stanley Bagg, Oliver Wait, Jules Quesnel and building contractor, Thomas Phillips. But when *La Minerve* announced that Daniel Tracey too was likely to offer himself as a candidate, the conservative press saw red.

Since he had taken charge again at the *Vindicator*, Tracey had given more and more space in his editorials to questions of a specifically economic nature. In mid-March, he gave considerable publicity to the new Canadian Commercial Establishment that was in the process of being set up by an association of businessmen with strong links to the Patriotes. Among the names cited were those of François-Antoine Larocque (one of the founders of the Bank of Montreal and a partner of Joseph Masson), Jean-Dominique Bernard, Léonard Bouthillier, Pierre-Louis Le Tourneux, Pierre-Dominique Debartzch, Côme-Séraphin Cherrier, Dominique Mondelet and Édouard-Raymond Fabre. Responding to one of the grievances expressed at a meeting of the association that the import and export trade of the province was practically the exclusive reserve of the British, Tracey wrote a strongly critical editorial on the defeatist attitude of many French Canadians who, he claimed, envied the prosperity of their industrious fellow-citizens while remaining "motionless as if wealth and honors were to flow into their laps spontaneously." Economic prosperity, he reminded his readers, was a pre-requisite if the political and civil rights of French Canadians were to be safeguarded.[7]

Tracey returned to the same theme in two editorials published while the Patriotes and the English party were still debating which candidates to support in the upcoming election. His hard-hitting opinions now placed him on a collision course with some of the most powerful figures in the Montreal business community. News from London had revealed that plans to form a joint stock company to be called the British American Land Company had been resurrected.[8] The intention of the company was to purchase large tracts of land in Lower Canada, improve their infrastructure by building roads and canals, and then divide the whole into smaller sections to be sold off to intending emigrants from Great Britain. Tracey was familiar with the project since he had been a vigorous opponent of it from the time it had first been proposed some years earlier. At the time, one of its main supporters in the province, James Stuart, had caused a major controversy by suggesting that the land be made available only to Scottish and English settlers, since "Irish Roman Catholics would coalesce with the people of Canada and the political intentions of the company be thereby frustrated."[9] The renewed interest in the project, Tracey suspected, was linked to a sudden resurgence in the activities of the Orange Lodge in Lower Canada.

The reference was an odd one. The columns of the *Vindicator* were regularly filled with accounts of the Orange lodges in Ireland but never before had the paper referred to their presence in Montreal. The reason for their mention now was due entirely to George Perkins Bull, an Orangemen of some repute and a recent arrival in the province from Ireland where he had served time in jail for libelling a priest. Not only was he in charge of a lodge but he had become Montreal's most recent newspaper editor, having founded the *London and Canada Record* as a support for the interests of his lodge. The paper also served as a means of establishing communication with Orangemen among the rank and file of the 24th Regiment stationed in Quebec and with the large Orange faction among the ranks of the 15th in Montreal.[10] Tracey was not alone in voicing his misgivings about Bull—even the conservative press in Montreal had expressed alarm—but it was an exaggeration to claim that the renewed interest in the creation of a British American land company owed its origin to Montreal's Orangemen.

The commercial enterprise had originated in London but with the active support of two prominent Montreal merchants, George Moffatt and Peter McGill, both of them recent appointees to the Legislative Council. It was McGill's London partner, Nathaniel Gould, who was one of the principal organisers behind the scheme. At stake was one of the biggest private land deals the province had ever known, involving over a million acres of undeveloped agricultural land in the Eastern Townships. The Land Company would eventually pay the British government £110,321 sterling and appoint Moffatt and McGill as the company's commissioners in Lower Canada.

Tracey's opposition to their plans reflected the strong sense of injustice the Assembly had long felt over the way the British government intended to dispose of Crown Lands in Lower Canada. The Assembly's London agent, Denis-Benjamin Viger, had been reassured by the government some years earlier that its fears were unfounded but Tracey now suspected that the government was about to go back on its word. In his editorial, Tracey called for absolute control of crown lands to be given not to a "set of London bankers and jobbers," his term for the Land Company, but to the province. With an outlay of some thousands of pounds each year, the legislature could establish the lands and open them up to the young people of the province. "This would be an excellent means of preventing monopoly," he stated. "The money thus employed would return to the advantage of the country. We would not see thus speculators, greedy and without attachment to this colony spending among strangers the immense profits which they will accumulate amongst us at our expense."[11]

The selection of candidates

It was inevitable that Tracey's opposition to the Land Company would antagonize large sections of Montreal's merchant class and indirectly the Legislative Council. For many merchants the Patriotes' persistent calls for political reform represented more of a hindrance than a support for the commercial prosperity of Montreal. In view of the strong majority the Patriotes enjoyed in the Assembly, the merchants knew they had little chance of reversing the trend in the near future. The loss of John Fisher's seat to a Patriote candidate was a prospect that few merchants were prepared to stomach and none less so than George Moffatt. His appointment to the Legislative Council in 1831 following the death of John Richardson, the leader of Montreal's merchant class, gave him the opportunity to assume the same anti-Patriote role that his predecessor had filled for over a generation.[12]

As the leading spokesman in the council for Montreal's merchants, Moffatt had jumped at the chance to establish his credentials with his fellow councillors in voting for criminal charges to be laid against the *Vindicator* and *La Minerve*. That decision had now returned to haunt him. If Tracey were ever to be elected, he would represent an even greater danger to the financial interests of the merchants than he did as editor of the *Vindicator*.

The possibility of Tracey standing in the West Ward election concentrated the minds of the English party which was still revelling over Berthelet's victory in the East Ward. It recognised the need for a united front against Tracey and that meant presenting a strong candidate. Within a very short time most of the potential conservative candidates had withdrawn their names leaving just two, Bagg and Phillips, to battle it out together for the prize of running against Tracey. The first of a series of meetings of the electors of the ward was held on Monday, April 9. It was evident from the beginning that strong divisions existed in the ward over the desired outcome of the election. The first meeting, held in the Nelson Hotel, a regular haunt of the Patriote party, ended inconclusively, and was followed by a larger gathering three days later at Lavoy's Hotel, Main St, St Lawrence Suburbs.

The meeting was chaired by Pierre-Édouard Leclère, superintendent of the Montreal police and a man who had little sympathy for Tracey. Robert Armour, editor of the *Montreal Gazette,* opened the debate and he was followed by Austin Cuvillier, the city magistrate and Assembly member for Laprairie County. Cuvillier had gone from being one of the most prominent politicians in the Patriote party to one of its most determined opponents in the space of three short years. In 1828 he had accompanied Denis-Benjamin Viger and John Neilson to London where he had spoken before the Canada committee of the House of Commons. However, when the Assembly finally chose Viger and not Cuvillier as its agent in London in March 1831, Cuvillier broke with the party.[13]

There was little surprise, therefore, when Cuvillier rose to speak in support of Bagg and Phillips and against Tracey. The first two, he said, were known for their industry and integrity. Tracey, on the other hand, was unworthy to represent the West Ward. Although he possessed undeniable talents, Cuvillier conceded, Tracey was still a stranger in Montreal and had no real stake in the country. What the West Ward needed was a merchant with strong roots in the country.

Cuvillier's remarks had brought the meeting to life. He was constantly interrupted by applause from one section of the meeting and protests from the other. A lone voice spoke up in defence of Tracey: Côme-Séraphin Cherrier, one of the lawyers who had successfully defended Jocelyn Waller, the Irish editor of the *Canadian Spectator*, in 1828 against the charge of libelling Governor Dalhousie's administration. Cherrier had little difficulty in countering Cuvillier's biased opinion of Tracey. The Irishman had always been a friend to the country, Cherrier insisted, and of all the English newspapers published in the province, the *Vindicator* was the only one that defended the cause of the French Canadians. The Irish had a right to expect support from French Canadians as they had always shown themselves to be friends of the country at times of crisis.[14]

By now, the din was so deafening that the next speaker was unable to be heard. The chairman decided that nothing more would be gained by prolonging the discussion. On his recommendation it was decided that each candidate would hold separate meetings at different venues in the city as a means of calming passions. Accordingly, the following evening, Bagg's supporters met at Boulet's in the Hay Market while Phillips' defenders returned to Lavoy's.

The meeting at Boulet's under the chairmanship of Leclère served in part to blacken even further Tracey's character. Horatio Gates, an American-born entrepreneur, chairman of the Champlain and St Lawrence Railroad and one of Montreal's leading exporters, was scathing in his attack on the Irish editor. Judging by the politics of his paper, Gates argued, Tracey was too violent and would be dangerous in the House of Assembly where he would act merely as the tool of the Patriote party. John Fisher was equally dismissive of Tracey: "we must consider him as a man unfit for that situation, he

Côme-Séraphin Cherrier, a lawyer related to the Viger and Papineau families who had distinguished himself in several political trials. He acted as Tracey's right-hand man during the by-election. He was elected to the Assembly for the riding of Montreal in 1834. (McCord Museum – M22336)

would be a *burning coal* in the House of Assembly, he would do injury to the country, and we would feel it in the end."[15]

By the end of the week, buoyed up by the support they had both received, Bagg and Phillips felt confident enough to announce their formal candidatures for the West Ward seat. Statements to that effect were released on April 16.[16] The *Montreal Gazette*, which had refused to report what had been said in favour of Tracey, was now convinced that Tracey would not stand.

Tracey in fact had by now given up any idea of standing in the election. Nevertheless, he pointed out to his readers that Cuvillier's criticism of him had more to do with a personal grievance that Cuvillier harboured against him than with any supposed lack of commercial expertise on Tracey's part. Cuvillier had come in for severe criticism from the *Vindicator* following a previous prorogation of Parliament over the stand he had adopted in favour of indemnifying members for attending the Assembly. Even the *Montreal Gazette* had joined in the criticism of Cuvillier at the time, wrote Tracey. However, what rankled most with Cuvillier, Tracey insisted, was the fact that an Irishman had seen fit to criticize him.[17]

Cuvillier's outburst against Tracey, however, had the opposite effect to the one he had intended. Tracey's candidature suddenly became a real possibility, though it was likely that the idea had originated in the inner sanctum of *La Minerve*. If some Patriotes still entertained doubts about him— Dr Robert Nelson was opposed to his candidature—the continuing attacks on him by the English party turned opinion in his favour. Édouard-Étienne Rodier, a dynamic young lawyer closely linked to *La Minerve*'s editorial team and Côme-Séraphin Cherrier, a Montreal lawyer related to the Papineau and Viger families, both testified later that Cuvillier's outburst had been a determining factor in persuading them and others like them to support Tracey.[18]

The Patriotes called their election meeting on the same day that Bagg and Phillips announced their candidature. A number of influential members of the party met at the house of Pierre-Louis Le Tourneux, situated in the St Joseph Suburbs. In the chair was Louis Roy Portelance, the venerable vice-president of the Constitutional Committee of 1827, while La Fontaine acted as secretary. The one item on the agenda concerned the replacement of John Fisher as representative for the West Ward. Tracey's name was proposed by Joseph Valois, the long serving Assembly member for Montreal and seconded by Augustin Tulloch. A delegation of one hundred men then set off for Tracey's house on St Antoine St where they formally invited the Irish editor to offer himself as a candidate. Tracey put up little resistance. In his acceptance speech, he stated that he would offer himself to the electorate as a defender of the Patriote policy on the Civil List, on the need to reform the Legislative Council and as an opponent of the proposed land company.[19]

Some days before, Neilson's *Gazette de Québec* had forecast that Tracey would eventually stand and had even suggested that he would be elected because of the Irish factor. But this was by no means a foregone conclusion given the large number of Ulstermen who had settled in Montreal. For the *Montreal Herald* it was Tracey's Irish background that made him most vulnerable. In a bitter editorial the paper sought to discredit Tracey in the eyes of potential Irish voters by accusing him of "shutting the door in the face of his fellow countrymen and excluding them from the advantages which they might find, and he has found, in Canada."[20]

Tracey was only too aware that in the coming by-election the Irish vote was likely to play a pivotal role. It was crucial therefore that he scotch the suggestion that he was attempting to put a stop to Irish immigration to Lower Canada. In a forceful editorial Tracey claimed that the *Montreal Herald* was concerned less with the lot of Irish immigrants than with protecting the British American Land Company. Surely Irish people could comprehend his position on this question, he wrote. The company was planning to implement the same system that had been used in the colonization of Ireland, "which policy, as Irishmen, we should dread as the main cause of the calamities of our native country." The aim of the land company was to impose on the province a system of absentee landlords similar to that still prevailing in Ireland. It would be far better, Tracey counselled, to allow emigration take its natural course and to make land available to new arrivals without the intervention of a set of London speculators. Only local government could guarantee to settle the land in the most judicious fashion.[21]

Now that Tracey had agreed to contest the West Ward election, the Patriotes organised two rallies in his support. One was held at Bellamy's Hotel in the Old Market district for his English-speaking supporters. *La Minerve* reported that the meeting presided over by Stephen Field, Montreal's leading wholesale shoe and boot manufacturer, drew some two hundred Irish and American voters.[22] The main rally, however, took place on the evening of April 17. Nearly three hundred supporters turned up and crowded into Papineau's former home at the entrance to the St Joseph Suburbs. Once more Roy Portelance was in the chair. La Fontaine as acting secretary read out Tracey's acceptance speech. Other prominent Patriotes were there in force to speak in favour of Tracey: Jacob de Witt, John McDonell, Alexis Demers, member for Vaudreuil, Sabrevois de Bleury, the unsuccessful candidate in the East Ward, La Fontaine, Édouard-Étienne Rodier and Côme-Séraphin Cherrier. As was to become the practice,

Cherrier acted as Tracey's main spokesman. Tracey's credentials as an active supporter of the Patriotes were solid, he reminded everyone. In 1827, before founding his newspaper, Tracey had been strongly committed to the work of the Constitutional Committee, as Roy Portelance was there to confirm. His commitment was characteristic of the Irish in the province and it was time, Cherrier insisted, for all French Canadians to recognise their support by showing solidarity with them in the forthcoming election.

Much to the surprise of many, Charles Mondelet also attended the rally and even agreed to speak, though his support for Tracey was at best lukewarm. His few references to Phillips and Bagg were designed to avoid offending their supporters. As for Tracey, Mondelet told his listeners that the Irishman was reputed to be a violent person but it was to be hoped that Tracey's talents, education and good sense would serve him well in the Assembly. He then informed his audience that he was a busy man and would not be taking any further part in the election.[23]

Supporters of the two Tory candidates were now in a quandary. As Mondelet may well have confirmed to them, Tracey had the strong backing of the Patriotes. To defeat him, the English party had to choose just one of its two candidates. Several meetings between the two sets of supporters ended inconclusively. Finally, negotiations began in earnest on the morning of Thursday, April 19, when a committee made up of six friends of each candidate met at Luckin's Hotel. After a short discussion, it was agreed to adjourn the meeting till the evening. The deliberations went on until late in the night but no decision was reached. Next morning the committee sat again with each candidate represented this time by twelve supporters. After a further prolonged discussion, the two sides remained deadlocked.

It was Phillips who eventually conceded defeat. His supporters announced that he was standing down in the interests of "the public good." In reality he had no choice. It was Bagg who was able to count on the more influential supporters of the likes of Horatio Gates, John Fisher, Alexis Laframboise, Pierre-Edouard Leclère, Jean-Baptiste Castonguay and Robert Armour Jr, the sort of people the *Montreal Gazette* liked to describe as "respectable Canadians." Phillips had bowed to the inevitable but the *Montreal Gazette* nevertheless praised his willingness to step aside. The paper also gave this warning to its readers: "To the electors of the West Ward, we have only to say, that if by their supineness, or by their indolence they permit Mr Tracey to be returned, upon their heads must fall all the discredit which cannot fail to be the consequence of such a result."[24]

In normal circumstances, Stanley Bagg would have been elected with no difficulty. The Bagg family originated from Durham, England, but had emigrated to the United States at the end of the eighteenth century. Stanley and his brother Abner had moved to Montreal in the early part of the nineteenth century and had become involved in a number of business ventures. Both had prospered as merchants and were prominent members of the Montreal business community. Abner owned a brewery at Laprairie while his brother was involved in the wheat and flour staple trade with the United States and had been associated with the founding of the City Bank of Montreal in 1831. In the early 1820s, along with Oliver Wait and Thomas Phillips, Stanley had been one of the principal contractors in the digging of the Lachine Canal. It is doubtful whether Montreal's Irish Catholic community held him in much affection.

In contrast to the Baggs, Tracey, despite the fame of the previous three months, was probably known to only a small proportion of the inhabitants of West Montreal. In an attempt to improve his profile among the electors of the constituency, he had towards the end of March moved the office of the *Vindicator* from St Lawrence Hill to the corner of Notre Dame and McGill. By late April, he realised that a more personal approach was needed.

To counter Mondelet's unflattering comments about him, Tracey disclosed certain details about his early life in Ireland. Orphaned at an early age, he had been raised by his maternal uncle, Daniel Manifold. He had later studied medicine at Trinity College Dublin where some of his former professors remembered him well as a very accomplished scholar. Tracey printed two of the references he had received from his alma mater. The one written by Professor Kennedy a few weeks before Tracey sailed for Quebec in April 1825 was particularly flattering: "I have always found him a person of a gentleman-like deportment and moral conduct—and that his literary character was one of very high respectability." [25]

The two candidates published their political manifestoes in the week leading up to the election. Tracey's was the longer and more detailed of the two. In content, it aimed at winning over the Irish and Patriote vote. For the benefit of both groups, Tracey concentrated on the strong links he had once had with Jocelyn Waller, the Irish editor of the pro-Patriote *Canadian Spectator* whose sudden death in 1828 had led to an outpouring of grief in Patriote circles. Tracey had been part of the great struggle of 1827 against Lord Dalhousie; he had been on the Constitutional Committee along with Waller and he had taken part in all the events connected with it at the time. Tracey's name had been among the first on the list of some 86,000 names attached to the petition of that year and it was Tracey who had drafted the petition presented to the House of Assembly by the citizens of Montreal in the James

Stuart affair. In a clear warning that his principal objective was political and not commercial, Tracey wrote: "The smallest inroad on the rights of the people, tolerated by the representative body, is a dereliction of duty towards the Constituents and the country. Only when these rights and liberties are secured will it be necessary to turn to other matters such as various improvements of the country and education." He pledged therefore that as a matter of policy he would, if elected, concentrate on three major questions: the Civil List, the composition of the Legislative Council and the proposed activities in Lower Canada of the British American Land Company.

Stanley Bagg, as befitting a candidate who was confident of victory, issued a manifesto that was as brief as it was vague. His appeal to the electors rested on the fact that he had been engaged in commercial pursuits in Montreal for some twenty-four years and that he was aware of the best interests of the country in relation to commerce, agriculture, internal improvements and political rights. Consequently, he pledged to promote the city's prosperity, the cause of education, the improvement of commerce, the extension of internal communications, the protection of religion and the liberty of conscience.[26]

On the eve of polling day, Tracey published a long editorial that expanded on the commitment he had given in his manifesto to oppose the plans of the British American Land Company. It was a grievance with which regular readers of the *Vindicator* were already familiar but it had clearly become the main plank of his electoral platform. The editorial spelled out in the clearest terms the extent of the territory that could fall into the hands of the speculators. The British government had at its disposal two large tracts of land, the Crown Reserves and the Clergy Reserves, amounting to a total of almost one million acres. If the government were to offer this land as an option to the land company without first submitting the matter to the province's legislature, it would prove that the local legislature was "a mere cypher (*sic*), of no power, weight or value—a bauble thrown to us, grown up colonial children, to tickle our ears, and to keep us in good humour." As for the argument that the scheme would be beneficial to the province by introducing capital and clearing and settling the new lands, Tracey expressed doubts over the land company's ability to accomplish what it was promising. He also suspected that the money raised would not be put to proper use. "Is it certain, we ask, that it will not be spent in pensioning more parasites, and in providing further for hungry dependants?" A comparison with the way funds from the Upper Canada Land Company had been appropriated, Tracey maintained, would offer some clue as to what would happen in Lower Canada:

> We cannot but fear that it will form the nucleus for a party whose wealth, power and influence may be sufficient to neutralize, if not to overpower, the efforts which are making (*sic*) at present, by the people to establish their constitutional rights on a firm footing; and we clearly foresee that the capital thereby introduced into the company will but serve as food for pensioned idlers and salaried sinecurists, whose chief recommendation has hitherto been their virulent opposition to the people's wishes.[27]

For many of the leading members of Montreal's commercial élite it was Tracey's pledge to oppose the British American Land Company that represented the greatest danger to their collective interests. Two merchants in particular, George Moffatt and Peter McGill, both of them legislative councillors, had been founding members in 1825 of the failed Lower

Canada Land Company, the forerunner of the new company. Tracey never lived to see the result of the company's huge land purchase but a list of its Canadian proprietors published in London in 1835 showed that some of Tracey's fiercest opponents must have viewed with alarm any attempt to sabotage the company's speculative venture. Among the names, were those of Samuel Gerrard, Benjamin Holmes, Peter McGill, Adam L. McNider, George Moffatt, John Molson, William Robertson, and Joseph Shuter, all of them Montreal magistrates and all of them responsible for policing the upcoming election contest between Tracey and Bagg.[28]

Later in 1838, during Lord Durham's time in Lower Canada, Charles Buller's inquiry into crown lands and immigration in British North America discovered the remarkable fact that just 105 individuals or families owned 1,404,500 acres outside of the seigniories as a result of the largesse of the provincial and imperial governments. Again some of the largest speculators were names that would have been all too familiar to Tracey: Sir John Caldwell of the Legislative Council (35,000 acres), Charles Ogden, the solicitor general (25,000 acres), Chief Justice Sewell (6,500 acres) and Stanley Bagg (4,000 acres).[29]

It is clear that the determined opposition to Tracey's candidature on the part of Legislative Councillors and magistrates had more than mere politics at its origin. Tracey's sworn promise to campaign actively against the plans of the British American Land Company placed in jeopardy the future economic development of the province and the vast profits that would accrue for those able to invest in the speculative venture. Bagg was not the only one who felt that Tracey had to be stopped at all costs.

For the time being, Tracey's immediate concern was the election itself. Fearing there might be trouble, he thought it

George Moffatt, a successful Montreal businessman, magistrate and member of the Legislative Council. He instituted criminal charges against Daniel Tracey and Ludger Duvernay in January 1832 for their remarks about the Council. He was on duty in the Place d'Armes on May 21 and called for military intervention. (McCord Museum – I-4703.0.1)

appropriate to remind the returning officer of his responsibilities as laid down in the law on elections in Lower Canada.
Every returning officer, the statute read, had the power and
authority to maintain and enforce order and keep the peace
at an election, "and if any person or persons shall commit
violence, or be engaged in any affray or riot, or be armed with
clubs, staves, or other offensive weapons, or wear or carry any
flag, ribbons, or cockade, or other badge or mark whatsoever,
to distinguish him or them as supporting any particular
candidate or candidates, or in anywise disturb the peace or
order at such election, or wilfully prevent or endeavour to
prevent any elector or person from coming to vote thereat, or
in anywise interrupt the poll" the returning officer had the
power to arrest, confine or commit to prison anyone who so
offended."[30] Over the coming weeks, it was to be the most
neglected law on the province's statute books.

3

The Heated West Ward Contest

The 1791 Constitutional Act had conferred on Lower Canada, though not intentionally, a political system that gave certain women the right to vote, a right unknown outside of British North America. Voting rights depended on property qualifications and as the act did not specifically disenfranchise women they enjoyed the same rights as men. The one restriction applied to women married under a regime of community of property—in such cases only the husband was entitled to vote.[1] Voting was a public affair. An election lasted as long as it took eligible voters to cast their votes, provided at least one vote was cast each hour until closing time each day. Electors had to announce the name of the candidate of their choice to the returning officer who then entered the vote and personal details of the elector into the poll book. Each candidate had the right to challenge an intending voter if it was suspected that he or she did not fulfil one or more of the requirements set down in the statutes. Five oaths were available to be administered to voters about whom doubts existed as to their age, their place of abode, their status as a property owner, their length of residency as a tenant or the possibility that they had received a financial inducement to vote.[2] The system was open to abuse and in a tightly fought campaign an official challenge could be used as a means of intimidating those wishing to vote for the other candidate. The West Ward election proved to be a prime example of such abuse.

The opening days

The opening formalities began on the morning of Wednesday, April 25 at the Hay Market, a large open space at the end of St James St. A large crowd had gathered as well as the two candidates and their close supporters. At precisely 11 o'clock, the returning officer, Hypolite Saint-George Dupré, a Montreal lawyer, read out in English and French the election writ and called on the electors to nominate a candidate to represent them. Bagg and Tracey were both proposed. Dupré then asked the two men whether they were willing to have the election decided on a show of hands, as the law allowed. Neither was willing. Whereupon, three electors stepped forward and asked that a poll be taken. Two of them, John Fisher and Pierre-Édouard Leclère, represented Bagg. The third man was Tracey's supporter, Édouard-Étienne Rodier. Dupré announced that voting would commence at 1 pm in the vestibule of the American Presbyterian church, situated at the corner of St James St and the Hay Market.[3]

In the time left to them before the first votes were cast, the candidates were allowed to address the assembled crowd. Wearing the medal he had received after his release from prison, Tracey spoke first but he was soon interrupted by a group of hecklers, many of whom appeared drunk. Tracey pressed on with his speech but he had great difficulty in making himself heard over the din. Only when one of the troublemakers was identified as Joseph Monferrand, the legendary boxer, did Tracey's supporters realise that a group of *fiers-à-bras* or bullies had turned out in force for the election.

The Montreal American Presbyterian Church at the northeast corner of St James St and McGill St across from the Hay Market. Voting took place in the vestibule during the first three days of the by-election. For the next five days, voting took place in the house at the back of the church. (McCord Museum – I-1555l)

Employing bullies during an election to intimidate and prevent electors from voting for one's opponent was commonplace in Montreal and Bagg appeared to have recruited between twenty and thirty of them. Standing next to Tracey were his principal legal advisors, Côme-Séraphin Cherrier and Louis Roy Portelance. As it appeared that the bullies were intent on drowning out Tracey's words, Cherrier appealed directly to Bagg to impose some order on the bullies. The appeal worked. Bagg intervened and Tracey was able to finish his speech with fewer interruptions. Bagg then addressed the crowd followed by his principal supporter, John Fisher, who translated Bagg's words into French.

The *Vindicator* later reported that Tracey had said that he bore Bagg no ill will but had insisted that the two men differed on questions of principle concerning the civil list, the Legislative Council and the new land company. Bagg for his part produced an amazing volte-face by claiming to be in large agreement with the Assembly on the question of the civil list and even on the reform of the Legislative Council but he had been careful to make no reference to the British American Land Company.[4] For Cherrier, the most worrying aspect of the disruption was the attitude of the returning officer. Dupré had clearly witnessed the incident but had made no attempt to intervene, Cherrier said later. It was an ominous sign since his inaction merely encouraged the trouble-makers, Cherrier added, and it convinced Tracey's supporters that Bagg had already won over Dupré to his side.[5]

When voting began, the bullies went into action, positioning themselves around the entrance to the church vestibule where Dupré and his assistant waited to record the first votes. Those electors who were known to be supporters of Tracey were threatened, jostled and even chased away from the polling sta-

Hypolite St George Dupré, a lawyer and the returning officer for the Montreal West by-election. He failed to impose his authority on the magistrates and drew criticism from all sides. (Service de la gestion de documents et des archives, Université de Montréal. Collection Louis-François-George Baby (P0058). 1FD00166. Dessin de Pierre-Hypolite St-Georges Dupré. 1834.)

tion before they were able to vote. The few who resisted were assaulted, some of them badly. At the earliest opportunity, the *Vindicator* gave more details of the organised violence: "a number of persons known in this city under the designation of bullies, apparently under the direction of a son of Austin Cuvillier MPP excited considerable disturbance and grossly ill treated some of our most respectable citizens, among whom was William Campbell who received a severe injury."[6]

The paper reported that the bullies, who had been paid ten shillings each for their services, had also badly injured John Brennan, an inn keeper and a Mr Carroll who remained in a critical state. The violence produced the required result. When polling finished for the day at 5:30 pm Bagg had taken an early lead having received seventy-three votes to Tracey's fifty.

Although the bullies had undoubtedly deterred a number of Tracey supporters from voting, nevertheless a certain pattern in the distribution of votes was already discernible. Thirty-one French Canadians had voted, twenty for Tracey and seven for Bagg. The Irish vote was also clear-cut: twenty-seven votes for Tracey and seven for Bagg. Four Americans had voted, three of them for Bagg. Fifty-four other voters were classed in the poll book as "other nationalities." Of these, Tracey had secured the support of just two. The first woman, Isabella McIntyre, had also turned up to vote but she was found to be ineligible on account of her marital status. The two candidates had also been active in challenging the eligibility of other voters. Bagg had objected to six Irishmen and to two French Canadians causing one Irishman and one French Canadian to withdraw without voting. Tracey had objected to two French Canadians, one of whom had withdrawn, and to three other "nationals," one of whom, an English labourer, had withdrawn.[7]

As the events of the day had shown, Tracey had been caught off guard by an opponent who had benefitted from the active support of Austin Cuvillier, an experienced fixer of elections. Some six months earlier, with the help of the same bullies, he had helped Dominique Mondelet win his Montreal seat in a by-election. Tracey called an emergency meeting of his advisers that evening to devise an appropriate riposte. They came up with a plan to meet force with force, a strategy made all the easier in view of the support Tracey could call upon in the Irish community.

Next morning, Thursday, April 26, Bagg's bullies returned to the Hay Market and positioned themselves once more close to the polling station. Tracey's people also turned up in large numbers and the inevitable clash took place. The returning officer recorded in the poll book that he was unable to open the polling station at the designated time of 10 am because of the disorderly scenes that were taking place outside. This time it was the bullies who came off worse and in particular, Bill Collins, reputedly one of the toughest of that group of rough-necks. Among the people who had turned out that day for Tracey was Montreal's strongest man, Antoine Voyer. When Collins attempted to repeat the same strong-arm tactics of the previous day, Voyer knocked him out cold. The blow was so strong in fact that many thought that Collins had been killed. A priest suddenly appeared from nowhere and pro-ceeded to baptise the unconscious bully. The combined efforts of Voyer and the unnamed priest were enough to send the terrified bullies scattering in all directions.[8]

The disorder had lasted twenty-five minutes but it had ended to Tracey's satisfaction. With calm restored, voting remained brisk and undisturbed all day. Tracey received seventy votes in contrast to Bagg's twenty-five. Tracey's sup-port that day had come mainly from French Canadians (44) but the Irish vote had remained firm (25). Bagg had once more relied on English and Scottish voters for the majority of his votes. In the absence of his hired bullies he had been forced to resort to the challenge as a means of intimidating the opposition. He raised objections to twenty-seven voters and was successful in barring just one: Mrs Collins, a widow, the only woman to turn up to vote that day.

After just two days it was still too early to forecast the final outcome but the city's conservative press remained quietly confident of victory. The *Montreal Gazette* carefully omitted any mention of Bagg's apparent last-minute support for a reform of the province's political structure but found space for a letter signed simply "A Merchant." In tone and content it was as vehement as the paper's own anti-Tracey editorials. Tracey was described as "almost a stranger in the Province; quite unknown to us (at least for any good quality) except as the Editor of a Newspaper, violent and rancourous (*sic*) in its politics, opposed to every measure, which does not meet the approbation of a kind of soi-disant Patriotes." An indication of the danger that Tracey represented for the business community came at the end of the letter in the form of a desperate rallying cry: "I would appeal to the commercial part of the community, and entreat of them, to use every effort which they constitutionally may, to effect the return of Mr Bagg."[9]

The second day of voting had not been to the liking of many of the magistrates. Cuvillier in particular was incensed. He called a court of special sessions of the peace for that evening to discuss what he termed a matter of great urgency.[10] Nine magistrates responded to the call. Cuvillier informed them that a serious disturbance was likely to arise in the vicinity of the poll and that he had received reports that certain people were arming themselves with clubs and other arms. Cuvillier offered no evidence for his allegations but the majority of those present were prepared to trust his judgment. All but one of them were Bagg supporters. Two of them, George Moffatt and Toussaint Pothier, were members of the Legislative Council. Also present were Moffatt's fellow harbour commissioner, Jules-Maurice Quesnel, Benjamin Holmes, the Dublin-born general manager of the Bank of Montreal, John Fisher, the former incumbent of the West Ward seat, and Scotsman Dr William Robertson. Robertson, the senior magistrate, was one of Montreal's leading citizens and was the owner of a large house on St James Street a short distance from the Place d'Armes. As a very young ensign with the 73rd Foot he had seen action during the 1798 Irish rebellion. He had then gone on to study medicine at Edinburgh University but left without completing his degree, preferring instead to continue his military career in British North America. He eventually served as a surgeon in the 41st Foot during the War of 1812 before being placed on half pay in Montreal. His current position was that of head of the medical faculty of McGill College.[11] Tracey's lone supporter was Joseph Roy, one of Montreal's most prominent merchants.

Cuvillier persuaded the magistrates to send for the returning officer. When Dupré eventually turned up, Cuvillier offered to provide him with assistance in the form of a large number of special constables. To the evident displeasure of the magistrates, Dupré declined their offer and returned home. Not to be outdone, the magistrates decided on their own initiative that they would swear in one hundred special constables regardless of the wishes of the returning officer.[12] Early next morning, the new constables were duly sworn in and were each supplied with a blue wooden stave as a mark of their authority. They were then ordered to march to the American church and to position themselves close to the poll. Tracey's immediate reaction when he saw them arrive was to protest to the returning officer and demand that they be kept well away from those intending to vote. This time Dupré had little choice in the matter. He ordered the specials to return to the court-house and to turn in their arms. Tracey was proved right. The rest of the day remained trouble-free. One woman turned up, an English widow by the name of Elizabeth Summers, who voted for Bagg. It was also another good day for Tracey who finished the day with a lead of forty-eight votes. The French Canadians were turning out in force for Tracey and the English and the Scots for Bagg.

Nevertheless, the sudden appearance of so many constables at an election clearly rankled with Tracey. He had recognised in their ranks the same bullies that Cuvillier had recruited in support of Dominique Mondelet's successful bid for his seat in the Assembly. He accused the magistrates of flouting the law and suggested that Dupré was partly to blame: "we may be permitted to question this *coup d'autorité*," he wrote in the *Vindicator*, "as it was not requested by the returning officer himself, who made no application to the magistrates for their aid, and whose authority is sufficiently extended if properly applied."[13] He also expressed astonishment at the decision to place the constables under the command of Horatio Gates, an American-born loyalist and undisputed leader of Montreal's merchant community. But it was downright provocation, he wrote, to have recruited Emmanuel-Xavier d'Aubreville and William Flynn to be at the head of the special constables, two of the principal bullies involved in the disruption of the poll and against whom warrants had been issued for assault.[14]

The d'Aubreville family was well known in Montreal. The head of the family, Louis-Nicolas-Emmanuel de Bigault d'Aubreville, had left France during the French Revolution and had eventually reached Montreal as an officer in a Swiss regiment sent to support British troops. In 1818 he had been appointed captain of the Montreal night watch that served as the city's police force under the supervision of a number of police magistrates and justices of the peace. The position eventually became too much of a burden for him and he was dismissed in October 1827 following a charge of drunkenness and neglect of duty. Even the support of the *Montreal Gazette* was of no avail to him. A month later, one of his sons, 21-year-old Emmanuel-Xavier, was in even more serious trouble when he and William Flynn were convicted of rioting and destroying the property of a young woman. Both were fined five pounds and d'Aubreville was also sentenced to a month in prison.[15] That incident had clearly not disqualified him in the eyes of certain magistrates for he was the first bully to be sworn in as a special constable on the second day of voting.[16]

The events of the first three days finally wore down the patience of the administrators of the American Presbyterian church. A request was made to the returning officer to find a new venue, and a house belonging to a member of the Donegani family at the back of the church and facing onto the Hay Market was designated as the new polling station. Before voting began at the new address, Dupré took the unusual step of writing to the magistrates at 6 am on the Saturday morning to request the presence at the poll of between 150 and 200 special constables under the orders of Benjamin Delisle, the high constable, to maintain order. Dupré specified that the majority should be either French Canadian or Irish and that in no case should any of the d'Aubrevilles be included in the numbers. He gave no hint that he was expecting trouble and there was no reference to past trouble justifying such a high number of special constables.[17]

The magistrates were called to a court of special sessions early that same morning to consider Dupré's request. The magistrates who had deliberated two days earlier were now joined by six others. Except for Pierre Lukin, they were all confirmed Bagg supporters. Two of their number, Jacques-Philippe Saveuse de Beaujeu and Pierre de Rastel de Rocheblave, were both members of the Legislative Council. One other, John Molson Sr, had only recently joined Stanley Bagg and a number of shareholders from New York State in founding the City Bank in Montreal. Over the previous two days, 130 special constables had been sworn in. The magistrates decided to add Montreal's four full-time constables and the night watchmen to their number and to send them all off to the poll with the high constable. As a precaution, they also decided to swear in an additional number of specials.

At the same court of special sessions, a man by the name of Pierre Jacques Beaudry came before the magistrates with an alarming tale to tell. He had been present the previous evening at a meeting during which he had heard La Fontaine and Cherrier propose taking over the polling station early the next morning and driving the special constables away if they turned up without a requisition from the returning officer. Coming so soon after Dupré's first official request for police help, Beaudry's allegations arrived at an opportune moment for the magistrates who made no attempt to investigate the matter further. The mere suspicion that trouble might occur was enough for them. As a precaution, they ordered Beaudry to provide a sworn affidavit at some future date.[18] Their fears however proved groundless. The day passed off peacefully with 149 people voting, the highest number to do so on any one day of the election. Twenty-three of them were women. By 5 pm Tracey's lead had increased to seventy-five.

The second week saw no great change in the pattern of voting. On three days, Bagg received more votes than his opponent but Tracey maintained his lead, even going ahead by eighty-nine votes on May 1, the biggest lead of the whole campaign. The *Montreal Gazette* attempted to reassure its readers by claiming that Bagg still had a number of votes in reserve and was confident of ultimate success. If their candidate was behind in the voting, the paper hinted, it was because of the intimidation his voters were forced to endure:

> The place of election has been for several days the scene of the most disgraceful riots and disturbances. Several of our most respectable citizens have been most violently assaulted, beaten and otherwise maltreated by a number of individuals who have no right of voting, many of whom have been supported all winter by the *Emigrant Society* and in the *Montreal General Hospital*. It is somewhat annoying to see these poor misguided people so far deficient in common gratitude to their benefactors, but they will no doubt experience in future, from the Patriotic benevolence of Mr Tracey and his partisans, more liberal support and attention than from those they are now opposing with disgraceful violence.[19]

The reference to emigrants was the *Gazette*'s coded term for the Irish whom it constantly blamed for much of the violence. Tracey admitted that some of Bagg's friends had been assaulted and he condemned the assaults unequivocally. But he also pointed out that his own supporters had been victims of assault at the hands of hired bullies who were being paid ten shillings a day by the party supporting his opponent.[20]

Voting was suspended on Friday, May 4, the date that the governor had decreed as a day of fasting and prayer in the hope of preventing the onset of a cholera epidemic in the province. The returning officer took advantage of a free day to organise yet another change of venue. The choice of the Donegani house on the Hay Market had proved unsuitable and fighting remained a constant problem in the neighbourhood. Early on Saturday, May 5 he wrote to the clerk of the peace informing him that voting would take place, beginning later that morning, in the fire engine office on the corner of St James St and the Place d'Armes. He added that in view of the various reports he had received of people being assaulted near to the previous polling station, he requested the magistrates to "adopt prompt and efficient measures for maintaining order, peace, and tranquility" in the area around the new venue.[21] The magistrates met in special session and ordered all the special constables and watchmen to assemble in the courthouse yard under the direction of two magistrates and the high constable.

The Place d'Armes

When voting began as usual at 10 am, the magistrates were shocked at how few special constables had turned up for duty. It was easy to understand, however. Instead of a simple three-day affair as in the recent East Ward by-election, the West Ward by-election was proving more troublesome and looked likely to last for at least another week if not longer. Many of the special constables had no stomach for the daily confrontations. The twenty who did show up as ordered took fright and refused to serve. Eighteen of them signed a petition protesting at their lack of numbers and presented it to the high constable.[22] Nevertheless, voting in the Place d'Armes passed off without incident. The number of people who voted was only slightly down compared to figures earlier in the week. Thirteen of the sixty-one people who voted were women. Over half had supported Tracey who now finished the week with a lead of sixty votes.

That evening, eleven magistrates attended the second court of special sessions of the day to discuss the implications of the constables' petition. After three hours of discussion, the magistrates came up with new proposals: the number of special constables should be increased to 250 men, of whom 150 would be stationed from the Monday onwards in front of the parish church of Notre Dame, on the opposite side of the Place d'Armes from the polling station. They would remain under the immediate orders of three magistrates and a similar force would assemble at sunset each evening to act as a night patrol.[23] This was by any standards an exaggerated response to Dupré's request for measures to maintain peace and tranquility and several magistrates came to that conclusion over the weekend. The special court reconvened on the Monday to adopt the measures in an atmosphere of some tension. When Robertson moved that the measures discussed earlier should be put into execution, William Charles Grant left the room before the voting began. Pierre Lukin, Joseph Roy and John Molson then voted against the motion.[24]

The presence of so many special constables in the Place d'Armes was just one of the problems preoccupying Tracey. His constant attendance at the election gave him other material on which to comment in his editorials. After the first five days of voting during which time well over six hundred people had cast their votes, Tracey was convinced that Bagg was deliberately intimidating his supporters by requiring needlessly the qualification oaths from the vast majority of them. He denounced the practice in an editorial.[25] The accusation brought an angry riposte from the *Montreal Gazette*. Mr Bagg was merely exercising a right conferred on him by the law, the paper said. But there was more: "The class of voters for Mr Tracey are not so notoriously entitled to the elective franchise, as to allow their vote being taken without discrimination—the appearance of the great majority is sufficient to cast doubt upon their claim." It was Tracey's reliance on the working class of Montreal that convinced the paper that he would not win the West Ward seat:

When all the riotous conduct of Mr Tracey's partisans is considered, the present feeble majority in his favour, gained as it has
been by force, is the best proof of the weakness of his cause, and
if he were possessed of the ordinary feelings of our nature, he
must feel how low he stands in public opinion, when he finds all
the intelligent, wealthy and influential inhabitants of Montreal,
whether Canadian, Irish, English, Scotch or American, with a
few exceptions, are ranged against him, and that he owes his
support to club law.[26]

When voting opened on Monday, May 7, Tracey had a lead
of sixty votes. Five days later, at the close of voting on Saturday,
May 12, Bagg had drawn level with him. The *Montreal Gazette*
continued its personal vendetta against Tracey and accused
him of harbouring "low radical designs." It even found an
unexpected ally in the person of one of Jocelyn Waller's sons
who issued a statement denying there had been any connection between his late father and Tracey other than a slight
acquaintance.[27] At the beginning of the election campaign,
Tracey had made much of the continuity of thought and
action that existed between him and the late editor of the
Canadian Spectator. This intervention by Jocelyn Waller of
the Royal Navy at such a crucial point in the election was
intended to embarrass Tracey and discredit him in the eyes
of his fellow countrymen. For good measure, the *Gazette* even
cast doubt on Tracey's medical qualifications and questioned
whether he was entitled to call himself a doctor.

Tracey refused to be drawn on the personal attacks, preferring instead to concentrate on what he denounced as the
systematic cheating on the part of his opponent's supporters.
The frustration and disillusionment he felt as his opponent
drew closer led him to question the very electoral system in
force in the province: "We have learned enough from this
election," he wrote, "to deprecate the whole system of the

elective franchise according to the present form; and certainly if anything stands in need of alteration, this system above all others demands it." As for the accusation that he was a radical and a supporter of revolution in Lower Canada, Tracey insisted that his strong opposition to the idea was well known. He was conscious of the advantages the inhabitants of the province enjoyed and he had no wish to change the situation. But the word "revolution" had more than one meaning: "if the *Gazette* means by 'revolution' an annihilation of the existing abuses, none will go further than we are disposed to do to have them done away with. Such 'low radical' designs we openly avow, and in the avowal we feel the utmost pride."[28]

After fifteen days of voting, 1266 votes had been registered. It was obvious to the candidates and their close supporters that the election was nearing its end. The poll list for the riding indicated that the vast majority of people eligible to vote had already done so. With Tracey and Bagg running neck and neck, tactics now became the order of the day. Each team had voters in reserve ready to be called out at a moment's notice whenever the returning officer's official announcement to close the election after an hour put its candidate in danger of losing the election. On Monday, May 14 first Bagg then Tracey called on their reserves to stay in the race as the total number of people who voted that day amounted to a mere twenty-two. By the end of the day, Tracey had pulled slightly ahead by two votes. It had been a day with its share of drama. A woman, one Charlotte Curote, had come to vote, Tracey reported in the *Vindicator*, and when asked for whom she had voted, she twice stated very distinctly that Tracey had been her choice. As she was about to depart, someone told her that she should have voted for Bagg. She then turned to the returning officer and told him she had changed her mind. Dupré erased her

name from the list of Tracey's voters as registered by the clerk
and transferred her vote to Bagg.[29] It was later discovered that
the woman was related to Dupré.

As the week progressed, the lead fluctuated between the
candidates. On the Tuesday, Tracey was in the lead by one
vote; the next day, the two men were tied; on the Thursday
Tracey regained the lead by five votes and by the end of voting
on the Friday, Bagg had the lead for only the second time in
the election. The lead was just one vote. The small number of
voters who now turned up at the poll were subjected to the
closest of scrutiny by both sides. Thus far into the election,
over 150 people had withdrawn without voting after being
challenged over their eligibility. Both sides were convinced
that certain individuals had perjured themselves and voted.
The *Montreal Gazette* reported that several of Tracey's voters
had been arrested for perjury but without naming them.[30]
Tracey admitted that two of his supporters, Sabrevois de
Bleury and John Donegani, had in fact been arrested but
wrote that he was confident that the two men would be exonerated. If his opponents were really interested in investigating
bribery and perjury, he continued, then they need look no
further than Horatio Gates whom Tracey accused of providing the funds to buy votes on behalf of Bagg.[31]

The law was not clear on some points of voting qualifications, Tracey conceded, and both sides were taking advantage
of the loopholes. However, in the case of a Mr Wells, owner
of a plot of land in St Anne's suburbs, Tracey said there was
a clear case of abuse:

> He caused to be nailed together a few boards, and put a chimney
> at the end of them, a week or two before he came to the poll. All
> this he was obliged to admit. Yet this *gentleman!* swore he had
> a lot of ground and *dwelling* house thereon, *six* calendar months
> before the date of the writ of the election! This man was cau-

tioned before he voted, and even had the law read to him. He said, however, it made no matter—he was ready to swear.[32]

Deception at the poll was not the only matter troubling Tracey. As the tension increased at the poll, so did the intimidation in the street. Tracey complained that the vicinity of Luckin's hotel represented a serious danger to his supporters. On Saturday, May 12, close to the hotel, one of his supporters, Michael Hughes, a tailor, had been confronted by a party of Bagg's friends, one of whom, a man by the name of McKenzie, had fired on him and wounded him in the arm.[33] Five days later, Rodier was attacked at night in the same place.[34] The most serious attack occurred, however, late in the evening of Friday, May 18. Returning home to St Joseph St (Saint-Sulpice) from a choir practice in the Récollet church between 9 pm and 10 pm, Charles Curran, a blacksmith, was hit in the legs, arms and body when a neighbour of his fired upon him with his blunderbuss from an upper window in St Joseph St.

The aggressor was Robert Cooke, a shoemaker by profession and, in the words of Jacques Viger, a "violent Orangeman." He had voted for Bagg on the opening day of the by-election and was among the first special constables brought into service the following day. He was not sworn in, however, until May 10 when Cuvillier administered the oath. It came out later that for several days before the attack on Curran, who had voted for Tracey on the opening day, Cooke had loaded a firearm saying that "he would have the life of one of those 'damned Tracey-men'." This time he had almost succeeded. Pierre Lukin ordered the night watch to arrest Cooke but after a fruitless search lasting over four hours, it was clear that Cooke had escaped.[35] He was arrested eventually some time later. After facing the grand jury in September, he was sent forward for trial.

When polling opened on Saturday, May 19 tension was running high. News of Cooke's attempt on the life of Curran spread quickly and reports indicated that the victim was close to death. Tracey received three votes in quick succession and took a two-vote lead. Suspecting that Bagg had few if any voters in reserve to keep the election open, Tracey requested the returning officer to read his proclamation. The designated hour was almost up when Susanna Holmes, wife of John McDonald, voted for Bagg. Again Tracey called for the proclamation. This time, two women came to Bagg's rescue: Marguerite Viger, a widow and Marie-Claire Perrault, Austin Cuvillier's wife. Bagg had regained the lead by one vote.[36]

The next two voters declared for Tracey: Thomas Horne, an Irish surveyor and Jacob Bigelow, an American merchant. At 1.32 pm, Dupré was again required to read the proclamation, the fifth time that day. Several minutes went by before Pierre Bibaud turned up and voted for Bagg, bringing the two candidates level again. Bibaud had no sooner voted than two other Bagg supporters, Pierre-Édouard Leclère and Matthew Campbell, suddenly joined him. All three asked Dupré to adjourn voting until the following Monday. Dupré later said that he allowed two minutes to go by before declaring the vote adjourned at precisely 1:45 pm, the time recorded in the poll book.[37]

There was consternation in the Tracey camp. The poll had closed over three hours earlier than usual despite the fact that Tracey had supporters waiting to vote. A heated discussion began between Dupré and a very angry Tracey. John Donegani intervened saying that he and several other electors were waiting to vote. Pierre Auger from the office of the clerk of the peace then turned up and insisted that his vote be taken. Dupré told the two men that they were too late and that polling had finished for the day. Three electors had requested an adjournment as the law stipulated, he told the protestors, and that left him no option but to obey.

The slow response of Bagg's supporters to cast their votes during the course of the morning had created an expectation in the Tracey camp that its candidate was on the verge of being elected. When word reached Tracey's supporters outside the polling station that their expected victory had suddenly been snatched from them, there was an explosion of fury. One irate Irishman rushed into the room where Dupré was presiding and remonstrated with him. Worried lest they lose control of the situation, Tracey, Cherrier and La Fontaine went outside and addressed the crowd. Tracey described the returning officer's action as an act of injustice directed against him personally and he called on all Irishmen to unite in demanding justice. Cherrier reiterated Tracey's words and said that Dupré's decision to adjourn voting for the day had been illegal but they were obliged to abide by it. Finally, La Fontaine prevailed upon the crowd to disperse peacefully but urged them to return in large numbers on the following Monday morning.[38]

Dupré was in a state of panic. The reaction of the crowd and his face to face with the Irishman had produced his most frightening experience of the election. There still remained the Sunday for tempers to cool but Tracey was keeping Cooke's attack on Curran to the forefront of people's minds much to the displeasure of the English party. The *Montreal Gazette* was particularly incensed at Tracey's tactics: "An infamous Bill from the Vindicator office," it wrote in its next edition, "calling Cooke a murderer has been posted round town, with no other tendency than to excite the people to riot."[39] Dupré had no confidence in his own ability to control what might turn out to be another explosive situation when polling recommenced on the Monday morning. As a further complication, Tracey had refused to agree to the usual 10 am opening of the polling station. The new time would have to be much earlier.

By the Saturday evening Dupré had decided that a show of strength on the part of the magistrates and constables was the only solution. He wrote to the clerk of the peace informing him that polling would open at 8 am on the Monday and that he required a strong presence of constables to be in position by that time. The next day, Sunday, three magistrates, Rocheblave, Masson and Holmes, considered Dupré's request and were only too happy to accede to it. They issued an order for the constables to assemble next morning at 7:30 am.

Meanwhile, Dupré came under new pressure when he received a letter dated May 20 and signed by Bagg, Pierre Bibaud, Charles T. Greece, William Ryan and Pierre-Édouard Leclère. The contents were designed to increase the returning officer's alarm:

> In consequence of the acts of violence committed yesterday at the poll, and of the *certain* information which we have received from Captain Spence (*sic*), who lives opposite to Mr Tracey, that Mr Tracey intends to place himself to-morrow at the head of a numerous party of persons disposed to commit the most violent outrages, we find ourselves under the necessity of calling on you to take the measures necessary for our protection.[40]

The letter called for an imposing force of constables to be sent to the Place d'Armes otherwise lives would be in danger. For good measure, the authors of the letter added: "It is even currently reported in this city, and the opinion of all the respectable persons who support Mr Bagg, that greater attempts at violences will be made to-morrow, than have yet been made since the commencement of the election."

The accusations were as flimsy as those contained in the anonymous letters sent to the garrison the previous February when Tracey and Duvernay were in prison. The final sentence even suggested some collusion between the magistrates and the signatories to the letter: "In case you should deem it necessary to call a meeting of the Magistrates, we are ready to testify on oath to the insulting manner in which you have yourself been treated by Mr Tracey, and there is no doubt that they will be ready to employ all the means which the Law has placed at their disposal, to support you in the exercise of your functions." What should have alerted Dupré, the lawyer, to the vacuous nature of the letter was the fact Bagg and his four supporters were prepared to testify on oath only to Tracey's "insulting manner," hardly a matter requiring the combined attention of all the magistrates.

Encouraged by what he took to be Bagg's sympathy with his plight, Dupré decided to communicate once more with the magistrates, including as a form of justification his own version of what had happened the previous day at the polling station:

> Having, yesterday evening, refused to submit to the pleasure of Mr Tracey and his partisans in my interpretation of the law, a tumult was the consequence and I was very near being attacked, as the high constable who was present can inform you. Mr Tracey himself insulted me as a public officer, and threatened to compel me by force to do what he wished, as did also an Irishman who leaped into the Poll room.

In reference to the letter he had received, Dupré repeated his earlier fear that it would be impossible to continue the election unless he had a sufficient number of constables in the poll room armed with their staves and led by at least one or two magistrates.

At 7 pm that same evening, eleven magistrates met in special session to consider Dupré's two letters. The meeting quickly decided to send seventy-five constables to the polling station the next morning with the high constable, to position a hundred constables under the command of two magistrates in front of the parish church, and to have the watchmen in attendance all day. Moffatt and Masson were required to be on duty in the morning, and Holmes and Lukin in the afternoon. For some of the magistrates, stronger measures were needed: nothing less than military assistance. It was a controversial suggestion since the returning officer had made no such request and no attempt had been made to verify Captain Spencer's information. Two of the magistrates, Joseph Roy and Pierre Lukin, both of them Tracey supporters, objected to any interference by the army but the mood of the meeting was against them. Roy refused to have anything more to do with the meeting and went off home. A motion was then put to the remaining magistrates: that the commandant of the local garrison be requested to reinforce the main guard with a company of the 15th Foot under the command of a captain and to hold himself in readiness to act when required to do so by a magistrate "for the purpose of aiding the civil power in suppressing any riot which may arise in consequence of the election." All except Lukin voted in favour. Robertson and Moffatt were then delegated to call upon the commandant and communicate the magistrates' wishes in person.[41]

The two magistrates arrived at the garrison at 10:30 pm and put their request to the commandant, Lieutenant Colonel Alexander F. Macintosh. The 37-year-old officer, whose introduction to army life had been the Peninsular War against Napoleon on the Iberian Peninsula under Wellington, needed little persuasion.[42] He told them that a captain's guard, consisting of a captain, a subaltern, a sergeant, a bugler and forty-two rank and file, would replace the usual main guard at the head of the New Market next morning. If the need arose, he reassured them, the rest of the regiment would be ready to turn out at a moment's notice. The magistrates on their own initiative had effectively—and ominously—placed the city of Montreal under military control.

4

The Polls Close…
and the Troops Open Fire

On Monday, May 21, Montreal woke up to find that the rain that had fallen over the weekend was continuing unabated. On the Place d'Armes, some fifty people had already gathered when polling opened at 8 am. Numbers then gradually increased as workmen and other labourers made idle by the persistent rain turned up in the square. For the first hour, voting was brisk. Pierre Auger who had been prevented from voting two days earlier was the first to register his vote. By 9 am Tracey was in the lead by five votes and the returning officer had made his first proclamation of the day. Tracey's hopes that Bagg was unable to muster fresh support were dashed when at 9:46 farmer James Watson turned up and voted for Bagg. Over the next four hours, the proclamation was read five times but each time Bagg received a vote and stayed in the race. Despite the fears of the returning officer and the magistrates, the morning passed off calmly without a single incident being reported.[1]

The Riot Act

The afternoon might well have remained as peaceful as the morning had it not been for a minor incident that escalated into something more serious in mid-afternoon. At around 2:45 pm, Dieudonné Perrin, a Bagg supporter and one of the many special constables who had been sworn in on April 27, completed his business in the bank on St James St and set off across the Place d'Armes in the pouring rain. As he neared the enclosure wall of the parish church, he spotted a fellow merchant, John Jordan, a Tracey supporter, coming in the opposite direction. For reasons that were not immediately apparent, Perrin traded insults with Jordan and then struck and damaged Jordan's umbrella with his own. Three Irishmen who were standing nearby overheard Perrin insulting Tracey and intervened. The quarrel quickly attracted the attention of some special constables nearby who intervened and put an end to the fray. A general skirmish then ensued. The two magistrates on duty, Robertson and Lukin, arrived on the scene together with some of Tracey's friends and managed to restore order. The incident had lasted barely ten minutes.[2]

John Fisher, however, had observed the incident from some distance away and had concluded that the planned violence by Tracey and his supporters had begun. Without consulting his fellow magistrates, Fisher took it upon himself to fetch the military detachment stationed at the New Market. Captain Henry Temple reacted immediately to the summons and arrived on the Place d'Armes with his men around 3 pm. Surprised as anyone by the presence of troops on the square, Robertson and Lukin approached them. Temple informed them that if they required military assistance they would have to provide a written requisition signed by both of them. The two magistrates could easily have declined his offer and ordered him to return to the New Market on the grounds that his troops were not needed. Instead, they handed Temple a signed document that read: "Sir, We require that you advance with the picquet under your orders to the Place d'Armes for the purpose of aiding the civil power to maintain the public peace of the city."[3]

In the meantime, Macintosh had arrived in the square to assess the situation. Many in the crowd were angry at the sight of troops so close to the polling station and it appeared to Macintosh that trouble was brewing. Robertson and Temple were deep in conversation when Macintosh approached them. Robertson told him that the only way he could deal with the volatile situation in the Place d'Armes was by reading the Riot Act. With that, he headed off in the direction of the polling station with his copy of the provincial statutes tucked under his arm. It was about 3:15 pm. A short while later, he returned and told the officers that the Riot Act was in force.[4]

According to the act, once the declaration had been read, those guilty of "riotous assembly" had one hour to disperse and return to their homes. Failing that, the magistrate could if necessary call for military backup to enforce the order. Was a riot in progress in the Place d'Armes? The subsequent behaviour of Robertson and Macintosh suggested that such was not the case. Neither appeared concerned by the large crowd still milling about in the Place d'Armes seemingly oblivious to the obligation they were under to disperse. Macintosh's only concern was with reinforcing the troops already present. Robertson agreed that some were needed and a short while later, the Light Infantry Company arrived from the Champ de Mars under the command of Captain Smith. Heavy rain continued to fall prompting Macintosh to order the troops to shelter under the porch of the parish church. No attempt was made to disperse the people already present in the square. And no one thought to inform the returning officer.

There had been little activity at the polling station during the various incidents on the Place d'Armes. A married woman, Sarah Wurtele, had registered her vote at 1:36 pm and at 1:49 pm Dupré had read his proclamation. Ten minutes later, Dr Timoléon Quesnel had arrived to vote and Bagg called for him to take the property oath. Bagg was trailing by one vote and Quesnel was not known as a supporter of the Patriotes. Quesnel stated that his property adjoined that of Horatio Gates but he declined to take the oath and left without voting. The next vote to be recorded was at 3:34 pm when Margaret Louisa Hoyle, a widow, voted for Bagg.[5]

No vote had been recorded for almost two hours and more than one hour had elapsed since the proclamation had been read. Dupré should have declared the election over and Tracey the victor, but minds had been distracted by the appearance of the troops.

Tracey received the next vote and moved back into the lead. Then Dr Quesnel turned up again but this time it was Tracey who raised an objection. Quesnel took the property oath and voted for Bagg. It was the last vote that Bagg was to receive in the election. The next to arrive was Josephta Latrémouille, a married woman, who declared in favour of Tracey. At 3:52 pm Dupré read the proclamation for the seventh time that day. Two minutes later Tracey received two more votes. The timing of these votes is significant. Two women and four men had turned up to vote less than twenty minutes after a riot had supposedly broken out, one so serious that a magistrate had felt the need to read the Riot Act.

Bagg had no more voters in reserve. Fearing the returning officer might read his declaration once again with just over one hour left before the poll closed, he tried a new ploy. At exactly

4 pm, Abner Bagg, Pierre-Édouard Leclère and Thomas Barron approached Dupré and requested an adjournment on the grounds that the poll had been open for eight hours. Not daring to risk another explosion of anger on the part of Tracey's supporters, Dupré refused their request—Bagg had survived but only just.[6] The poll closed at 5 o'clock with Tracey three votes in the lead. This time his supporters were jubilant. He still had voters in reserve while Bagg once more had resorted to dubious tactics in order to keep his hopes alive.

New incidents

In the Place d'Armes the two sets of supporters gathered close to the polling station, as they did each evening, ready to greet their respective candidates and escort them home. As usual, the order of departure was decided after intense discussion. This time, it was decided that Tracey would leave first. Normally, Tracey would have emerged into the Place d'Armes via a small opening in the fence that the returning officer had erected in front of the polling station and the Fabrique and then turned right in the direction of St James St. However, as he emerged flanked by his closest advisers, he ignored the opening in the fence and chose to turn left and walk inside the fence as far as the exit opposite Henderson's liquor store, the unofficial meeting place for Bagg's supporters and many of the special constables. Was this an act of provocation or simply a move forced upon him because the gap in the fence was impassable as a result of the rain that had fallen over the weekend and all day? For the demoralised special constables assembled in front of Henderson's store, there was no doubt in their minds. There was some pushing and shoving between the two groups as Tracey's party moved out into the square and then headed back towards St James St.

Bagg allowed Tracey's group time to clear the Place d'Armes before emerging with his supporters. In the square a small group of young men that had detached itself from Tracey's main party and had remained behind close to the polling station began to chant Tracey's name. Their premature celebration was noisy and good-humoured. But for some of the constables it represented an added act of provocation. Brandishing their staves, they charged the small group of revellers and began clubbing one of them. Some of his companions managed to escape and attract the attention of the tail end of Tracey's party which went back to investigate. The solitary victim, later identified as William Creed, an Irishman and a carpenter, had received a severe beating and his body lay prostrate on the ground. Shouts rang out for the main body of Tracey's group now heading along St James St to return to the square and rescue those under attack. A number of them did so. Recent work to lay down macadam in the street had left a plentiful supply of stones lying about. The constables suddenly found themselves under attack and the target of a hail of stones thrown by the Tracey group. The constables responded at first by throwing the stones back at their attackers but realizing they were outnumbered decided to beat a swift retreat. Some gained access to Henderson's store while others ran off to the safety of the enclosure wall in front of the parish church.

The magistrates on duty behind the wall had their first inkling of trouble when the sound of stones striking the windows and metal shutters of Henderson's store resounded across the square. Moments later the special constables who had failed to gain access to Henderson's reached the enclosure gates. Following close behind were two very frightened magistrates. Joseph Shuter could be heard shouting that people were being murdered and that property was being destroyed.

"Bring out the troops," he yelled. George Moffatt who only minutes earlier had taken a group of special constables to investigate the trouble was also in full retreat and gesticulating wildly. Robertson concluded that nothing less than a full-scale riot was in progress. He turned to Macintosh and requested him to bring out the troops. Macintosh responded by ordering muskets to be loaded. The troops then formed a column of two divisions and marched out into the Place d'Armes.[7]

The stone throwing in front of Henderson's store had ended after just a few minutes. Once the special constables and magistrates had disappeared from view, most of the stone throwers began heading back along St James St. La Fontaine had also come back and had persuaded the few remaining stragglers to return with him and rejoin the main Tracey group which by now had reached the Hay Market. The troops meanwhile had advanced to the north-east corner of the Place d'Armes and had come to a halt outside Dr Arnoldi's house at the corner of St Joseph St and Little St James St, just twenty yards or so from Henderson's store. From there, Macintosh had a clear view as far as the Bank of Montreal. There was no trouble to be seen and apart from a few bystanders who had collected at Dillon's corner, the Place d'Armes was almost deserted. If Macintosh believed that the Riot Act was still in force two hours after it had been read, he was able to see that the crowd had finally dispersed and that there was no further need for military involvement. He could have ordered the troops to return to barracks but indecision ruled the day.

Suddenly, on the other side of the square, the special constables who had earlier sought refuge inside the church enclosure but now reinforced by a large group of Bagg supporters were seen running in the direction of St James St. At their head was a magistrate, Joseph Shuter. Macintosh immediately ordered his men to advance to the entrance of St James St but they were too late to cut off Shuter and his men who were in hot pursuit of those who had stoned and humiliated them just minutes earlier.

Vengeance was now uppermost in the minds of the pursuers. Magistrates, special constables and Bagg supporters all joined in throwing stones at the last group of Tracey supporters who were heading away in the direction of the Hay Market to the west. Some of the latter turned about and threw stones back at their attackers but the sudden appearance of the troops behind the attackers changed the situation and added further to the confusion. Mere bystanders who were caught up in the confrontation ran off along St François-Xavier St in both directions. The troops came to a halt outside the Methodist church at the corner of St James and St François-Xavier streets and were then ordered to advance another seventy-five yards (about seventy metres) until they drew level with Dr Robertson's house. Stones continued to be thrown by both sides though how many people were actually involved at this point became a point of contention in the days and weeks that followed.

Macintosh and some of the magistrates later claimed that they advanced at different times towards the crowd and attempted to persuade it to disperse, threatening that otherwise the troops would open fire. How Macintosh and the magistrates managed to avoid injury when confronting a stone-throwing crowd was never explained. None of them ever reported an injury in later affidavits. At some point, but no later than ten short minutes since the troops had emerged from under the portico of the parish church, Robertson turned to Macintosh and told him to do his duty. Without further ado, the officer ordered the troops to open fire. Less than one round from the first division, according to

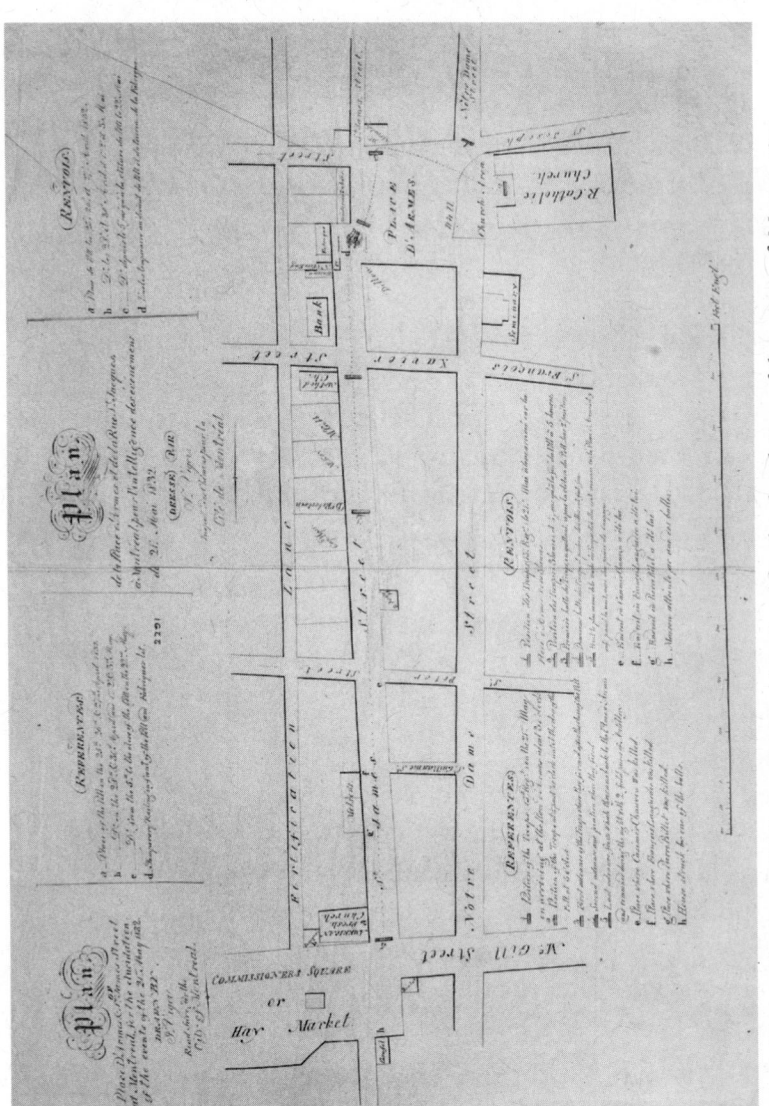

Plan of Place d'Armes and St James Street at Montreal for the elucidation of the events of May 21, 1832. Drawn with a keen sense of detail by Jacques Viger, road surveyor for the City of Montreal, and future mayor of Montreal. (See pages 301 and 304 for close-ups of St James St.) (McCord Museum – M2291-P1)

Macintosh, was discharged.[8] Three men fell, mortally wounded. All were standing some considerable distance away. Casimir Chauvin, an apprentice printer, fell at the corner of St James St and St Peter St, François Languedoc, a carpenter, died opposite St Guillaume St and Pierre Billet, a shingle maker, was killed between the Molson house and the American Presbyterian church, respectively about 125, 185 and 256 yards away from the troops.

As Macintosh and the troops continued their advance to the end of the street, people came to the aid of a number of people who had received bullet wounds. Philippe Groulx and Charles Mongras had both been wounded in the thigh. A Mr Voyer had part of his upper lip shot away and a Mr Dubé was hit in the shoulder.[9] Meanwhile, at the corner of St James St and the Hay Market, Macintosh had drawn the troops up in a line across the street in a defiant show of strength but by then the crowd had long dispersed.

First reactions

There was stupefaction among Tracey's supporters. None of them had imagined that the army would ever use real ammunition against a crowd. It quickly became known that the three victims had had no direct involvement with the election and were in the street at the time of the shooting by pure chance. François Languedoc had arrived in the street only minutes before he was struck. Pierre Billet, a carpenter, had been returning home after working all day and was carrying a few pieces of wood when the single lead ball struck him. Both men were married and in their late fifties. The third victim, Casimir Chauvin, a young man aged about twenty, the only one to have a connection to Tracey, was a printer in the *Vindicator* office. The only support of an elderly mother, as the newspapers later recounted, he had left home a mere ten minutes before being shot through the head.[10] Their bodies remained lying in the street while people ran off to inform the coroner.

The coroner immediately sent word to Benjamin Delisle, the high constable, to assemble a jury of twelve men ready to begin sitting that same evening. He also gave instructions for the bodies to be brought to the Place d'Armes. It was at this point that someone thought to inform Papineau. He had held one of the West Ward seats since 1814 but unlike John Fisher, he had played no active part in the election and had refused to endorse publicly either candidate. He had not even been aware that troops had been called out earlier that afternoon. Several of his friends went to his home and begged him to attend the inquest. Papineau arrived at the Place d'Armes shortly before 7 pm at the same time as the coroner. Already assembled there were Sabrevois de Bleury, Cherrier and La Fontaine in a group of some thirty people. A short distance away, Macintosh was standing with his military detachment. Sabrevois de Bleury suggested to Papineau that they ask the officer on whose orders he had opened fire. Papineau replied that Macintosh would refuse to reply. He would be well advised to tell us, answered Sabrevois de Bleury, and with that he walked over to Macintosh and asked him bluntly:

— Colonel, will you allow me ask by what order the troops have fired on the people?

— I might be inclined to answer if you were not followed by so many and such people, he replied.

Sabrevois asked those around him to move away and then put the question to him again, adding:

— It is for your own sake and for the ends of justice that I renew the question.

— Gentlemen, I will not answer but to superior military authority.

The arrival of two pieces of artillery from Île Sainte-Hélène put an end to the conversation. The troops were still on edge reacting aggressively towards bystanders who came too close to them.

A short time later, the high constable arrived with just nine jurors. The rain was still falling and it was growing dark. The coroner announced that it was now too late to begin the inquest and that he preferred to adjourn proceedings until 9 am next morning. Papineau spoke to him saying the three deaths were not some ordinary suicide or drowning cases but rather a matter of some political importance, that it was essential that the coroner ensure that the jury members were impartial. The coroner turned to the chief constable and said that he hoped that that would be his practice. He then had the bodies taken inside the small chapel adjoining the Fabrique to await the opening of the inquest.[11]

The magistrates

Three of the magistrates who had witnessed the shooting, George Moffatt, Pierre Lukin and Benjamin Holmes, had earlier hurried back to the court house and held a short meeting to decide on their next move. The time was 6 pm, barely forty minutes after the shooting. Their primary responsibility was the maintenance of law and order but the military intervention had proved the inadequacy of their efforts. Their only option was to summon the other magistrates for what they termed "business of pressing importance." At 7 pm fifteen magistrates assembled in their room at the court house. Among them was André Jobin, a committed Patriote, who had been absent from Montreal for most of the election. The most significant absentee, however, was the chief magistrate, Dr William Robertson.

St James St, Montreal, looking west where the three bystanders were killed. The first building on the right is the Bank of Montreal. The next is the Wesleyan Church. Dr Robertson's house is the third one after the church. (John Murray, 1843-44. McCord Museum – M970.67.21)

Security was the only item on the agenda. Joseph Masson proposed that the garrison commander provide a strong piquet to patrol the streets during the night with the support of a mounted section supplied by Major Gregory and suggested that three magistrates should be in attendance. Roy and Jobin expressed their strong disapproval of the motion, arguing that such measures far from preserving the lives and property of their fellow citizens might actually have the opposite effect, especially since the election was not yet over. Cuvillier proposed that the election should be closed forthwith. Moffatt advised caution and suggested that they consult legal counsel, adding as an afterthought that it might also be advisable to send for Dupré.

The first to arrive was Stephen Sewell KC (King's Counsel), brother of the Chief Justice and one of Montreal's leading jurists. He was also a committed supporter of the English party and a man known to harbour anti-French sentiments. On this occasion he was of little help to Cuvillier. Cuvillier pleaded that if the election were allowed to continue it would pose an immediate danger to the city. Sewell answered that on purely legal grounds he could not agree with the motion: neither the magistrates nor the returning officer had the right to stop the proceedings.

When Dupré arrived, Cuvillier asked him whether he thought he could continue with the election after all that had happened that day. Dupré replied that his first reaction had been similar to Cuvillier's but that on reflection he did not think that it was possible to discontinue an election. Cuvillier then offered to provide him with a force of special constables but Dupré replied, "Gentlemen, I know that will do more harm than good." All he needed, he told the magistrates, was just one magistrate to accompany him the next morning to the poll and to remain with him for as long as it was necessary. He suggested the name of Joseph Roy. "I think it would be better than any force," he said. For once, Dupré had shown some mettle in the face of the combined authority of the magistrates but it had come too late. Roy said that he was willing to volunteer provided there were a second magistrate with him and that they go not as magistrates but as ordinary citizens who simply wanted a peaceful end to the election. Jobin agreed to be the second magistrate.

Cuvillier was still dissatisfied. He attempted to persuade the two magistrates to accept the services of his special constables but again Roy refused. "But the constables will remain under the portico of Notre Dame," Cuvillier assured him. No, retorted Roy. It would be too dangerous if they were seen standing in the very place where the troops had waited all afternoon. Far better if they were not seen at all. At this point, Dupré intervened and tentatively suggested that perhaps five or six constables might prove useful after all at the poll, but Roy would not hear of it. That would just be another irritant for the people who turned up to vote, he told Dupré. Don't forget, he continued, that there are three bodies lying at the door of the polling station where the Coroner's inquest is to take place tomorrow morning. "I will only go," Roy said, "on condition that none of the people involved previously in maintaining order show their faces." Dupré told the meeting that the plan might just work but he asked that some constables be kept in readiness just in case. After he left, Louis Malo, a constable and well-known troublemaker, came in and reported that there had been talk in the Place d'Armes earlier that day that an attempt would be made to set fire to the town. However, news that Macintosh had sent for a unit of the Royal Artillery and two six-pounders from the garrison on Île Sainte-Hélène to be positioned close to the Fabrique and Henderson's store and covered by the Light Company of the

15th was sufficient to calm the nerves of the majority of the magistrates.[12]

Victory

Throughout the night the streets of Montreal were patrolled by a party of the Montreal cavalry under Major Gregory and all remained calm. By 6 o'clock next morning, the cannon had been withdrawn and the troops had returned to their garrison. Two hours later the poll opened. It was later reported that some three hundred people turned up to witness the final moments of the election. Dupré sent word that he was sick and was unable to attend. His poll clerk, Etienne Guy, deputized for him. Stanley Bagg also failed to turn up. Instead his brother Abner accompanied by two public notaries arrived. They informed Guy that Bagg had decided to withdraw from the election for reasons that were set down in a document they had brought with them. The news was of little interest to Tracey. He was leading by three votes and had more people waiting to vote for him. First in line was Joseph Roy, the magistrate. The poll clerk registered the vote and then announced that there was little point in taking any others. Following the usual procedure he read the proclamation. One hour later, at 9:15 exactly, he declared the poll closed and announced that Tracey had been elected by 690 votes to 687 to represent Montreal West in the Assembly.

Tracey addressed the crowd outside and thanked them for their support. He spoke about the three deaths, singling out Chauvin for special mention: the young man had been in his employ and had been an excellent worker. La Fontaine cautioned the crowd against any public display of rejoicing as they escorted Tracey to his home. They were in a period of mourning but if they wished to express the horror they all felt at the killings, they should all attend the funerals that would soon take place for the three victims. With that, Tracey, La Fontaine, Cherrier and Rodier set off for the St Antoine suburbs followed by a huge crowd that walked behind them in silence.[13]

Bagg's decision to withdraw from the contest rather than concede defeat was an attempt to salvage some honour from what had been the most violent election in the history of Lower Canada. He was also determined to pin all the blame for what had happened on Tracey and his followers. The announcement of his withdrawal had come in the form of a statement issued by two public notaries, H. Griffin and G.D. Arnoldi on behalf of Stanley and Abner Bagg, Pierre-Édouard Leclère and Benjamin Hall. Tracey was accused of having resorted to "divers illegal means" in order to be elected. These were itemised as organising people to vote for him who were not legally qualified to do so, intimidating Bagg's electors and preventing them from casting their votes, and "apparently by connivance and premeditation" as evidenced by his supposed rallying calls on the previous Saturday and Sunday, assembling a large body of people at the polling station that resulted in an affray, a riot and the intervention of the military. This had prevented Bagg's electors still in reserve, and in his opinion more than sufficient to ensure his election, from coming forward. Bagg had no option but to retire from the contest. But as the returning officer had refused to close the poll at 4 pm the previous afternoon as requested by three electors when the votes were equal, the statement concluded, Tracey could not be considered the free choice of a majority of the electors of the ward.[14]

For all its bluster, Bagg's statement lacked any real substance. Accusations of intimidation and of perjury by voters had been made regularly by the two rival camps during the election. The claim that Tracey had incited his supporters in speeches over the previous weekend had come from the magistrates and was based on dubious sources. The final objection that the returning officer's refusal to close the poll at 4 pm had invalidated the election was based on a misunderstanding of the statutes governing elections in the province. It was true that by 4 pm the previous day, the poll had been open for eight hours, longer than on any other day but this was perfectly legal. The relevant statute stated that the returning officer was "required to keep the Poll at every Election open eight hours at least in each day subsequently to the first day of Election, between eight of the clock in the morning and five of the clock in the afternoon, unless otherwise determined by the unanimous consent of the Candidates, or their Representatives."[15] The returning officer had acted properly and no doubt wisely in refusing to close the poll before the usual time of 5 pm.

The election figures

The election had produced a very narrow victory for Tracey, one that highlighted the deep divisions that existed both in the French Canadian and Irish communities. Voting had taken place on twenty-three days and 1533 men and women had turned up to register their votes, some on more than one occasion. Altogether, 155 individuals, twenty-six of whom were women, had been refused or had withdrawn when challenged on some aspect of their eligibility. Nevertheless, 199 women had voted and their votes had been crucial.

Tracey owed his victory to the strong turn out of French Canadian and Irish voters. The call by Patriote leaders for French Canadians to place their trust in an Irish candidate had borne fruit and 500 of them had voted for Tracey. It was a cause for concern, however, that ninety-three French

Canadians had opted for Bagg. Jacques Viger referred to them as traitors when he drew up his own personal summary of the election. The vast majority of the 210 Irish votes registered had gone to Tracey with just sixty in favour of Bagg. Tracey, however, had made little impression on the other two ethnic categories. Just eleven Americans and thirty other 'nationals' had given him their support.

Bagg had managed a more even balance in his support from the various ethnic groups. Almost two-thirds of his votes (428) had come from other nationalities, mainly English and Scottish, and in receiving 106 American votes Bagg had almost achieved a clean sweep of that section of the electorate. When the voting figures are analysed according to the number of property owners (730) and tenants (648) who took part in the election, there are some surprises. It was Tracey who garnered most of the property votes (440) but only just over one third of the tenant votes.[16]

Tracey's reaction

Tracey was in no mood to celebrate. Having been escorted back to the offices of the *Vindicator* by a sombre group of supporters, he spent the rest of the morning preparing his paper's Tuesday edition. In his editorial headed "Horrible Massacre!!" he gave vent to the strongest condemnation of his journalistic career: "Canada has just now to witness the most foul and barbarous murder of several of her citizens! and Montreal is to become no less famous than Manchester, in the annals of military despotism, outrage and assassination." There was no doubt in his mind who was responsible for the deaths: "The Magistrates have become partizans (*sic*) from the commencement, and to this may be attributed almost all the evils which spring from the contest. They have lost sight of their public duties in gratifying private resentments; and in giving their support as they have done, no justice can be expected at their hands."

There were equally harsh words for the returning officer who was blamed for his lack of firmness. But the strongest language was reserved for the party that had hoped to take the Montreal West seat: "A desperate faction, resorting to every foul and base means to accomplish its ends finds itself foiled by the simple will of the people. This faction becomes enraged, and stops at no mischief to effect its purposes. Incapable still of succeeding, it applies the last resource of depravity and consigns to destruction peaceably disposed citizens."[17]

Two days later, on Thursday, May 24, the Patriotes organised one of the largest funerals the city had ever witnessed for the three victims. Four thousand people turned up for the service, according to the *Vindicator*, five thousand according to *La Minerve*. In an emotionally charged ceremony, the bodies of the three victims which had been in the care of their families were brought back to the chapel of the Fabrique and then taken across the Place d'Armes to the parish church of Notre-Dame. Almost all of the priests from the nearby seminary of Saint-Sulpice were in attendance for the Requiem High Mass celebrated by their fellow Sulpician, the Rev. Jean-Baptiste Roupe. Most of the stores in the city closed for the duration of the funeral. At the end of the service, the organising committee lined the mourners up four abreast for the funeral procession. At its head walked Tracey and three other Assembly members, Papineau, Joseph Valois and Jacob de Witt. The mourners crossed the Place d'Armes and proceeded along St James deliberately retracing the route that the troops had followed three days earlier in their pursuit of Tracey's supporters. Having reached the Hay Market, the procession then moved slowly along Bonaventure St and St Antoine St until it reached the French burial ground. There the bodies were laid side by side in a single grave.[18]

The following day, Tracey's editorial returned to a theme that he had often exploited in past but which now became all the more urgent in the light of the voting figures for the election. The Patriotes, he wrote, deserved the support of the whole Irish community since the struggle for justice and political reform in Quebec was no different from the path the Irish had pursued for centuries in their own country:

> We have often exposed on the columns of our Journal, the horrible scenes which have occurred in Ireland, and the massacres perpetrated there on the people. We can assure the people that there is not much difference between the spirit which dictated and encouraged the late transactions in this city and those recorded crimes; and that but little remains to render this country as liable to this baneful influence, if the people do not, by strenuous, but legitimate means, endeavour to prevent it.[19]

The English party was equally determined to win over the Irish to its side and the one means at its disposal was by discrediting Tracey in the eyes of his fellow countrymen. The Tory press thus began a concerted effort to pin the blame for the events of May 21 squarely on the Patriote party and its Irish candidate.

5

The Official Investigation Leaves Many Questions Unanswered

Details of the shooting became known as early as the next day when *La Minerve* printed a special one-page edition and the *Vindicator* published its regular Tuesday edition. The Tory newspapers saw no need to disrupt their normal twice-weekly pattern and were content to wait till the Wednesday in the case of the *Canadian Courant* and the *Montreal Herald* and the Thursday for the *Montreal Gazette* before making their first comments. The papers were aware of the wild rumours that were circulating but they had no means of verifying the information. After publishing a long account of the shooting, the *Canadian Courant* admitted that it had "had to rely entirely on hearsay and may have been on some points misinformed."[1] All placed their hopes in the coroner's inquest confident that their version of the facts would be substantiated in the end.

The Coroner's Inquest

Jean-Marie Mondelet had been Montreal's coroner since August 1812, one of the many government posts he had held during a long career of service to the province. Between 1804 and 1809 he had represented first Montreal West and then Montreal East in the House of Assembly when in general he voted with the nationalist Canadian party. His failure to be re-elected to the House led him to distance himself from nationalist politics and to accept an increasing number of lucrative government posts. In 1822 he had returned to the nationalist fold when he opposed plans to unite Upper and Lower Canada but his allegiance to the party was never more than lukewarm unlike the more radical politics of his two sons, Dominique and Charles-Elzéar. The apparent support of the two brothers for the Bagg campaign led the Patriotes to suspect that Jean-Marie's allegiance had also shifted back to the English party.[2]

As Mondelet made his way to the Fabrique early on Tuesday, May 22, he had a chance meeting with Côme-Séraphin Cherrier on the street. Cherrier told him that some members of the jury were Bagg activists, in particular, the foreman of the jury, Pierre Charles Dubois, who had told people that he had already made up his mind on the verdict he would return. Mondelet replied that he was not worried since a simple majority from the jury would be enough.[3] At the Fabrique, Mondelet was approached by Papineau who told him Dubois should be recused. There were witnesses prepared to swear that they had heard Dubois the previous evening express his satisfaction at what had occurred in St James St and state that French Canadians would only calm down when several hundred of them had been killed. Mondelet refused to consider the objection. In all his long career as a coroner, he told Papineau, he had never recused a single jury member and he was not going to start then. In any case, the point was irrelevant since a coroner's jury did not need to reach a unanimous verdict—seven out of the twelve would be enough to reach a proper verdict. Was he sure? asked Papineau. Mondelet said he was, since it was exactly the practice he had often followed in the past.[4]

Inside the Fabrique the twelve jurors were sworn in at 8 am just as the final vote in the Montreal West Ward was being recorded next door in the polling station. In a short address to the jurors, Mondelet urged them to use moderation in their search for justice and the truth and then announced that he was adjourning the proceedings to the more spacious surroundings of the Quarter Sessions room in the courthouse.[5] On leaving the Fabrique, Mondelet and the jurors inspected the three bodies and then set off for the short walk to Notre Dame St. Among those who set off with them were Papineau and an unexpected ally, William Walker, a distinguished barrister whose name had once been cited as a possible candidate in the West Ward election. The two intended to keep a very close eye on the proceedings in the coroner's court.

Mondelet's early morning confrontation with Cherrier and Papineau reflected the serious misgivings the Patriotes had over the likely outcome of the inquest. The high constable was supposed to have selected twelve jurors who had had no connection with the election but he had made no real effort to do so. As he later admitted, he had merely stepped outside the Fabrique and selected nine men from the crowd gathered outside. After Papineau's intervention the previous evening, Delisle had been forced to go as far as the Quebec suburbs on the edge of Montreal to find three suitable jurors but it was too little and too late as far as the Patriotes were concerned. Cherrier's cousin, Jacques Viger, soon discovered the political affiliations of most of them. As census commissioner for Montreal County since 1825, no one knew the private details of his fellow citizens better than he. According to Viger, at least four jurors were Tracey supporters and two had voted for him. Bagg had similar support on the jury but the two who had voted for him had other connections. Pierre Charles Dubois was reported to be related to one of the magistrates implicated in the shootings while Alexander Dewar was a business partner of John Fisher.[6]

The clerk of the peace, John Delisle, the high constable's brother, had been asked to prepare a list of potential witnesses for the inquest but it was the magistrates who supplied him with the list. Not surprisingly, it comprised names of people who had voted for Bagg or who had strongly favoured his election. They included people such as Dr William Caldwell, Scottish born and like William Robertson, a former student of medicine at Edinburgh University, a former army staff surgeon, and a professor at the medical faculty of McGill College, George Perkins Bull, a recent immigrant from Ireland, leader of the Orange Lodge in Montreal and editor of the *Canadian Record*, Dr Daniel Arnoldi, an ardent loyalist with strong business ties to Peter McGill and Horatio Gates, Alexander Carlisle Buchanan, nephew of the British agent for emigration at Quebec, Olivier Berthelet, the recent victor in the East Ward election and James Sommerville, a farmer from Lachine, as well as other doctors, merchants and lawyers.[7] Not a single name had been drawn from the Tracey camp. Not all of these witnesses were called to testify before the jury, but the suspicion lingered that a deliberate attempt had been made by the magistrates to influence the outcome of the inquest.

Before calling the first witnesses, Mondelet reminded those present that the object of the inquest was to discover how, when and by whom the three men had been killed. He would therefore not allow any evidence that strayed from those strict parameters. It was a ruling that Mondelet would find more and more difficult to impose as the inquest progressed.

The first witnesses to be heard were Robert Nelson and Guillaume Vallée, two of the doctors who had performed the autopsies. There was no doubt, they told the jury, that all three victims had died from gun-shot wounds: Pierre Billet had received a wound an inch and a half above the clavicle and had died instantly; François Languedoc had been shot in the right side of the chest and Casimir Chauvin in the head.[8] Some of the other witnesses who followed had little to say other than that they had been in St James St by chance and had been taken completely by surprise when the firing began. They said that the three victims had been mere bystanders and had been shot at some distance from each other between St Peter St and the Hay Market.

Other witnesses had observed the constables, the magistrates or the soldiers at some point on the Monday afternoon. In spite of the coroner's warning, a few witnesses spoke of the heavy-handed actions of the special constables in the Place d'Armes and suggested that this had a bearing on the subsequent events in St James St. Alexander Noon, a tailor, had seen Louis Malo around 4 pm wielding his stick at a man and he himself had been attacked when he had tried to intervene. Michel Jacques, a clerk, spoke of the violence meted out by several special constables on a lone Tracey supporter shortly after the candidates had left the polling station. It was this incident, he said, that had prompted some of Tracey's supporters to return to rescue the man which in turn had led to the scuffling and stone throwing. When yet another witness, Joseph Constantineau, began to describe the assaults carried out by the special constables in the Place d'Armes, Mondelet's patience snapped. He interrupted the witness and asked him whether he could say how the three French Canadians had been killed. When Constantineau replied that he could not, Mondelet told him to withdraw.

The next witnesses had no choice but to concentrate on the events that had occurred from 5 pm onwards. John Mondelet, a law student, had been present as part of Tracey's escort from the polling station. He testified that at about 5:15 pm he had reached the bank when he heard other supporters shouting, "They are killing our friends! Help, help." He left Tracey and ran back to the Place d'Armes where the two sets of supporters were engaged in throwing stones at each other. He stated that he managed to persuade most of his own party to desist from fighting and to return to St James St with him. When they arrived level with Robertson's house, Mondelet saw that Bagg's supporters were pursuing them and throwing stones. There was also a detachment of the 15th Foot with them.

Other witnesses also spoke of the large number of Bagg supporters positioned both at the rear of the troops and on their flanks and who threw stones. Hypolite Voyer, a mason from the St Lawrence suburbs and Édouard-Étienne Rodier, one of Tracey's close collaborators, agreed with Michel Jacques in stating that the appearance of the troops and those who were throwing stones caused the crowd to flee along St James St. They also testified that many of those fleeing had thrown stones at their pursuers but, as both Voyer and Mondelet pointed out, the distance between the two groups was too great for the stones to have hit their intended targets. Pierre Lukin, the magistrate on duty with Robertson on the Monday afternoon, confirmed that the special constables and Bagg supporters at the rear of the troops had thrown stones at those fleeing along St James St despite his best attempts to restrain them.

Details of the final minutes before the shooting came from a few of the witnesses. Jacob Abdella, a Montreal trader who had voted for Tracey, was alone in claiming to have overheard John Fisher say, shortly after the poll had closed, that the troops should clear the ground of the "rebels" and that there would be further orders when they were level with Dr Robertson's house. Other witnesses stated that the order to shoot was given when the troops were indeed drawn up opposite Dr Robertson's. Both Rodier and Jacques saw an officer position himself at end of the first rank of soldiers and give a signal with his sword. The troops then fired on those who fled. Richard Fogerty, a labourer who happened to be in St James St when the troops arrived, heard a sergeant reply to the officer in command after he had given the order to take aim, "But, sir, the mob is dispersing." The officer had remained undeterred. John Mondelet was the only one to name Macintosh as the officer who gave the order. He said that he saw him say something to the troops and then lower his sword. The troops presented their muskets and fired at Tracey's supporters who were at this time in full flight. Each witness who had been in a position to see was adamant that he had heard two discharges of fire. Each was equally convinced that when the officer gave order to fire, the lives of his soldiers were not in danger.

For certain people present in the court room, the first day's proceedings did not go according to their liking. Few of the names on the clerk of the peace's list had been called to testify and little or no evidence had been offered in justification for the shooting. The coroner was informed that there were a number of competent witnesses ready and willing to testify that the troops were fully justified in opening fire on the crowd in St James St. Despite his earlier ruling, Mondelet agreed that they could be heard. Next day, a succession of witnesses followed one another offering a defence of the officers and of the troops under their command. Five of them, Caldwell, Arnoldi, Robert Armour, John B. Finlay and John Jones, had voted for Bagg. The coroner provided them with even further latitude in allowing the vast majority of them to read previously written depositions that dealt with events that had occurred hours before the shooting. There was an objection in the room that the coroner would not be acting impartially if he were to allow on Wednesday what he had denied to others on Tuesday. Campbell Sweeny, counsel for the two officers, then spoke up and insisted that Mondelet had a duty to listen to all the testimony that would establish the truth. Though reluctant initially, Mondelet eventually allowed himself to be swayed by Sweeny.

Most of the new witnesses had been in the vicinity of the troops when the shooting began but all were adamant that Tracey alone was ultimately responsible for the deaths that had occurred. Four witnesses suggested that the decision of Tracey and his supporters to leave the polling station by walking past Henderson's store and out into the Place d'Armes had been a deliberate act of provocation. It was done, said John Beekman Finlay, "with an intention, I have no doubt, from their gestures, of insulting and striking the Constables who were peaceably standing in the square." John Jones, a merchant, was of a similar opinion: it was done with intent to threaten Bagg's friends, he said. Alexander Robertson observed that Tracey's group of supporters appeared to be "in a state of great excitement, pushing anyone in their way violently aside and flourishing sticks and umbrellas about." Even the few stragglers who remained behind in the square after Tracey had left, Robertson stated, continued their provocative behaviour by using "vituperative language to their opponents."

Unusual but significant was Alexander Robertson's description of one particular constable who had attacked the small group of stragglers with his baton, knocking unconscious one of the young men. Another constable had attempted to drag his colleague away but without much success. This was what had caused the real trouble, suggested Robertson: "it would have been more judicious on the part of the above Constable had he at once retired among his fellows and allowed the ebullition of feeling on the part of the few individuals with whom he had brought himself in contact to expend itself in words, which it probably might have done."

Robertson was attempting to assist the injured man when some of Tracey's supporters suddenly appeared with stones in their hands. Robertson had then decided to beat a hasty retreat.

For several witnesses the subsequent stone fight between the constables and the group of Tracey supporters outside Henderson's store was a crucial turning point in the events of the day. From the inside, the sound of breaking glass suggested that the store was under attack. Thomas Mitchell Smith, a local merchant, testified that he was inside the store at the time and was convinced he was going to be murdered. Only the arrival of the troops had saved his life, he said. Dr William Caldwell had been standing at the door of Henderson's shop when the fighting began. The mob, he said, threw stones at the windows and the door and he himself was struck more than once. He had heard shouts such as, "Have at their heart's blood," which had convinced him that every individual in the shop would have been killed had the military not advanced and driven back the rioters.

Dr Daniel Arnoldi had been standing at the door of his house on the Place d'Armes at the corner of St James St and St Joseph St and claimed to have had a clear view of the attack on Henderson's shop. His description of the incident closely resembled Caldwell's: "The infuriated populace assailed the house with sticks and stones, etc, broke the glass in the windows, and endeavoured to force their way in, to beat the persons who had run there for protection; and I firmly believe that if the crowd had entered, murder would have been committed; and it was only when the cry was made for soldiers that they desisted."

Mondelet's apparent deference to the likes of Robertson, Caldwell and Arnoldi meant that he showed more forbearance in allowing them to dwell on the fighting in the Place D'Armes than he had when Constantineau attempted to testify. Both sets of witnesses were convinced that the events in the square and those in St James St were inextricably linked but it was only the witnesses for the defence who were allowed to develop their theory. Their intent was to show that Tracey's supporters, whether attacking Henderson's store or confronting the army in St James St, were fuelled by the same murderous intent and therefore the troops had been justified in opening fire to defend themselves and to suppress a riot. Alexander Robertson spoke of the "coolness and forbearance of the troops up to the time they fired, notwithstanding their being exposed to showers of stones." Finlay stated that the discharge of firearms against the rioters was the only measure capable of putting an end to the riot. George Perkins Bull had been on duty that day as a special constable and had seen both officers and magistrates struck by stones, he said. In his opinion, the lives of the soldiers had been in danger. Dr Caldwell had seen the same violence directed against the military. Neither had noticed any magistrates or constables throwing stones.

The one witness for the defence to suggest that the violent confrontation in St James St was a two-way affair was Caldwell's fellow Scot, Robert Armour Jr, editor of the *Montreal Gazette*. He had seen everything, he said, from the vantage point of his house in St James St. He had watched the troops advance along the street behind a group of constables and other people, all of whom were throwing stones at the retreating crowd. Gradually, the crowd was forced back in the direction of the Hay Market. When the troops came level with Dr Robertson's, they stopped. Stones continued to be thrown from both sides. Finally, there remained just one or two individuals in front of the troops continuing to throw stones in the direction of the crowd. Armour then heard an order ring out for the individuals to move out of the way and for the soldiers to take aim. Confirmation of this last detail came from Dr Arnoldi. He had seen Mr La Fontaine step out in front of the crowd and attempt as best he could to stop the stone throwing. He would most likely have been shot there on the spot, Arnoldi stated, had it not been for the stupidity of a constable who was taking his time retreating behind the troops, apparently unable to understand that he was supposed to get out of the way. The troops eventually opened fire but by then La Fontaine had managed to take cover.

Before concluding his evidence each witness stressed that the troops were justified in firing since a riot was in existence and their lives were in danger. In his testimony Armour specifically used the language of the Riot Act when he insisted that the incident in St James St represented a clear and immediate danger to the lives and property of his fellow citizens. When Dr Arnoldi stated his opinion that the town was saved from murder and pillage "as the description of rioters was almost entirely composed of the lowest class of Irishmen," he not only betrayed a prejudice that was shared by many in the English party but he undermined the credibility of the rest of his evidence.

The verdict

After two and a half days of testimony from twenty-three witnesses, the coroner decided that he and the jury had heard enough and that further evidence was unnecessary. The jury concurred. The inquest, however, had not run as smoothly as Mondelet had hoped. The presence of Papineau inside the

Louis-Hippolyte La Fontaine, brilliant young advocate and contributor to *La Minerve*. The Assembly member for Terrebonne since 1830, he played a leading role in managing Daniel Tracey's campaign during the Montreal West by-election and risked his life in St James St on the afternoon of May 21. (McCord Museum – M981.207.4)

room had been controversial from the outset. Mondelet's uncertainty at times about the correct procedure to follow allowed Papineau to intervene on numerous occasions, correcting Mondelet and forcing him to change some of his decisions. Papineau later wrote that he had saved Mondelet from making a number of stupid mistakes but the thousand others he had committed were done knowingly and voluntarily.[9] For Campbell Sweeny, this was a blatant act of collusion between the coroner and Papineau to reach the verdict the Patriotes wanted. However, in one sense, the verdict was a foregone conclusion. No one during the inquest had suggested that the three victims had died other than as a result of the lead balls fired by British troops. The problem was whether the jury would find the shooting justified. Was there a riot in progress and were the lives of the soldiers in danger when the soldiers opened fire? Had the crowd already dispersed when the shooting occurred? The evidence had been contradictory.

One defence witness had, however, unwittingly provided a piece of evidence that supported the prosecution case. Arnoldi's contention that a constable had been able to amble back unscathed towards his own lines behind soldiers who were supposedly being assailed by a riotous mob suggested that the evidence of his fellow witnesses had been less than accurate.

Before sending the jurors out at 12:30 pm, Mondelet read his charge to them informing them that a simple majority would be sufficient for them to deliver a verdict. Campbell Sweeny sprang to his feet and objected to the coroner's ruling. He said that Mondelet's interpretation of the law on jury verdicts was wrong and that he could prove it. Mondelet agreed to look at a document that Sweeny handed to him. After a few minutes, a clearly embarrassed Mondelet once more addressed the jury. It seemed that Mr Sweeny's objection was well founded and that he the coroner was wrong, he told the twelve jurors. Their verdict needed to be unanimous.[1] Sweeny was either bluffing or was honestly convinced that the law was ambiguous on the matter. Whatever the case, his tactic benefitted his clients. The law in fact allowed as many as twenty-three jurors to make up a coroner's jury but twelve was the minimum number. Where a jury failed to agree, the coroner could take a majority vote, subsume the minority opinion into the majority and declare the verdict to be that of all. A simple majority thus became a unanimous verdict. Mondelet's characteristic uncertainty once more let him down and he allowed himself to be swayed by the force of Sweeny's arguments.[10] That decision was to have far-reaching consequences.

The jury retired to a room where it remained under lock and key and provided with just bread and water for the rest of the day. The Patriotes had been hoping for a rapid decision, but as the hours passed, they grew apprehensive. By late evening there was still no news from the jury room. Deliberations continued throughout the night and on through Friday morning. Finally, at 11 am, the jurors came back into court and reported that they were unable to agree. Two of their number were holding out. The *Vindicator* informed its readers that the two in question were closely linked to the magistrates involved in the events under investigation.[11] The coroner ordered the jurors to return to their deliberations. Another sleepless night ensued.

At midday on Saturday, May 26 the jury informed Mondelet that it was still divided and consequently had produced two verdicts. The majority view, signed by nine jurors, stated that Languedoc, Billet and Chauvin had been killed in St James St on Monday, May 21 between 5 and 6 o'clock in the evening "from the discharge of guns loaded with ball, on the people who were dispersing at the adjournment of the poll, in the said St James St, by a detachment of troops of the 15th Regiment, now in garrison in this city and who were then commanded by Colonel McIntosh (*sic*) and Captain Temple."

The three dissenting voices were those of Dubois, Dewer and Edward Talon L'Esperance. In their version of the verdict they eliminated the words "on the people who were dispersing at the adjournment of the poll, in the said St James St," and replaced them with the following: "after a riot after the adjournment of the Poll for the Election of a member for the West Ward of this city held near the house of the Fabrique in front of the Place d'Arms."[12] The nature of the gathering—a riot or not—that day on St James Street after Polls closed had thus become the heart of the issue.

The coroner was in a quandary. The verdicts carried no legal weight since neither was unanimous but Mondelet had already committed himself. At 11:30 am he had gone to the office of the clerk of the peace and handed Delisle a warrant for the arrest of Macintosh and Temple for wilful murder. Had he expected a unanimous verdict from the jury? Dubois had given no indication that he was going to change his mind and was reported to have said that he would rather spend six months on bread and water than give in to the rest of the jury. Mondelet later wrote that the evidence he had heard in court had convinced him there was a case to be heard but he may have decided on the arrests ahead of time as a means of defusing a potentially explosive situation in the city.[13] At 2 pm Mondelet adjourned the proceedings. He told the jurors that they were free to return home but ordered them to reconvene the following Monday morning at 10 am.

Informed of the coroner's warrant against them, the two officers had arrived some time before 2 pm at the courthouse where the high constable placed them under arrest and confined them to the barristers' room. There they were able to mingle freely with Robertson, Moffatt and other magistrates they knew. Their lawyer, Samuel Gale, an American-born loyalist and former protégé of Governor Dalhousie, turned up with a mass of papers and entered into discussion with the Chief Justice Reid and another judge in chambers. A short time later, Papineau and Walker also turned up at the court-house and discovered that Gale appeared to be in the process of applying for a writ of *habeas corpus* for the two officers. Alarmed at the secrecy of the proceedings, Papineau barged in on the judges and asked to be allowed to witness what was going on.

An embarrassed Chief Justice Reid said he had nothing to hide. He and his fellow judge had examined the evidence taken at the coroner's inquest and Gale had just finished read-ing to them new depositions that he had submitted on behalf of his clients. Papineau suggested that in a matter of such importance a King's Counsel should be in attendance. Gale suggested Stephen Sewell, brother of Chief Justice Sewell in Quebec City and speaker of the Legislative Council, the same lawyer the magistrates had consulted on the evening of May 21. Sewell arrived at 4 pm and was asked to read the pile of depositions that Gale had submitted. As he set to work, Papineau protested that Sewell should not be allowed to work alone on the case since he had had just learned that Sewell had spent the previous day advising the two officers on legal matters. There were two other KCs available, Frédéric-Auguste Quesnel and Michael O'Sullivan, he told Reid. Chief Justice Reid gave his assent and announced that to give everyone a chance to read the new depositions, he would hold the matter over till the following Tuesday morning.[14] The officers were released on bail. Two sureties of £1000 each were provided by two of the magistrates present, John Forsyth, a prosperous Scottish businessman and member of the Legislative Council, and Samuel Gerrard, the Anglo-Irish former president of the Bank of Montreal.

When the coroner's court reconvened on Monday, May 28, Mondelet told the jury that after due reflection he felt unauthorized to make a final return. Instead he was adjourning proceedings to the next criminal term of the Court of King's Bench. The jury was therefore required to return on August 27. It was not a decision that was welcomed by Tracey's Patriote friends. While the jury was deliberating, Walker had twice urged Mondelet to consider discharging the jury if it failed to return a unanimous verdict and to empanel a new and larger jury. A petition to the same effect with twenty-six names including those of Dr Robert Nelson, John Donegani, Dr Guillaume Vallée and Édouard-Raymond Fabre had been handed to the coroner after the jury had announced its split verdict. Mondelet remained deaf to their appeals.[15] Mondelet probably made the correct decision from a purely legal standpoint but it might have been more prudent to follow the advice of the petitioners. Once more he was reluctant to be seen siding with the Patriotes at this time.

The Magistrates' version

The opening day of the inquest had troubled the magistrates. The accusations levelled against them by the early witnesses and the denunciation Tracey had published in the columns of the *Vindicator* required some action on their part. A court of special sessions was hurriedly organised for 8 pm that same evening at which the magistrates voted to provide material for the coroner's court. However, nothing that was said the following day at the inquest satisfied William Robertson. Having consulted Benjamin Holmes, he convened another court of special sessions for the evening. Fifteen magistrates turned up. Robertson announced that he and Holmes had each prepared a report on the events of the previous Monday and they intended to read them into their records. Roy and Jobin protested strongly that a court of special sessions was not an appropriate place for such an exercise but Robertson brushed aside their protests as irrelevant. The two magistrates knew that their actions on May 21 were likely to come under even closer scrutiny as the inquest progressed. The court of special sessions was the only forum where they could justify their actions for the time being.

Robertson's version of events begins on the Monday afternoon, at 2:20 pm, when he arrived to relieve Benjamin Holmes who had been on duty with Lukin and the special constables within the precincts of the parish church. Except for some occasional shouting or cheering, the crowd, Robertson said, was peaceable. At 2:45 pm, fighting suddenly broke out on the opposite side of the square, close to the polling station. A large number of people then came running across the Place d'Armes towards the wall enclosure of the church. One man in particular was receiving a severe beating. Lukin, Robertson and a few special constables ran out into the square and rescued him. The constables then came under attack as fighting broke out in different parts of the Place d'Armes. Robertson stressed that the magistrates present endeavoured to restore order but it was an impossible task as they too were jostled and assaulted. It was a riot, he said, that lasted for some fifteen or twenty minutes during which several people including some constables were severely beaten.

Robertson and the other magistrates eventually escaped to the safety of Henderson's house. Within minutes, a party of soldiers arrived on the Place brought there by John Fisher. Robertson and Lukin went over and spoke to the commanding officer. He informed them that if military assistance were required to keep the peace he would need a written requisition signed by two magistrates. Robertson and Lukin conferred and agreed that they were unable to maintain order with the force of constables under their command. Accordingly, they signed the requisition. Despite the military presence, Robertson claimed that the disturbance continued unabated. It was at this point that Robertson decided that drastic action was needed. At approximately 3:15 pm, he said that he read the Riot Act in the presence of Holmes and Lukin. Heavy rain was falling and gradually calm returned to the square. Robertson told the soldiers to take shelter under the church portico and to remain there until voting ended.

A few minutes after 5 pm, Robertson heard the noise of fighting and wild yelling coming from the direction both of the bank and of Henderson's store. Stones started to fly and the sound of breaking glass and of iron shutters being struck could be heard. Robertson caught sight of a man lying on the ground, apparently dead, close to the store. Then he spotted a fellow magistrate, Mr Shuter, who was running across the square shouting, "For God's sake, bring out the troops, the mob are murdering the people, and have commenced an attack upon the houses." At the same time, he saw Moffatt running towards him and waving as if he wanted the military and magistrates to advance. Robertson turned to Lt Col Macintosh and told him that his help was needed. He could not remember his exact words but it was to the effect that the troops were needed to quell a riot and to protect people's lives and property since the civil authority was powerless to act. He then described how the troops advanced across the Place d'Armes first to Dr Arnoldi's house and then to the bank where stones were thrown at them. The troops continued to advance along St James St as the mob withdrew in the direction of the Hay Market. When the mob noticed that the constables had positioned themselves in front of the military and were leading the advance, it turned about and began throwing showers of stones at both constables and soldiers. When the troops reached a point some one hundred yards past St François-Xavier St, they fired a volley and the crowd dispersed.

Robertson's report considerably minimised his own role on the afternoon in question. According to the magistrate, it amounted to reading the Riot Act at 3:15 pm and ordering the troops to go into action shortly after 5 pm. But where was he in the minutes before the troops fired? Did he tell Macintosh to order the soldiers to fire? Did he consider the commanding officer to be still protected by the terms of the Riot Act even though it had been read two hours earlier and in a different place? Robertson had remained silent on these points though it was surely central to proving the legality of the army's action on the day. His claim that he had read the act at 3:15 in the presence of Holmes and Lukin raises certain questions. The Riot Act of 1714 stated that any group of twelve or more people involved in riotous assembly had to disperse within an hour of the order being given by a justice of the peace. At the time, the Place d'Armes was packed with people. Robertson claimed that trouble had broken out in various places in the square. Who exactly was involved in an illegal riotous assembly? Did Robertson have in mind the whole of the Place d'Armes when he read the act? Did he intend to clear everyone from the square? Since an election was being held there, it was the returning officer and not the magistrates who had ultimate jurisdiction.[16] Was an attempt made to inform Dupré that the Riot Act was in force? When Shuter claimed two hours later that another riot was in progress, did the magistrates think that the act was still in force? Robertson's account had left many questions unanswered.

Benjamin Holmes's version provided important new details. Holmes stated that Robertson had relieved him at 2.40 pm, not 2.20 pm, when all was quiet. Heavy rain was falling but Holmes said he was still afraid that the situation could change for the worse at any moment. He told Robertson that he could provide him with a new requisition for military assistance once he got back to the bank. No sooner had Holmes reached his office than Robertson arrived in urgent need of the requisition. There was trouble in the Place d'Armes, he told Holmes, and he needed help. Holmes told him he might have to read the Riot Act and agreed to fetch Robertson's copy of it while the magistrate returned to the Place d'Armes. At 3 pm Holmes found Robertson close to the parish church and handed him the copy of the act. A short distance away, troops had just arrived. Within a few minutes a disturbance broke out in the square and the officer in command informed the magistrates that he would not engage his troops without a signed requisition. Uncertain what to do, Robertson thought first of having the election adjourned and asked Holmes and Lukin to see whether the returning officer was willing to cooperate.

The two magistrates conveyed Robertson's request to Dupré, adding that there was increased disturbance in the square and that they feared that serious rioting would erupt now that troops were present in the square. La Fontaine had been present and had told the two magistrates that he disagreed with their view of the situation and said that he would oppose any attempt to close the poll prematurely. In the circumstances, Dupré decided it would be more prudent to allow voting to continue. When Holmes and Lukin reported back to Robertson, the chief magistrate fell back on his second option. Holmes and Lukin then escorted him back towards the polling station where Holmes said he heard the Riot Act

Benjamin Holmes, general manager of the Bank of Montreal and one of the magistrates on duty in the Place d'Armes on May 21. He failed to inform the returning officer that the Riot Act was about to be read. Later in life he supported the Reform administration of La Fontaine. (McCord Museum –I-7840.1)

read "at about a quarter past three o'clock in the midst of the crowd near the poll." Holmes maintained that this enabled certain individuals to separate the two rival groups of supporters and to restore order.

The magistrates then returned to the church enclosure. Within minutes of arriving, Holmes was approached by two of Tracey's supporters, Mr Desrivières and Mr Normandeau, who complained that Louis Malo had been deliberately targeting their side. If he were not removed, the two men said, he was likely to create more trouble. Holmes returned to the area of the polling station and ordered Malo to leave the Place d'Armes immediately. The constable was reluctant to leave but eventually did so. Holmes lingered for another fifteen minutes before returning to the bank.

Shortly after 5 pm noise from the street drew him to the windows of his dining room. He saw Bagg and his supporters leave in the direction of Notre-Dame St while Tracey's party walked on past the bank. All was quiet, he said. Two minutes later, he noticed a man on the Place d'Armes acting in a violent fashion and surrounded by several stragglers. Blows were being struck. Two men ran into St James St and beckoned for Tracey's party to return. A number of men ran back shouting and throwing stones. The fray intensified as the special constables joined in the fighting. One man appeared to be dead. Holmes had seen enough. He ordered the blinds to be shut and went downstairs to secure the front door. It was then that he heard a volley of small arms fire.[17]

Holmes's recollection of the afternoon of May 21, though more detailed than Robertson's report, still leaves many questions unanswered. He too is imprecise about the original disturbance that led to Fisher calling out the military. Was there a riot in progress at the time? Why did Holmes not tell Dupré when he and Lukin spoke to him that Robertson was about to read the Riot Act? Was it because the disturbance did not warrant such an extreme measure? Did Holmes and Lukin really follow Robertson into the middle of the crowd where he was supposed to have read the act? Why did the magistrates and the army make no attempt to disperse the crowd as required by the act? Was it simply the appearance of soldiers on the Place d'Armes that had restored order in the mid-afternoon? Holmes's decision to expel Malo from the square shortly after the disturbance seems to suggest that part, if not most, of the responsibility for the trouble on the Monday afternoon lay with the leader of the constables. Even if Holmes did not witness the shooting, his testimony suggested that very little time elapsed between the fighting after the poll closed and the soldiers opening fire.

The Conservative press

Montreal's pro-government newspapers had no need to await the outcome of the coroner's inquest to apportion blame for the events of May 21. All claimed that Tracey had set events in motion when he had addressed his supporters on the morning of Sunday, May 20. The *Canadian Courant* accused him of having used violent and inflammatory language.[18] The *Montreal Gazette* claimed that he had called on the crowd to rally in a body the next morning in order "to beat down by physical force that determined opposition which had been manifested to his return by the respectable portion of the community," and to have asked them "to persevere in the violent conduct they had on former occasions manifested, and cost what it may, to seat him among the freely chosen representatives of the people." Most significantly, the paper said, Tracey had offered to lead the crowd himself and had "announced his determination to fire the town and to procure an illumination in honour of his return from the blazing residences of his opponents."

The paper spared its readers none of the details of the physical appearance of the "mob" that assembled at dawn next morning: "the half suppressed murmurs, the gestures, and the infuriated eyes of his partisans, sufficiently indicated that the poison had been instilled, and that in a few hours the effects would be decidedly visible." There was little sympathy for the victims and utter disdain for Tracey: "We also regret with many, that those who were perhaps innocent of riot should have fallen, but a discrimination between guilty and innocent cannot take place on such occasions. Those who urged the mob to violence were the first to take to their heels, and none was more distinguished for the expedition with which he retreated, than the redoubtable Mr Tracey who had volunteered to lead them."[19]

The *Montreal Herald* absolved the army of all blame and had nothing but praise for the discipline of the British soldiers. The description it gave of the final minutes before the shooting began owed more to the editor's imagination than to any eyewitness account: "The forbearance of the officers and the troops, under the complicated provocation of insult, violence, and a drenching rain, was truly admirable—a calm good-humoured smile (which might, perhaps, conceal their contempt) sat upon the countenances of the men, and Colonel Macintosh endeavoured with soothing and condescending language, to avert the exercise of a painful though imperious duty."

The newspaper's principal target however was not Tracey but the Patriotes in general and in particular its leader:

Mr Papineau, and his political adherents resident in Montreal, have, in our opinion, the whole weight of this disgraceful scene, with its tragical results upon their shoulders. We speak not of Mr Tracey, (for he is the known *tool* of Messrs. Papineau and Viger) any further than this, that when the clique found how totally inadequate their influence was for the *fair* return of a member to represent the West ward, they employed Mr Tracey to invite the Irish violently to uphold their cause.[20]

Tracey and his Irish supporters were also the targets of a similar vitriolic onslaught in the pages of a small pamphlet that appeared less than a week after the end of the election. Entitled *Quelques réflexions sur la dernière élection du Quartier-Ouest de la cité de Montréal* (Some thoughts on the recent election in the West Ward of the City of Montreal) and dated May 26, the work claimed to have been published on the order of a "Comité composé de Canadiens, amis de la justice et de la vérité."[21] It was more than likely the work, at least in part, of Michel Bibaud, the former editor of the reform newspapers, *Le Spectateur canadien* and *Le Courrier du Bas-Canada* and of his brother Pierre, one of Bagg's close supporters. There was no trace of the reformist-minded editor in the angry diatribe directed at Tracey and the Irish. Bagg was a "respectable citizen both in character and conduct;" while Tracey had given ample proof "of the violent and vulgar nature of his style and language." With little to go on except the conflicting accounts in the Montreal newspapers, the Bibauds nevertheless decided that the trouble on the Place d'Armes had all been the fault of the Irish and "of French Canadians for the most part from the lower classes or uneducated."[22] In a final appeal to their readers, the authors called for the founding of a newspaper in French that would counter the influence of *La Minerve* and promote what he termed liberal and constitutional ideas. They had not long to wait. The Sulpicians, who just two days earlier had conducted the funeral service for the three victims, were about to fulfil their dream.

Tracey was stunned by the charge that he had been, directly or indirectly, responsible for the fatal outcome on May 21. The accusation was libellous, he wrote, and he intended to take legal action. Nothing he had said on the Sunday morning in question could justify what had been written about him by his opponents. He had indeed spoken publicly on the Sunday morning—it had been around 9 am when a small group of five or six people had gathered near his home on the corner of Notre-Dame St and McGill St. As he discussed the state of the poll with them, numbers increased to some twenty or thirty people. He had criticized the returning officer for closing the poll early the previous day and had revealed that some of Bagg's friends had later proposed that the two candidates should retire from the election and submit to a new one at a later date. Tracey had turned that offer down suspecting that Bagg had used up his reserve of voters. He had asked his supporters to turn up in large numbers next morning to forestall any attempt at perjury on the part of Bagg's supporters. He had also accused Bagg of being responsible for all the trouble at the polling station saying it was his actions that had tended time and time again "to inflame the town." It was these words, Tracey insisted, that had been twisted to concoct the rumours that had circulated in Montreal on the Sunday evening.[23]

It was not a theory that the Tory press was likely to accept but there was some truth in what Tracey claimed. Bagg and his close circle of friends had been quick to react to the unsubstantiated allegations made by a special constable against his close neighbour, Tracey, and to relay them as fact to the appropriate authorities.[24] The conduit was an obvious one. After his frightening experience the previous day, Dupré was ready to believe the worst about Tracey. The returning officer in turn had little difficulty in persuading the majority of the magistrates that the Irishman was planning murder and mayhem for the following day. Robertson in particular still suspected there was more than a grain of truth in the accusations contained in the anonymous letters sent to Major Grierson three months earlier. One way or the other, Bagg was probably convinced that he had done enough to turn the tide in his favour.

6

Trials Raise the Stakes

Matthew Whitworth-Aylmer, or Baron Aylmer to give him the Irish title he had inherited in 1785, had arrived in Lower Canada in October 1830 to replace Sir James Kempt as governor-in-chief. As a soldier he had served under Wellington and had been awarded the Military Cross. Later he had spent nine years as adjutant general of British forces in Ireland. Conscious of his lack of experience as a civil administrator, the new governor adopted from the outset a deliberately conciliatory attitude with regard to the Canadian population. Though he was not prepared to give in to the demands of the Patriotes for an elected legislative council, he was successful in gaining the trust of the likes of Papineau and Tracey. The events of May 21, however, put an end to any pretence of goodwill between him and the Patriotes. His mismanagement of the crisis exposed his political inexperience and led to a serious breakdown in his relations with the Assembly and ultimately to the disastrous end of his own career as a colonial administrator.[1]

On the morning of Tuesday, May 22, before setting off to attend the coroner's inquest, Papineau had written an urgent letter to Lord Aylmer.

You will have learned [he wrote] the disastrous events which
yesterday stained our streets with blood. His Majesty's subjects
have been shot by the troops sent to protect them. I have seen
the dead bodies of three of them, and am assured that a fourth
was killed on the spot by the same fire, and that four or five
others are dangerously wounded. Until that day Canada had
never been afflicted by a similar misfortune.[2]

He urged Lord Aylmer to travel to Montreal immediately
and set in motion an investigation into the shooting. He even
proposed the names of John Neilson and Philippe Panet, both
members of the Assembly, who might accompany the governor. Papineau's request fell on deaf ears but it did succeed
in gaining Aylmer's complete and undivided attention.

The Solicitor General

Macintosh spent the same Tuesday morning writing up his
official report on the incidents of the previous day. His justification for the decisions he had taken was that he had acted
on the basis of information received. When he had arrived on
the Place d'Armes he had been informed by Dr Robertson
and Captain Temple that many acts of violence had been
committed, that many people in the crowd were in possession
of firearms, and that the "rioters were in the act of murdering
a man on the side of the place opposite St James St." He had
acted accordingly, he wrote.[3]

In Macintosh's mind, the close involvement of the magistrates was enough to protect him from legal prosecution, a
point he underlined in his report: "For fear of misunderstanding, I consider it proper to observe that I received distinct
authority from Doctor Robertson, for 'firing' before it was
resorted to." The impending coroner's inquest, however,
was giving him cause for concern. As an extra precaution,

Macintosh decided to join Moffatt, Robertson and some other magistrates in retaining legal counsel in the person of Campbell Sweeny to protect his interests during the inquest.

Sweeny's report of the proceedings shocked Macintosh. Sweeny told him that he had been horrified by the indecorum and partiality of the court and what he described as its "legal informality." He had no confidence in the jurors, most of whom "were violent political partizans (*sic*), swayed by the same passions and prejudices which so strikingly characterized the leaders of Mr Tracey's party." Most ominous in Sweeny's eyes, however, was the presence in court of the leader of Tracey's party: "It is impossible to conceive greater indecorum, nay! indecency, than that which marked the conduct of Mr Papineau and his party during the whole of the Inquisition." He had seen Papineau whisper into the coroner's ear and some of his followers exchanged "looks of intelligence" with members of the jury. The coroner had accepted evidence that was illegal and had refused what was legal. In a word, Papineau and the coroner were either grossly ignorant of the law or corrupt.[4]

Macintosh had placed his trust in the governor and was now anxious to receive official approbation of the military action. Aylmer, however, had decided to await the outcome of the coroner's inquest before making a public statement. When news reached him on Sunday, May 27 of the arrest and release on bail of the two officers, he had immediately set about organising a legal defence for the men. He sent a letter that same evening to Charles Richard Ogden, the solicitor general, ordering him to leave for Montreal by the first boat next morning. Ogden's instructions were to communicate with the King's Counsel in Montreal and to take measures with them "for controling any irregular or unlawful proceedings which may be going forward with a view to implicate criminally the

Magistrates or the King's troops in consequence of the recent events which have taken place in Montreal."[5] Ogden set off as ordered and arrived in Montreal at dawn on the Tuesday morning. He was relieved to discover that the application by Macintosh and Temple to be discharged from arrest had been postponed yet again and was now scheduled to be heard the next day at 12 o'clock.

Ogden was no friend of the Patriotes. He had represented Trois-Rivières in the Assembly almost continuously since 1814 and had always voted with the English party. His appointment as solicitor general in 1824 had been achieved with the backing of Governor Dalhousie.[6] Aylmer was confident that he had no better man for the task of extricating the two officers from the predicament they now found themselves in.

After disembarking in Montreal, Ogden made contact with the three KCs who had been brought in for the first bail hearing. All were agreed that the two officers were entitled to be bailed but they were uncertain how to achieve it legally. Doubts were also expressed about the advisability of granting them an absolute discharge at a time of heightened tension. In the end, they decided that Ogden would take the case on behalf of the Crown. Next day, he appeared before the Court of King's Bench and asked for the case to be held over until he had time to read all the depositions. The chief justice gave him until the end of the week.[7]

Ogden's arrival in Montreal was less reassuring for Macintosh than some might have imagined. Ogden had not brought the expected communication from the governor. Fearing that his commander-in-chief did not fully understand the gravity of the accusations levelled against him during the coroner's inquest, Macintosh wrote him a long letter in which he detailed the criticism that Sweeny had made of the inquest. "I feel called upon to state," he wrote, "that much

Charles Richard Ogden, solicitor general of Lower Canada, was dispatched by the governor to defend the two British officers implicated in the three deaths in St James St. As attorney general he faced stiff questioning at the inquiry over the manipulation of the grand jury. ((McCord Museum – I-28425.0.1)

appearance of partiality on the part of the Coroner and of party spirit on that of the jury was evinced during the Inquest." He complained that the coroner had confined the evidence to the simple fact that the fire of the troops had killed the deceased instead of investigating what had occasioned that fire. He added that he had been assured by counsel who had attended the inquest that "the most conclusive evidence came before the Coroner's Court, and proved that the troops acted against the Rioters *during a riot, by order of the Magistracy*, and were by them empowered to fire, to which they would have been at any rate compelled in self-defence."

Before ending his letter, Macintosh thought it prudent to add a piece of information that had come into his possession. He had received a visit from a friend, a Mr Forbes, who had recently been visited by Jacques Viger. Viger knew of the friendship between the two men and wished Forbes to act as an intermediary between Macintosh and the Patriotes. If Macintosh were willing to divulge the name of the magistrate or magistrates who had ordered him to fire, the proceedings against Macintosh and the military under his command would be brought to a halt. Forbes had told Macintosh that he understood the proposal to have come straight from Papineau himself, an indication in his view that the executive was always ready to acquiesce to whatever was suggested by its leader.[8] Macintosh clearly hoped the information might be used to discredit any attempt by the Patriotes to exploit the predicament in which the army now found itself.

On the morning of Saturday, June 2 the Court finally heard the new bail application. Gale again appeared for Macintosh and Temple. He informed the court that he had brought with him some forty affidavits sworn by his clients and by a variety of other people both military and civilian. On the basis of this evidence, he argued, it was clear that the two officers had been called out by the civil power and had acted under it. For this reason he called for an absolute discharge. Ogden said that he too felt that the men were entitled to bail and that he was supported in this by the learned counsel present in court, Sewell, Quesnel and O'Sullivan. As far as the Crown was concerned, he said, there was no charge against the officers and had it not been for the coroner who had issued the arrest warrant and adjourned the inquest to August 27, the men would have received an absolute discharge. The court therefore had no difficulty in admitting Macintosh and Temple to bail in the sum of £200 each and two sureties of £100.[9]

The officers' defence

Two of the affidavits presented in court by Macintosh and Temple, those of Robertson and William Caldwell, had already been made public but for those following the affair closely, the real interest of the affidavits was that for the first time they had the army's version of events.

Macintosh provided two affidavits which expanded on the report he had sent to the governor. In the first, he stressed that much of the responsibility for the day's events lay squarely with the magistrates. Two of them, Robertson and Moffatt, had come to see him on the Sunday night at 10:30 and told him that they expected a serious breach of the peace the next day after polling finished. They had suggested that the main guard at the New Market be replaced by a captain's guard, but Macintosh had decided instead to mount the main guard at 11 am as usual and to keep the rest of the regiment in the garrison ready to turn out at a moment's notice. At 3 pm Captain Temple had received a signed requisition to go to the Place d'Armes. Macintosh had gone there a short time later and found an ill-disposed crowd of individuals assembled there.

Robertson and Temple told him that "many acts of violence had been committed by them, and that many were in possession of firearms." Robertson had a book in his hands and told Macintosh that he was going to read the Riot Act. He went off and then came back claiming that he had read it. As this appeared to have had no effect on the crowd, Macintosh suggested reinforcing the military presence. Robertson and the other magistrates agreed. Captain Smith was ordered to bring up some additional troops from the Light Infantry Company. This had more effect, Macintosh said, and as it was raining heavily, he gave orders for the soldiers to take up their station under the church porch nearby.

All was quiet until 5 pm when a serious fight broke out, continued Macintosh. The constables became involved but they were driven back inside the enclosure wall and were even followed by some of the rioters. Macintosh said he immediately ordered the troops to load with ball cartridge and to advance into the square in a column of two divisions. Informed that the mob was murdering a man close to St James St, he headed in that direction and progressed some quarter of a mile along the street.

> Perceiving, however, that the dense crowd in front, which appeared to be composed of many hundred persons, and a numerous portion of which appeared to have recently arrived in a body on the spot, and to be led in a systematic manner, was becoming nearer and nearer, and as we advanced, was throwing quantities of large stones, on the civil authorities, and military force around me by two of which Lieutenant and Quarter Master Dewson received severe contusions, and several struck the troops and my own person, it became necessary to order the troops to fire after I had at different times advanced in front, and by word and action, endeavoured to prevail upon the crowd to retire, loudly giving notice beforehand, that it was intended to fire if the attack and riot continued.

Macintosh said that it took less than one round from the first division of the main guard, consisting of sixteen file, to have the desired effect. Ensign Hay was dispatched to fetch the remainder of the regiment but they were not called upon to act. Macintosh then added, almost as an afterthought, "I had also within a few minutes before the firing, while the riot was going on, received directions from one of the magistrates to fire upon the rioters in case I should consider it necessary."[10]

Macintosh had sworn his affidavit on May 26, the same day that Mondelet had issued an arrest warrant against him. Some of the details he provided appear strange when compared to the reports Robertson and Holmes had given to the magistrates. Robertson had made no mention of the presence of firearms. It was not the sort of detail the magistrate would have forgotten so soon after the event. Why did Macintosh not insist that the Place d'Armes be cleared of people immediately? His description of the crowd that confronted him in St James St suggested that he was faced by more than just a localised riot. Claiming that a crowd of several hundred people had suddenly arrived in the street and was being led in a systematic manner was tantamount to saying that he was opposed by a military force. His justification for ordering the troops to fire seemed to be that he had a rebellion on his hands. The import of his account was that the initiative to fire was his and his alone, even though he had received permission to do so from a magistrate.

Whether on the advice of counsel or after due reflection on his own part, Macintosh saw fit a week later to swear a new affidavit before Moffatt.

The new affidavit was clearly intended to shift total responsibility for the deaths onto the shoulders of the magistrates. Macintosh recalled the Sunday evening when Moffatt and Robertson had first come to see him. He had warned them how dangerous it would be to use infantry against a mob and said how much he regretted that no cavalry was available: "So much better against a riot," he told them. The magistrates replied they were aware of the fact. The next day, before Macintosh used his troops against the rioters, Robertson had repeatedly told him that "the civil authorities had information of the most positive kind, that there was a plan arranged for firing the Town and the Suburbs in various places, so as to draw the military away in different and opposite directions, and in small bodies, that they might be more easily over-powered." After 5 pm, when he had ordered the troops to load their ball cartridges, several of the magistrates gave him a direct order: "Now Colonel, for God's sake, bring out the troops, the rioters are murdering the people and attacking the houses." There were new details. Macintosh now claimed that the "rioters" had marched back into the square. Fearing that they might attack the troops, he had headed in the direction of Dr Arnoldi's house having sent for the company of soldiers waiting in the Champ de Mars. When he and his men finally reached St James St, they were attacked with showers of stones some weighing between two and three pounds. But this time Macintosh made no mention of any injury done to himself, his officers or his men.[11]

Captain Henry Temple's affidavit reproduced Macintosh's almost word for word except for a few details concerning his commander's attempts to disperse the crowd. The troops had halted opposite the bank in St James St and had come under attack from some stone throwers. The colonel called out several times to them: "Give over throwing stones, or we shall fire at you." The troops continued their slow advance along the street till they were level with Dr Robertson's house where they halted again for several minutes. The crowd had increased in size and once more the troops were met with an even more ferocious hail of stones. The colonel again rushed forward and cried out several times: "I will fire if you do not give over." Temple shouted the same warning but neither officer was successful in quelling the stone throwing. Temple was also more explicit when referring to the tactics of those attacking the troops: "they continued to assail with increasing violence, kept in a body, and acted with great system in keeping up the shower of stones, as those in front posted themselves near enough to the troops to do them the greatest injury, and when they retired or advanced, ran through each other like troops skirmishing." It then became necessary to order the troops to fire: "Less than one round from the first division, consisting of sixteen file of the main guard party, was accordingly discharged and took effect." Temple's account reinforced the idea that the troops were confronted by military units rather than a disorganised mob caught up in a riot. But he too made no mention of any specific injury done to any of his men.

Several other members of the military also provided affidavits. Lt Jeremiah Wilkes Dewson's affidavit disclosed the identity of the magistrate who had ordered the shooting. Dewson, quarter-master of the 15th, stated that he happened to be crossing the Place d'Armes around 3 pm on May 21 when he observed people fighting. John Fisher had come running over to him, covered in mud and in a state of some anxiety. "What is to be done to preserve the peace?" he kept crying, "murder will be committed." Dewson told him that if he went to the main guard with a magistrate's order, Captain Temple would turn out with a party of men. Fisher followed his advice. Dewson remained on the square for the remainder of the afternoon, closely observing all that occurred after polling ended. He noticed that Robertson was standing close to Macintosh when the officer ordered the troops to load their ball cartridges. It was Robertson and Macintosh who walked at the head of the troops as they marched towards St James St, followed by a multitude of constables, magistrates and other individuals. When some were struck by stones, they called on Macintosh to open fire but to no effect. When the troops halted in St James St and were being pelted by a hail of stones—he admitted he himself received some contusions—, Robertson, who was still at Macintosh's side, turned to him and said in a very agitated tone, "Colonel Macintosh, do your duty." Whereupon, Macintosh ordered the soldiers to open fire.

Other affidavits came from a number of rank and file soldiers who had been part of the detachment that had fired on the crowd. Their accounts differed on minor points but all were adamant that they were faced by a large hostile mob of rioters who aimed volleys of stones at them. Private Thomas Lenham stated that the rioters were very numerous, fought with great fury and that "several of them turned round and pelted the detachment with large stones, without any cause or provocation whatever." Lenham thus confirmed what Macintosh and Temple had said about the violence of the crowd. However, nothing in any of their affidavits suggested that a single soldier, magistrate or constable had suffered any serious injury from the stones thrown. Lenham said that he was hit by a single stone as did Privates Henry Brass, Richard McGenniss and John Hancock. Private John Brown said he was struck on the leg and suffered an abrasion of the skin "although the blow had been much weakened by his front rank man's great-coat." Private Robert Hennessy swore two affidavits. In the first he said that he had been hit by a stone but in the second four days later he made no reference to being hit. Hancock, Brass and McGenniss all stated that a stone had hit Macintosh while he was standing out in front endeavouring to persuade the crowd to disperse. The fact

Macintosh made so little of being hit in his two affidavits suggests that no serious injury was done to him either. Sergeant William Gleeson also failed to report any injuries to his men. Indeed, the only serious damage reported was that done to Private Thomas Allcock's fire-lock which had split when a stone struck it. Armourer Sergeant Frederick even swore an affidavit stating that the damage had been caused by a heavy blow upon the barrel. It is certain that if any member of the military had been seriously injured as a result of the "discharge of stones," Macintosh and Temple would have made sure that a doctor swore an affidavit to that effect.

The other affidavits that Macintosh and Temple included with their petition to the chief justice came from a cross section of Bagg supporters, some of them special constables who had been on duty on May 21. The question as to whether the Riot Act had been read preoccupied several of the eye-witnesses. Henry Mackenzie was one of those who were certain it had been read. In his affidavit, he stated that he had spent most of the Monday in the Place d'Armes. Around 3 o'clock he had observed a disturbance near Henderson's store and had seen Robertson come forward and read aloud the Riot Act. Mackenzie stated that he then went about the crowd informing all and sundry that the act had been read and that they should disperse. George Fowler, a cabinet-maker and a special constable, was less certain of what he had witnessed: "I saw there a riot and a magistrate reading the Riot Act, as I was informed, not being myself near enough to distinguish the whole, although I heard some words."

Four other special constables were clear in their minds that Robertson had indeed read the act. Robert Howard, a merchant with a store in the Place d'Armes, stated that at about 3:30 pm Robertson advanced into the crowd with a book to read the Riot Act: "That I have no doubt, from what I understood, that he did read it—and my opinion was that it should have been read earlier in the day, the tumult was so great."

William Boston claimed that he had encouraged Robertson to read the Riot Act and had seen Robertson and Holmes go forward for that purpose but had not seen or heard it being done. Isaac Aaron was adamant that Robertson had read the Riot Act at about 3:30 pm: "He went into the middle of the mob and I followed and heard him read it aloud. Immediately after the Riot Act was read Dr Robertson withdrew from the mob and gave the book which he read the Riot Act from to some person in the door of Mr Henderson, the grocer, and told him to take care of it for him." James Carswell remembered it differently. It had been between 2 and 3 pm that Robertson and Lukin had gone to the spot where the disturbance was taking place. Carswell said that he had gone into the crowd with them and stood along side them and had "heard the said Dr Robertson audibly read the Riot Act and the Proclamation calling upon the people to disperse, and fixing one hour as the period within which they should do so." The only other affidavit to mention the Riot Act was that of William Carmichael, a blacksmith, who said he had been present at 5 o'clock in the Place d'Armes where he heard Robertson read the act and saw the troops move from the porch and march down St James St.

None of these witnesses a week or so after the event was able to say with certainty at what time Robertson read his proclamation. Carswell's and Carmichael's evidence can be dismissed as being too far wide of the mark. If Robert Howard and Isaac Aaron are to be believed, it would mean that Margaret Louisa Hoyle had been courageous enough to advance through a "tumultuous mob" of Tracey supporters in order to cast her vote for Bagg and had done so unscathed.

No clear picture emerges from these affidavits of what precisely occurred after polling finished for the day. Several eyewitnesses claimed that the trouble began when Tracey turned left on leaving the polling station and walked towards Henderson's store before heading back to St James St. This had brought Tracey and his party directly in contact with Bagg's supporters and large numbers of special constables who used the store as their meeting point. According to William Farquar, a special constable, Tracey was followed by "a great number of idle and disorderly persons" who took up almost half the Place d'Armes. William Fisher also claimed that Tracey led his supporters into the middle of the square. Not surprisingly, no affidavit made any mention of an attack by the special constables on the small group of Tracey supporters who had remained behind in the square. Instead, the affidavits concentrated on what was termed a riot when Henderson's store came under attack. George Fowler claimed the rioters intended to destroy the shop while James Breckenridge went even further in maintaining that without the intervention of the troops, every individual in Henderson's shop would have been massacred.

There was more unanimity about what occurred after the troops began their advance along St James St since this was where the riot was supposed to be in progress. George Fowler stated that during a halt of some four or five minutes the soldiers were assailed by stones. Macintosh called on the "rioters" three times to be quiet and to disperse, but his words had no effect and stones continued to be thrown. Fowler then heard "a person in authority" ask Macintosh to give the order to fire but the officer waited another two or three minutes. Only when the troops risked serious injury did Macintosh finally give the order to shoot, showing, Fowler added, "great coolness and forbearance on his part." Alexander McMillen, a Montreal lawyer employed by Bagg, had seen showers of stones aimed at the troops but none directed at Tracey's supporters: "I most solemnly depose that no return whatever was made by the citizens in the rear, they being mostly gentlemen and Special Constables." After repeated provocations, he said, the troops fired, but he made no mention of any warning being given by the magistrates or the officers.

A different version was provided by Charles Mittleberger who had followed the troops along St James St. He saw the special constables and other citizens who had placed themselves in front of the troops "engaged in a contest with the rioters, who were retreating with sticks, stones and other missiles." When the order to fire was given, a first discharge appeared to Mittleberger to have been levelled over the heads of the rioters, many of whom then dispersed. But when a new volley of stones was thrown at the soldiers, they replied with a second discharge. This version was supported in the affidavit of Thomas Barron, a lawyer from Trois-Rivières, who had accompanied Bagg to the polling station on May 21. Later that day in St James St, Barron had watched as the troops came under attack from stone throwers, several of whom appeared intoxicated. Macintosh drew his sword and ordered them repeatedly to withdraw but his efforts proved fruitless. He then placed himself on the right and ordered the front rank to fire. The effect, Baron said, was minimal but when the rear rank fired immediately afterwards, the assailants all dispersed. Macintosh then gave orders to reload and to advance along the street.[12]

The forty depositions that had accompanied the officers' request to be admitted to bail had produced the desired result in the short term but there was no guarantee that the many doubtful testimonies would hold up in front of a jury when the new criminal term opened at the end of August. Macintosh and Temple were faced with a three-month wait before they could learn their fate, a wait made all the more stressful by the lack of official support other than the occasional favourable articles that appeared in Montreal's conservative press.

Newspaper reactions

The Tory press was committed to defending the military intervention but at times this amounted merely to launching attacks on the two Patriote newspapers. The *Montreal Gazette* accused *La Minerve* and the *Vindicator* of "teeming with the most glaring falsehoods, and the most vile, low, dastardly, and slanderous imputations upon public and private character" and then proceeded to practise what it condemned by publishing a letter that that had been written supposedly by a fellow countryman of Tracey's. It was entitled "An Address to Irishmen" and was dated May 26. In form and content it was similar to letters the newspaper had printed at the outset of the election campaign, but this time the author, who signed himself "A True Irishman," concentrated on vilifying Tracey's character and dismissing him as nothing more than a hired hand of the Speaker of the Assembly, Papineau:

> As the innocent often suffer when associated with the guilty, the odium due to him has unfortunately extended to you, and the heartless unmeaning and polluted slanders of this political huxter, have caused the very name of Irishmen 'to stink among the inhabitants of the land' and this is the man for whom you had the temerity to insult and assault his Majesty's troops. What has Tracey ever done for you? He has betrayed you. Did he place himself between you and the troops? No, he *shewed the white feather*, he ran like a coward, and left you alone to suffer what every honest man regrets did not fall on the craven's own guilty head. If he enters the Assembly, will you benefit? No. Tracey alone will profit by your folly. He will pocket his blood stained

10 shillings per day, and for these unhallowed wages he will become a great SPEAKER's hack horse.[13]

Tracey dismissed such comments as mere "party defence" containing no information of any real substance. None of the papers, insisted Tracey, had been able to prove beyond doubt that the military had observed all the requisite formalities before opening fire. Was the Riot Act read immediately before the order to fire was given, he asked, and was the crowd at that moment intent on destroying lives and property? More importantly, should the soldiers have been anywhere near a polling station during an election? Crown lawyers might justify the intervention by appealing to the Common Law precept that all subjects of the king may be called upon to maintain his peace, Tracey wrote, but he deemed this an extremely doubtful presumption of law and pointed out that there was in fact a law in force, the Mutiny Act, that applied to all British troops stationed on garrison duty in North America. In Tracey's view, the only words in that act that might justify calling out the troops were those that referred to "the safety of the kingdom and its possessions." But this was not the case in the Montreal disturbance of May 21, Tracey continued, since the crowd was not attempting to bring about the slightest change to the current system of government or its safety. Nor could the disturbance be strictly called a riot since the people assembled in the Place d'Armes were lawfully convened for an election. As for the military, the relevant section of the act (8Geo.2.c.30) stated that soldiers should move from their quarters at least two miles from the place of poll a day before, and not return till a day after the election. Tracey deemed that there was legitimate reason to believe that the military intervention had been illegal from the outset.[14]

Strong support for Tracey began to build up outside of Montreal. Much to the displeasure of the governor, certain parishes organised rallies to press for action on the part of the authorities. On May 27 a meeting at Saint-Athanase 50 kilometres southeast of Montreal on the Richelieu River passed a resolution that described the action of the returning officer, magistrates and commanding officer as "evidently in opposition to the rights guaranteed by our constitution and deserving of being censured, prosecuted and punished."[15]

A week later, a similar meeting to consider the events of May 21 was held at St Rémi in the south shore county of Laprairie. The language of condemnation was even stronger than in Saint-Athanase. The first resolution stated that "the authors of this butchery are magistrates unfit to administer our laws and who daily stain the court of justice and that the military who have become the instruments of these audacious murderers have for ever tarnished the honor of the British troops." The meeting then went on to demand that "the authors of these premeditated murders be for ever devoted to public hatred, and that the cry of vengeance be repeated by every mouth until they shall be effectively reached by the laws and punished." Also condemned was Austin Cuvillier, the elected member for Laprairie County, for having "ignominiously abandoned the Canadian body to serve a party unworthy of the support of every honest Canadian." The St Rémi meeting also put into circulation the new name for St James St when it referred to the killings as "the butchery of Blood St."[16]

Conscious of the frequent accusations of sedition and rebellion levelled at the Patriotes, Tracey had to tread warily when encouraging similar reactions from other parts of the province. His reaction to the Saint-Athanase meeting was intended as much for Patriote sympathisers as for the authorities:

Let the country raise its voice, and justice on the loathed murderers of the slaughtered victims will yet be obtained. Let every
Parish of every County in Lower Canada proclaim its abhor-
rence of the barbarous deed, and let the venerated name of
religion be invoked to strike a deeper horror into the guilty. Let
these weapons be used and these alone, and no momentary
connivance will baffle the demands for a just retribution. The
people cannot hesitate for a moment. Their liberties, their rights,
their dearest privileges are at stake. Their very lives, perhaps,
depend on the expression of their opinions on the fatal 21st of
May.[17]

Support for Tracey also came from a variety of newspapers
published elsewhere in Lower Canada and even further afield.
Neilson's *Gazette* and *Le Canadien* had been swift to condemn the use of fire-power against unarmed citizens.[18] In a
later editorial, Étienne Parent in *Le Canadien* viewed with
real pessimism the long-term consequences of the killings in
Montreal:

[...] nothing will be easier, in future, than to create pretexts to
call out the military. It will be sufficient for one party to pay a
dozen *bullies*, under the name of special constables, who by their
conduct, will exasperate the people and, on the first head
broken, to call out the soldiers. Adieu, then to the liberty of
elections! All peaceable citizens will remain at their houses, and
the alarmists will have the day.[19]

Elsewhere, newspapers such as the *Acadian Recorder*
(Halifax, NS), the *St Francis Courier and Sherbrooke Gazette*,
the *Sapper and Miner* and the *York Freeman* published strong
condemnations of the military killings. The *Brockville
Recorder* wrote "we cannot see the necessity of ordering the
troops to fire. The act seems to us rather a wonton one on the
part of the Authority, who it will be recollected, were the

favourers of Mr Bagg." The *Cobourg Reformer* was even more scathing in its condemnation of the magistrates: "Three men have been murdered, and numbers have been dreadfully and dangerously wounded. There can no defence be set up to justify the unconstitutional stretch of magisterial authority in ordering the military to fire on the people."[20]

The most surprising reaction came from a New York newspaper, the *Old Countryman*, not generally reputed to harbour pro-Patriote sympathies. It derided the Montreal Tory press for ascribing all the blame for the tragic outcome of May 21 to Tracey:

> Now, if Mr Tracey, after so long a contest, had come off "second-best", there might have been some grounds for asserting, that, enraged at his failure, his friends under highly excited feelings, had hooted, hissed and stoned their successful adversaries; but we do not often hear of the *Victor* at an election, inciting on those who have gained him his triumph, to tumult and disorder. It would appear, however, if the Montreal Record, Gazette and Herald are correct in their statements, that it was the *Victor*, and not the *Vanquished* that was dissatisfied; that not content with besting Mr Bagg at the Poll, he was determined to best him in the streets afterwards: and not only Mr Bagg, but the Magistrates also; and not only the Magistrates but the Soldiery in the bargain. Why, this Mr Tracey must be a sad fellow; what say you, sir, Guilty, or not Guilty?[21]

Macintosh found the constant attacks on him in the two Patriote newspapers so intolerable that he sent a second desperate appeal to the governor for the mark of public support he had been expecting since his earlier letter of May 29 on the subject:

> I find myself, assailed as I am by the unbridled and disaffected press of the Province, with every variety of calumny and libel, held up daily to the Troops under my command as a murderer

and a coward; to be totally unfitted for doing what I believe to be my duty, and properly maintaining the discipline and efficiency of the Troops, until supported and reassured by the declaration of His Excellency's approbation.

He finished his letter by asking to be relieved of further professional responsibility until a judicial enquiry of a civil or military nature had passed judgment on his actions. As an example of the attacks on him, he included the previous day's copy of the *Vindicator* with his letter.[22]

In his reply on June 11, the governor for once showed some understanding for the plight of the lieutenant colonel: "His Lordship is fully sensible of the painful situation in which you find yourself placed as a consequence of the base attacks levelled against your character and conduct connected with events which have not yet undergone a thorough investigation."[23] This was as clear as the governor could be in admitting that there would be no public declaration on his part until the courts had given a final verdict. He also turned down Macintosh's request to be relieved of duty. He had far more serious problems occupying his mind just then.

Cholera

The arrival of the first cases of cholera from the United Kingdom had long been expected. Montreal's newspapers had prepared their readers with reports of the civil unrest that the outbreak of the disease had already caused in major cities in France and Great Britain. The province's slow response to the impending danger followed by the implementation of inadequate measures prompted criticism from all sides. Earlier in the year, Tracey had been contemptuous of the decision by the House of Assembly to appropriate £10,000 to set up a quarantine station on Grosse Île and to establish health boards:

It is only one of the ways of frightening the people into the Cholera Morbus, rather than preventing it, and should that disease unfortunately make towards our coasts, any Quarantine regulations will not be able to prevent it of coming amongst us. The fears on that head we would advise the people of Canada to laugh at. This appropriation is the most useless of the whole session.[24]

By May the epidemic was no longer a laughing matter. Graphic descriptions of the disease in Britain and France filled the pages of the province's papers. The *Vindicator* quoted from a private letter from Calais dated March 31 where the sudden outbreak of cholera had resulted in several deaths after just two days. It was noticeable, the paper remarked, that the principal victims of the disease had been people living in "habits of filth and drunkenness." The paper therefore advised its readers to insist on "ventilating the clothing of seamen and prohibiting the importation of old rags."[25] Then the first ominous notice appeared in Montreal's newspapers: the Carricks from Dublin had arrived at Grosse Île on June 2 and was reported to have lost "42 passengers, her carpenter and one boy from some unknown disease."[26] Four days later, the *Vindicator* reported, Quebec City was thrown into great alarm at the news that two people had died at the quarantine station of what doctors there had diagnosed as Asiatic cholera.[27]

The news from Quebec City grew more alarming by the day. Immigrants were said to be swarming the city and the disease was finally taking a hold. Typical was a letter from a doctor in Quebec City dated June 9 that appeared in the *Vindicator*: "I am just come from seeing a case of Cholera—the woman's name is Prendergast—who was quite well this morning." For the moment, Tracey adopted a cynical attitude to the lack of preparedness on the part of the authorities in Montreal: "Our

Magistrates have, now, as good an auxiliary as the bullets of the soldiers to help them to thin this population. We are anxious to see what exertion they will make to resist the progress of this calamity."[28] Advice from Quebec's newspapers to the general population was well meaning but at times verging on the fanciful. The *Quebec Gazette* suggested that cleanliness, temperance in drinking, regularity in all habits, warm clothes "and perhaps above all a manful determination to meet the worse, and indeed a kind of heedlessness about the disease, are the most useful preventatives."[29]

By mid-June, Montreal was in the grip of the epidemic. Tracey reported that there had been 169 deaths in the city attributable to the disease. But it was the rapidity with which it had arrived that most shocked the Irish-born doctor: "The sudden manner in which the unfortunate persons seized with this disease are carried off is truly terrific. Several have been seized in our streets and after three or four hours are turned into blackening corpses." Strangely, Tracey still clung to the idea that the disease affected the poorer classes and those who lead irregular lives. He even quoted one comment he had heard: "It is sweeping off all the old drunkards attacked by it."[30] Four days later it was a chastened editor who was forced to admit that "some of our most worthy and eminent Citizens have been already carried off."[31] Business in the city had almost come to a standstill. The *Vindicator* was barely functioning and was able to publish only a half sheet after Tracey and several of his hands were taken ill but managed to recover in time.

As June drew to a close there were the first indications that the worst of the epidemic was over for Montreal. There were still deaths but businesses were slowly returning to normal activity and the *Vindicator* was able to put out a complete edition. Some of the deaths reported in the *Vindicator* were of those who had in one way or another been closely associated with the events surrounding Tracey. In Quebec, Justice Taschereau of the Court of King's Bench for the district of Quebec and Jacques-Philippe Saveuse de Beaujeu of the Legislative Council died within days of each other, while in Montreal Stephen Sewell succumbed to cholera leaving Macintosh and Temple bereft of an important legal counsellor. Tracey's brush with the disease convinced him that part of the reason for falling victim to cholera was psychological: the disease had "leant with particular severity," he wrote, "on those whose lives were strongly addicted to indulgence in intemperate excesses. Either these excesses or fear may be said to be the predisposing causes to the disease."[32]

On July 9, a close friend of Tracey's, William Campbell, a man who had supported him throughout the long election process, died from the disease. Within a week, Tracey himself fell gravely ill. Crowds gathered outside his house waiting for news of his condition. At 5 am on Wednesday, July 18, he died. His funeral took place next morning in the same parish church he had attended less than two months earlier for the funeral of the three victims of May 21. After the church service, escorted by a large gathering of his fellow citizens, Tracey's body was taken to the Catholic cemetery and interred.[33] The *Vindicator* ceased publication immediately depriving the Patriotes of its main contact with the English-language community. It was now left to *La Minerve* to keep alive the memory of the three victims of May 21 until the coroner's inquest reconvened at the end of August.

The Tracey monument erected in Notre-Dame-des-Neiges cemetery Montreal in 1866 by Tracey's brother John to replace an earlier one erected by Tracey's personal friends Louis-Hyppolite La Fontaine, Dr Vallée and Charles-Ovide Perrault. (Photo 2009, Robin Philpot)

7

The Grand Jury

The decision of Jean-Marie Mondelet to adjourn his inquest to the first day of the new criminal term of the Court of King's Bench was deeply troubling to the Patriotes. The last thing they wanted was to have the coroner's inquest cancelled in favour of an investigation by the grand jury. The grand jury was an essential part of the Court of King's Bench inherited from the British criminal justice system but it held its proceedings in private and all associated with it were sworn to secrecy. The system was open to abuse as the Patriotes constantly reminded the population. Jury selection was the responsibility of the sheriff, a Crown appointee. Earlier in the century, only jurors from the city of Montreal were summoned, but even when the sheriff finally extended his choice to include the entire district of Montreal, he continued to follow a practice that the Patriotes deemed elitist and biased in favour of the English party. The vast majority of those summoned continued to be merchants and professionals despite frequent editorials in *La Minerve* denouncing the abuse.[1] In February 1832, a new statute came into force: an "act to regulate the qualification and summoning of Jurors in civil and criminal matters (2 Geo.4.c.22)." It was this statute that was supposed to regulate the selection of the grand jurors for the next Court of King's Bench but the Patriotes had no confidence in Montreal's sheriff.

Louis Gugy had been born in Paris of Swiss parents and had served as a lieutenant in a regiment of Swiss Guards before finally immigrating to Quebec in 1795 to take up a family inheritance. For twenty years he had served as sheriff at Trois-Rivières before being appointed to a similar post in Montreal in 1827 but it was his other post that caused most concern for the Patriotes. After twice being elected to represent Saint-Maurice in the House of Assembly where he supported the English party, he was appointed to the Legislative Council in 1818 and was forced to relinquish his Assembly seat. In January, 1832 he had been one of the councillors who had voted in favour of imprisoning Tracey.[2]

When the new criminal term of the Court of King's Bench opened on Monday, August 27, 1832, the Patriotes' worst fears were confirmed. It was revealed that the grand jury was going to investigate the May 21 killings. Preparations for the composition of both the grand and petty juries had begun at the beginning of the month when John Delisle, the clerk of the peace, had commanded Gugy to produce a panel of twenty-four "good and lawful men" to serve on a grand jury and sixty similar men for the petty jury. When the names of the twenty-four grand jurors were revealed, it became clear that the latest statute on jury selection had not modified Gugy's usual practice. Eight jurors were from Montreal, one from Côte-des-Neiges, three from Pointe Claire and twelve from Lachine. Seven were French Canadian and seventeen British. In contrast, the panel of the petty jury showed that there had been a clear intention to reach as wide a distribution as possible in the choice of the sixty jurors: there were forty-nine French names and eleven British and twenty towns were represented by at least one or as many as six jurors.[3]

Proceedings opened at 10 am when nineteen grand jurors were sworn in. Charles Penner (presumably the same Mr Penner whom the *Montreal Gazette* had described as the best candidate for the Montreal County Assembly election in September 1831) from Lachine was appointed foreman of the jury. Chief Justice James Reid then delivered his charge to them in both French and English concentrating almost all of his attention on the one event that was on everyone's mind. The jury would have to decide, he told them, whether the officers were guilty of murder or whether in discharging their duty they were justified in their actions. In considering whether there was justification, the jury had to consider

> whether at the time the military force was called in, there existed a tumult and riot, dangerous to the public peace and safety, that is, whether a great crowd of persons was assembled and united, and who in a violent and tumultuous manner, attacked, or threatened to attack, and injure the persons or property of others [...] and if the public and safety was here in such danger, that it became necessary to quell this riot, and disperse those concerned in it, by all possible means, and that in effecting this, [Chauvin, Languedoc and Billet], being in the riot, fell by the firing of the military, acting under the direction of a magistrate or peace officer, it cannot be considered murder.[4]

None of the depositions during the coroner's inquest nor any of the affidavits produced by Macintosh and Temple had ever hinted that the three men killed by the army had been anything more than innocent bystanders. Even the Montreal Tory press had agreed that the men were unfortunate to be standing in the wrong place at the wrong time. It was odd that the chief justice should now raise the possibility that the three were in fact guilty of riot. If the men died, the chief justice repeated, during "the necessary suppression of a dangerous riot, or in dispersing the rioters," the jury was "bound to protect the magistrate and those acting under him," and to reject any bill for murder. If on the contrary, the chief justice told the jurors, "it shall appear to you that the military force has interfered without necessity, even with the authority or consent of the Magistrates, or that it has been exercised imprudently, by firing upon the citizens when not in a state of riot and tumult whereby the deaths of any of these individuals has been occasioned, you ought in that case to find such a bill for murder."[5]

The reason for the grand jury's taking over the investigation of the killings soon became clear when Mondelet rose to address the court. He explained why he had adjourned his coroner's inquest to the first day of the new criminal term and then admitted that the original jury was unlikely ever to reach a unanimous verdict. A roll call of their names showed why: only seven jurors were present. More importantly, one of the five who had failed to turn up, Louis-Narcisse Roy, had died during the summer.[6] That was sufficient reason for the chief justice to dispense with the coroner's inquest altogether and to discharge the remaining jury members. It was then revealed that the solicitor general, less than three months after stating that the Crown had no charges to lay against the two British officers, had now prepared bills of indictment not only against them but also against Robertson and Lukin, the two magistrates who had signed the requisition form.

The second day of the new term brought a new development. François Perrin, a Montreal merchant who had been summoned for the opening day of the new criminal term, had not been called with the other grand jurors. As his name had been on the general list of grand jurors, he turned up in court on the Tuesday morning to investigate. Côme-Séraphin Cherrier volunteered to speak on his behalf and used the opportunity afforded him to criticize the choice of jurors. He launched into a speech that highlighted the under representation of French Canadians on juries over a period of forty years. Before he was able to develop his argument, Gugy interrupted him to tell him that the absence of Perrin's name had been a clerical error and that Perrin would be sworn in as a grand juror. Undaunted, Cherrier complained that the recent reform of jury selection had done little to change Gugy's choice of a grand jury. Why, he asked, were twelve men selected from the same parish of Lachine, one of the least populated in the district of Montreal? Justice George Pyke, who was presiding in the absence of the chief justice, interrupted Cherrier and objected to the insinuations he was making against Gugy. Cherrier replied that his objections were perfectly legitimate since the new law had been designed specifically to prevent the very odd anomaly that had come to light in the present make-up of the grand jury. Justice Pyke adjourned the court until 1 pm in order to seek the chief justice's advice. When the court reconvened, the chief justice had returned. He announced that the sheriff had added the name of François Perrin to the list of grand jurors and that the problem was now resolved.[7]

In the absence of any leaks from the grand jury's investigation, *La Minerve* was left to consider Chief Justice Reid's charge to the grand jury. Why, the paper asked, had Reid concentrated so much on commenting on the law pertaining to riots? Why had the learned judge not spent equal time discussing the necessity for the troops and their commanders to use all other means in their power to put down a riot before resorting to the most extreme? Why did Reid not draw the jury's attention to the question of the Riot Act—was it read, and if so, at what time and in what manner? Were the troops' lives in danger when they opened fire? Were citizens' lives and their property ever in danger? Had Reid considered these questions, the paper insisted, his charge would have at least given the appearance of being impartial.

The paper also decided to follow up Cherrier's references to the recent changes in the provincial statutes on the selection of grand juries. In order to draw up a general list of jurors, sheriffs were now required to take just the first name from the individual lists provided by each parish, seigniory and township. In the case of those lists that were twice the size of others, then the sheriff could take two names for every one on the shorter lists. *La Minerve* offered no prizes to the mathematicians among its readers for working out what percentage Gugy had used in selecting the current grand jury which had twelve jurors from a very small parish and all of them born outside the country.[8]

The verdict

On Saturday, September 2, surprise greeted the depleted grand jury as it came back into court to give its verdict. Missing were the six French Canadian jurors. Charles Penner, foreman of the jury, announced that a majority "having fully and impartially examined into all the circumstances of the case" found that there were no grounds for any criminal charges to be levelled against the two officers and two magistrates. In an unusual move so early in a new criminal term, Penner also announced that the grand jury felt impelled by a sense of duty to make a presentment explaining what had led the fourteen members of the jury to reach their verdict. The summary they offered of the facts as they understood them referred to "breaches of the peace," to "a disposition towards violence" and then to "an increased disposition to riot." Various acts of violence had been committed, the presentment stated, after

James Reid, Chief Justice at the Court of the King's Bench in Montreal.
La Minerve accused him of partiality in his conduct of the grand jury
investigation of the St James St killings and particularly in his instructions
to the jurors. (McCord Museum – I-3560.1)

the close of voting and a body of rioters had assailed Henderson's store with stones and other missiles with the evident design of injuring those who had taken refuge inside. It was to subdue this riot that the troops intervened. As they were assaulted and resisted, they were obliged to open fire. The final paragraph was an encomium to the authorities:

> However much the Grand Jury may deplore the fatal conse-quences, which followed from the introduction of an armed force on that occasion, they feel persuaded that it was fully justi-fied by the conjuncture, and its timely interposition in their belief averted the calamities which must have ensued, if the rioters had been suffered to pursue their impetuous and destruc-tive course. With this view of the case, the Grand Jury cannot withhold the public declaration of their opinion, that the con-duct observed, as well by the magistrates as by the military authorities, during these events, is worthy of commendation at the hands of those who love peace and respect the laws, while the inhabitants of the city of Montreal, in particular, are deeply indebted to the firm discharge by those gentlemen of their respective duties, for restoration to a state of security, and for the protection of their lives and property.[9]

The refusal of the grand jury to find a true bill against the accused came as no surprise to *La Minerve*. The paper blamed Reid's charge to the jury for influencing it in favour of the four accused, and for speaking as though he were addressing a petit jury rather than a grand jury whose sole duty was to decide whether the four had a case to answer. It was not for the grand jury to investigate the riot or to try the case—it had simply to decide whether people had lost their lives through violence and whether the authors of that violence had been identified. It would then be the task of a petit jury to decide whether a riot had taken place and in what circumstances. But Reid had been less than clear on this matter, claimed

La Minerve. He had first told the grand jury not to examine how or why the riot had started since public safety was the responsibility of all sides. However, he had gone on to say that if public safety was endangered as a result of a riot, any action taken by the military under the command of magistrates to quell the disturbances would be legitimate, even if deaths occurred.

La Minerve had other concerns about Reid's charge to the jury. It was possible to argue that the magistrates had spent several days engineering a riot and had constantly acted as *agents provocateurs* right up until the time of the shooting, that the troops had been called out illegally and had been warned days before to expect a riot. If all this were true, and *La Minerve* was certain it was, then a petit jury might have found the four guilty of murder. Reid's charge had led the grand jury to call witnesses who defended the action of the four and who had only a partial understanding of the circumstances surrounding the shooting. The two officers and the two magistrates had been acquitted on the grounds of justification, a verdict only a petit jury could return, maintained the editorial. And it had been returned by fourteen jurors, ten from Lachine and four from Montreal, who had all been born abroad, were all English speakers and were all sympathetic to the four accused.[10]

The *Montreal Gazette*, however, could hardly contain its joy. "The question was one of riot and anarchy against law and justice, involving the public security," it trumpeted. The magistrates needed to be protected by the law when carrying out their duty otherwise none would be found to assume their office: "it was a question between MOBOCRACY and LAW. Had the former obtained ascendancy, the devastations of BRISTOL might have been renewed at MONTREAL. Thanks to the firmness and public virtue of our magistrates, the law triumphed, and an honest and Patriotic CANADIAN GRAND JURY have vindicated the law's supremacy." What was to be done to the "intriguing leaders who incite to riot, by their seditious harangues?" the paper asked. It responded in the form of another question: "will the Government at length awake to the danger and institute prosecutions against the seditious agitators of insurrection and the libellors of justice?"[11]

The government's response was less drastic than the one proposed by the *Gazette*'s editor but it did bring considerable satisfaction to the English party. On receiving news of the grand jury's decision, Aylmer issued a general order couched in the language of the jury's presentment. The order stated that a detachment of the 15th regiment had been called out by the magistrates of Montreal to help in suppressing a riot which was endangering the lives and property of the inhabitants. When the magistrates failed to restore order by other means, the troops were required to open fire, killing three and wounding others. All regretted the loss of life, none more so than the officers and troops involved but their timely involvement saved the lives and property of very many peaceful inhabitants of the city. The two officers and the troops under their commanded having been absolved of all blame, the governor wished to convey to them "his approbation of the judgment, steadiness and discipline displayed by them in their respective stations on that occasion."[12]

The next day, September 3, Aylmer wrote to Dr Robertson in his capacity as the senior magistrate in Montreal and asked him to communicate to his fellow magistrates the contents of the letter. The governor stated that he had always been confident that the measures taken by the magistrates would be found to have been necessary and were adopted only when all other means of restoring order had failed. He regretted that public meetings had been held during which the magistrates and the military "were rashly pronounced guilty of the foul crime of murder." Now that all parties had been cleared of all blame, he thanked the magistrates "for the firmness, moderation and judgment displayed by them during the whole of the disturbances which agitated the city of Montreal." Their action, he claimed, had prevented a repetition of the scenes witnessed so recently in Bristol where so many lives were lost and so much property destroyed.[13]

Aylmer's dispatches containing news of the grand jury's verdict reached Horse Guards a month later. Lord Hill, commander-in-chief of the British army, was moved to send him a letter in which he expressed his complete satisfaction with the result. Lord Hill, the letter read,

> feels bound to say, after an an attentive perusal of all the papers bearing up the case, that he knows no instance in which Troops have been employed for the suppression of riots, when greater judgment, discretion, or humanity have been displayed, and if these officers have since been annoyed by accusations of murder, and by every proceeding which could tend to keep alive anxiety, they have at least the consolation of feeling that they have discharged a painful but imperative duty, with temper and moderation, and that by so doing they put an end to disorders which would probably have led to consequences most disastrous to the city of Montreal.[14]

The editor of the *Montreal Gazette* could easily have written the various statements from the military authorities except that the language was mild compared to the spleen that he now vented on Tracey and the Patriotes:

> History will record that the criminal instigators to riot and bloodshed, the vile abettors of lawless outrage, braving with reckless audacity the laws they had dared to violate, had the

shameless effrontary, openly and publicly, to attempt to poison and pervert the minds of illiterate multitudes, to cover their own iniquity, and cast the blame of blood from their own guilty heads upon the official defenders of the laws and the peace of society.

The editorial went on to consider the long-term implications for the future of the province in the light of what had happened in the city. The body politic was diseased but nothing that a "little wholesome purging" could not cure. But if the disease were to become malignant, then eradication would be more difficult to effect and the consequences disastrous: "Besides, the experience of ages should awaken us to a timely suspicion, that something like a settled and deep-rooted plan of rebellion and revolution is organised, the longer endurance of which is fraught with hourly encreasing (*sic*) danger to the peace of society, and the permanence of our institutions."[15]

The paper followed up its attack a few days later, incensed that *La Minerve* had produced a special single sheet to publicize the governor's public approbation of the military and the magistrates. In a long diatribe of an editorial, the paper analysed what it saw as the fundamental difference between its politics and that of the party it opposed: "there exists among the faction a deep rooted malignancy against our institutions and our laws, that will only be satisfied by their overthrow. Hence the constant, unremitting, incessant, persevering hostility to everything British." Aiding and abetting "the faction," it claimed, were two newspapers, *La Minerve* and *Le Canadien*. The first was described as "that official organ of treason, whence all the sedition that the demagogues concoct during their dark and filthy orgies, is poured out in disgusting, loathsome, and nauseating streams that taint and contaminate with political and moral defilement, all who are ignorant or weak enough to drink of the corruption," while the second was guilty of producing "a mass of low scurrility, intentional misrepresentation, vulgar abuse, disgusting defamation, libellous insolence, seditious malevolence and treasonable menace against the civil and military authorities."

The grand jury's presentment inspired the Tory newspaper to assign guilt even where no proof had been offered to support such allegations. Even the three victims of May 21 were not spared:

> The lives of rioters, it may be said, have been forfeited to the laws they outraged. True, but their deaths must be looked upon as an unfortunate sacrifice incident to the occasion, since these were the deluded victims of the guilt of mightier criminals who live at large, and still menace the peace of the country. A heavy weight of guilt rests somewhere. It is not with the civil or military authorities, for these have been justified, and commended. It must then rest upon the heads of the apostles of faction, of the reckless and restless disturbers of society, and against these justice now demands that weapons of the law should be directed.[16]

Support for *La Minerve*'s critical stance on the whole affair came from the *Quebec Gazette* which wrote that the public would surely view with suspicion the grand jury's decision:

> It will be satisfied, at any rate, that no real trial has taken place; that the accused were not confronted with the accusers; but that the proceedings upon which acquittal is alleged to have taken place, were (contrary to the very spirit of the English law of trial) carried on in secret, as it were; [...] The public can never overlook the fact that death has ensued by the fire of the troops, whose interference in civil matters they look upon with just jealousy; they can never overlook the fact, that the interference took place during a legally summoned assembly in the execution of the most solemn and important of their duties, at the instigation of

known partisans. They cannot therefore, we apprehend, consider the decision of the grand jury as a fair trial—as a fair acquittal;—and they are now fully justified in again seeking justice by all the means which the law and the constitution still offer them.[17]

New arrest warrant

On September 12, 1832 Joseph Roy received three affidavits that had been sworn before his fellow magistrate, André Jobin. They contained sufficient new evidence, he was told, to issue a warrant against Macintosh and Temple. The three witnesses were François Tavernier, James Magaughran and Samuel J. Pierce. Tavernier had already testified at the coroner's inquest and the other two had little to add that was new. Magaughran had been in St James St on his way home when he had seen a large number of people coming from the election. There was a sudden disturbance amongst the crowd and a short time afterwards the troops arrived on the street followed by many special constables who were throwing stones at Tracey's men. After the troops halted at Dr Robertson's house, he heard Macintosh give the order, "Make ready, present, fire." When they fired, Magaughran said, the troops were not in the slightest danger.

Pierce, a carpenter, was working in the fenced-off yard of Mr Wragg's house situated on the southern side of St James St about midway between Dr Robertson's house and St Peter St when Tracey and his friends made their way along the street. Pierce looked over the fence as a large group of Bagg's friends and many special constables first followed Tracey and then retired to the Place d'Armes. They returned preceded this time by troops under the command of Macintosh and Temple. When they reached Dr Robertson's house, the special constables and other people behind the soldiers rushed forward brandishing batons and throwing stones at Tracey's party as it continued its progress along the street. Pierce then watched as Macintosh came forward and ordered the special constables to retire to the rear of the soldiers. The troops came to a halt and then prepared to fire. When they opened fired they were not in the least danger.[18]

All three affidavits emphasised the fact that at the time of the shooting, there was no riot in progress and that the soldiers' lives were not in danger. Still, Roy was hesitant to act. Did the grand jury's decision mean that the officers could not be rearrested for the killings of May 21? He decided to seek William Walker's advice. Walker had followed the case closely since the time of the coroner's inquest and needed little time to form an opinion on the question. It was possible to argue, he told Roy, that when the two officers appeared before the grand jury they were not faced with legal jeopardy and consequently the outcome of the jury's deliberations offered them no indemnity against future arrest. The original coroner's warrant did not have the same effect as a magistrate's warrant. If the officers had been arrested under a magistrate's warrant, they would have been examined and either committed to trial or discharged but the issuing of a coroner's warrant had prevented the magistrates from taking action against them. Walker's advice, therefore, was that the officers could be arrested on the basis of the affidavits that Roy had received. He further advised that as the case involved a capital felony Roy should issue a special warrant so as to ensure that the constable executing the warrant brought the men before Roy.[19]

Roy pressed on with his investigations and on September 14 he received a visit from Theophile Bruneau, a Montreal lawyer and Papineau's brother-in-law, who provided the all important affidavit. Bruneau had spent most of May 21 at the polling station but his testimony offered no startling new revelation. It did, however, provide far more details about the final hours before the shooting than did the other three affidavits. In particular, it demonstrated how aggressively the special constables had behaved on the day. When the troops arrived on the Place d'Armes around 3 pm, Bruneau said, all was quiet as evidenced by the arrival of Mme Ladouceur who turned up to vote at the same time. She was followed shortly afterwards by several other women. It was close to 4 pm when the numbers of special constables suddenly began to increase noticeably. They were armed with their familiar blue staves which had been cut in two and appeared very agitated, ready to pick a fight at the slightest excuse with Tracey's supporters. The worst culprits in this matter were Louis Malo, Charles Try and Mr Farquar Jr but, so Bruneau noticed, the magistrates did very little to keep them under control. When Bruneau complained about the presence of the troops, the returning officer denied having called them out, saying all he asked for was an increase in the number of special constables. As for the events after 5 pm, Bruneau observed them from the Place d'Armes close to Dillon's corner and opposite the polling station.

After Tracey had left the polling station, about thirty of his party remained behind in the Place d'Armes shouting "Huzza, Tracey for ever." One of them, an Irishman who was shouting louder than the others, was suddenly attacked by Try and Farquar, two special constables, who beat him senseless. Malo was also scuffling with others and striking them with his stave. There then developed a general free-for-all between Tracey's party, the special constables and other Bagg supporters. Under the force of sticks and stones, Tracey's people were forced to retreat as far as the bank in St James St from where they began to defend themselves by throwing stones at their opponents. It was then the turn of the constables to retreat to the Place d'Armes but not for long. They soon returned behind a detachment of soldiers under the command of Macintosh and Temple, throwing stones at Tracey's supporters who were retreating along the street. Bruneau had become caught up in the crowd running away and had come level with Mr Molson's house when he heard the troops firing at them. He turned around and saw Casimir Chauvin lying dead on the ground. In his opinion it was an assassination, the murder of people who were running away.[20]

This was the confirmation Roy needed to issue a warrant against Macintosh and Temple. On September 15, the magistrate entrusted the high constable with the warrant and insisted that the two officers be brought to him in the first instance. Delisle met with Temple who agreed to turn up at the courthouse but Macintosh preferred to remain on the Île Sainte-Hélène where most of the garrison had been since the outbreak of cholera in Montreal and await the outcome of their legal appeal. Through their counsel, Samuel Gale, the men petitioned the chief justice for a writ of *habeas corpus* on the grounds that the arrest warrant had been issued for the same alleged offences for which they had been arrested nearly four months earlier, that the bills of indictment had been rejected by a grand jury and that in the end they had been discharged.[21] The chief justice and Justice Pyke were in discussion with Gale when William Walker and Cherrier turned up at the courthouse.

As soon as Walker understood what Gale was attempting, he intervened and suggested to the judges that they wait until Roy's warrant had been fully executed and the officers brought before him as the law stipulated. This would allow the magistrate to question them, Walker continued, and then to turn over the information to the court. He might even have information to which the judges did not have access. The chief justice refused Walker's plea, saying that the affidavits could be obtained from the magistrate later. When Gale persisted with his petition, Cherrier and Walker continued to argue that the magistrate's warrant took precedence over the current proceedings. Michael O'Sullivan KC then entered the argument objecting to what he described as an attempt by Cherrier and Walker to usurp the role of crown officers. They replied that they were entitled to have their say since they represented the injured parties in the matter but O'Sullivan would not give way. Instead, he stated that it was his opinion that the court should discharge the officers since the grand jury's rejection of the earlier bills exempted them from a second arrest. The chief justice eventually decided to adjourn the case till the following Monday.

Over the weekend there was a flurry of activity by the authorities. Aylmer learned of the existence of Roy's arrest warrant on the Sunday and immediately ordered the solicitor general to return to Montreal. Meanwhile, the judges made an attempt to have Roy hand over the affidavits he had in his possession. Roy was reluctant to accede to their request and once more he sought legal advice from Walker. Walker told him that as the accused had still not been brought before him, Roy was justified in not parting with his affidavits. Furthermore, Walker said, a writ of *habeas corpus* was intended to secure release from imprisonment and not from an arrest which had produced no imprisonment.[22] Early on the Monday morning, Roy wrote to John Delisle, clerk of the peace, to say that he would transmit the affidavits to the judges just as soon as his warrant had been executed.[23]

The court reconvened at 10 am with Walker and Cherrier once more in attendance facing the combined strength of Charles Richard Ogden, the solicitor general, Michael

O'Sullivan and Samuel Gale. Gale had drawn up a petition that played on the authorities' fears by suggesting that Roy's action was just the beginning of a new trend in attacks on the political allegiance of the province: "the same renewals of arrests might be repeated in endless succession, for the advancement of seditious and vindictive purposes, and a system of persecution will be established, under which no laws could long be enforced or Government subsist."[24]

The chief justice opened the proceedings by asking Ogden for his comments on the magistrate's warrant. Ogden said that he found Roy's behaviour both extraordinary and totally unjustified. The innocence of the two army officers had been conclusively established by the findings of the grand jury and by the presentment which had accompanied that verdict. Quoting from the Riot Act, which he said had been read on May 21, he pointed out that guilt was attached to the deceased and to all those who had not dispersed within the hour. Those who had neglected to disperse were guilty of a felony and that, he said, had been established by the grand jury.

Walker had spent the weekend studying various legal treatises in support of Roy's action and was about to address the court when Ogden demanded to know on whose behalf Walker was appearing. Walker replied that he represented the private prosecutors in as much as the law allowed a private individual to prefer a charge and to follow it up by an indictment. In this sense, he said, he represented the Crown. Ogden, however, insisted that there was no question of private prosecutors having a say in court. He was the crown officer and solely responsible for the prosecution. O'Sullivan concurred and argued that in fact the prosecution had already finished and, sounding more ominous, warned that Roy's issuing of an arrest warrant made him liable to pay the two officers the sum of £500 each in compensation. Walker asked to be heard as an *amicus curiae* but this too was refused. He was finally allowed to cite the authorities he had prepared but it was to no avail since the chief justice gave his decision before the judges had time to follow up the references: the rejection of the bills by the grand jury, he declared, for ever exempted the parties from arrest by a magistrate's warrant. Macintosh and Temple were accordingly discharged "without bail or mainprise."[25]

Macintosh wrote to the governor that same day informing him of the court's decision and including a copy of his petition to the chief justice. In an act of bravado, he also informed his commander-in-chief that he and Captain Temple intended to take immediate steps to recover from Joseph Roy the penalty for which Michael O'Sullivan had said the magistrate was liable.[26] In reality, Macintosh had decided to return to the United Kingdom at the soonest opportunity. He had been informed that a new grand jury might well find that he had a case to answer and he was not prepared to risk the consequences. A quick visit by Lord Aylmer to the Montreal garrison in late September had all the appearance of a public act of confidence in the men of the 15th Foot and their commandant, but the governor had decided on changes for the garrison. On October 6, he wrote to Sir John Colborne to order Lt Col McDougall and two companies of the 79th Highlanders to proceed to Montreal from York (Toronto). Later in the month he would order a detachment of Royal Artillery to move from Kingston to Montreal.[27]

Macintosh wrote on October 6 to Aylmer requesting fifteen months of leave of absence to proceed to Europe "on very urgent private affairs." In support of his request he pointed out that it was almost two and half years since he had last been to the United Kingdom on leave of absence and he had served a total of four years and two months abroad with his regiment.[28] The governor granted the request on October 9 and Macintosh left Montreal a few days later for New York.[29]

On October 20 he sailed back to England on the packet ship *Sovereign* in the company of Captain Piper of the Royal Engineers. After arriving in Liverpool, Macintosh made his way immediately to Brighton where King William IV was in residence at the Royal Pavilion. There Lieutenant General Sir Herbert Taylor, private secretary to the king, arranged an audience for the Scottish officer. The meeting lasted an hour during which the king, who appeared to have been well briefed concerning the events of May 21, "personally expressed his entire approbation of the Lieutenant Colonel, of Captain Temple, whose name the King mentioned, and of the troops under their command." The following day, Macintosh was invited to dine with the king. News of the officer's complete rehabilitation came some three months later when the *Montreal Gazette* informed its readers that "the King has been graciously pleased to confer on Lt Col Macintosh of the 15th the Third Class of the Royal Hanoverian Guelphic Order."[30]

The Viger reports

London had been made aware of the shootings in late June but it was only in mid-July when the Assembly's agent in the British capital raised the subject with the Colonial Office did the British government appear to take the matter seriously. On July 11, 1832 Denis-Benjamin Viger wrote to Lord Goderich, secretary of state for the colonies, and requested a meeting at the earliest possible opportunity.[31]

Viger was one of the leading Patriotes of his day. A lawyer by training and independently wealthy, he had become involved in politics at an early age. He was elected member

Denis-Benjamin Viger, the Patriote party's influential elder statesman
and its agent in London. He succeeded in gaining the ear of Lord
Goderich, secretary of state for the colonies, and won his support for
an enquiry into the shootings and the conduct of the grand jury.
(Les Éditions du Septentrion)

for Montreal East in 1796 and Montreal West in 1808, the same year that his cousin, Louis-Joseph Papineau, won his first election. He became a prominent member of the Canadian Party and had helped Jocelyn Waller to set up the *Canadian Spectator*. In 1828, together with Neilson and Cuvillier, he had made up the delegation sent to London where they each appeared before the House of Commons committee on Canadian affairs. The favourable outcome of that mission had led to Viger's appointment to the Legislative Council, a source of acute embarrassment for Papineau and the Patriotes. The problem eventually resolved itself in 1831 when Viger was appointed as the Assembly's agent in London where he was expected to liaise with the colonial office and seek support for the Patriotes in the House of Commons.[32]

Viger had arrived in London in June 1831 and had quickly established a good working relationship with Goderich. Nevertheless, the first twelve months had been difficult ones as in meeting after meeting Viger had had to defend the Assembly's accusations against James Stuart, Quebec's suspended attorney general. The killing of three unarmed French Canadians in Montreal by British troops threatened to be an even more controversial subject.

Goderich agreed to see Viger at the colonial office in Downing St and proposed Friday, July 13. The meeting was brief and to the point. Viger informed the minister of the death of the three French Canadians and expressed his serious misgivings about the way the authorities in Montreal were handling the affair. The minister listened but declined to make any comment for the time being.

A few days later, Viger put new pressure on the colonial office by providing specific details about the arrest of Macintosh and Temple and their subsequent appearance before the chief justice. Viger was critical of the way the proceedings had been conducted, he wrote. The chief justice and his two fellow judges had colluded with counsel for the accused to allow bail without any argument having been heard. William Walker, whom Viger described as counsel for the families of the deceased, had tried to gain access to the depositions supporting the two officers that had not been part of the coroner's inquest, but his request had been turned down by Stephen Sewell KC. Walker had then appealed to the solicitor general to be allowed to see the depositions and to speak against the application for bail but that request too had been denied. Everything was over in a matter of minutes and bail had been set at £200 with two securities of £100 until the two officers reappeared in court on August 27. Viger expressed surprise both at the summary nature of the proceedings in a matter of such seriousness and at the insignificant sums required for bail. Back in 1827, he reminded the minister, Waller and Duvernay had been accused of the lesser offence of libel and arrested but bail had been set at £1000 each with two securities of £500 each.[33]

Goderich took over a week to reply and then merely expressed surprise at the failure of the coroner's court to agree on a verdict. He dismissed the amount of bail required of the two officers as unimportant since it was highly unlikely, he wrote, that the officers would fail to turn up in court.[34] Undaunted, Viger kept up his discussion with Goderich via a series of letters he exchanged with the colonial office over the next month. The coroner should have summoned more than the minimum number of twelve jurors if he had wanted a majority verdict, Viger insisted. And when the coroner discovered that one of the jurors had already given his opinion on the killings before the inquest had opened, he should have summoned a new jury.[35]

News that Goderich had received reports from Montreal's magistrates prompted another letter from Viger requesting permission to see them. Goderich refused claiming the contents referred to matters still under judicial review. Viger replied pointing out that he was a member of the magistracy and was entitled to view their reports. Furthermore, he could not understand how his discussions with Goderich could in any way influence the courts in Canada.[36] Midway through August, Viger received new information from Montreal and again requested a meeting with Goderich. The minister saw him on August 29 but refused to react officially until Viger had given him a written account.

Viger wrote that same day, immediately after the meeting. For once he allowed his emotions to colour his language:

> Blood has been spilt in the streets of Montreal, on 21st of May last. Three of its inhabitants have been killed, several have been wounded. It has been spilt by a Company of a Regiment in Garrison, and it is the blood of those who but recently rivalling the army, repelled from their native land the enemies of England who had come to invade it.

Continuing in similar vein, Viger offered the minister a long detailed account of how the Montreal West by-election was conducted. He was particularly critical of both the magistrates and the returning officer. The election had been policed by a group of magistrates the majority of whom were known supporters of Stanley Bagg and some were even members of the Legislative Council that had condemned Daniel Tracey to prison only three months earlier. These same magistrates, Viger concluded, had constantly usurped the authority that was vested solely in the returning officer and had recruited hundreds of special constables, many of them Bagg supporters, against Dupré's express wishes. When the returning officer eventually requested the presence of constables, his reasons were specious and unjustified as were those that led to the calling out of the military on the penultimate day of voting.[37]

Goderich was careful not to become too embroiled in the controversy. He waited ten days before replying. His response was measured, even evasive. He expressed regret for the loss of life on May 21 but professed reluctance to express an opinion on the conduct of the various parties until the matter had come before the courts. The Government had no desire to screen the delinquency of any person, he wrote, "but it is its first duty to keep itself aloof from those party feelings which unhappily appear to be mixed up in this question." His hope was that the trial would be conducted with calmness and impartiality and that the jury would not allow itself to be influenced by what he termed "those angry publications" which he said had created a prejudice against the accused.[38]

Viger had little option but to wait. Eventually, in late October, news of the grand jury's verdict and presentment reached him. He hurriedly requested a new meeting with Goderich who agreed to see him on October 25. In a letter to Papineau written shortly after the meeting, Viger described the secretary of state as being honestly surprised by the news from Montreal. Informed of the manner in which the grand jury had been selected, Goderich knitted his brow, Viger wrote, and accused him of making a serious accusation against the sheriff. In Viger's opinion, Goderich's facial expression betrayed the minister's unease at what appeared to be a deliberate flouting of the law by those who were supposed to uphold it. To emphasize his point, Viger referred the minister to the recent law on jury selection that had been passed after a twenty-year campaign to bring about much needed reform. For years, he told Goderich, the Legislative Council had blocked the bills that the Assembly had sent to it to regulate the manner in which jurors were selected. The new law was now in existence but the sheriff had failed to obey it. Even if the act had not been passed, Viger had suggested, did the minister not think that the composition of the recent grand jury in Montreal was "evidently vicious and contrary to every principle of justice, and to the nature of the institution of the Jury?"

He reminded Goderich of something the minister had said: "That a sheriff might become criminal not only by violating the provisions of a positive law, but also by abusing the discretionary power which the law gave him." Viger said that the sheriff of Montreal had done both. He then drew a historical analogy of the sort that Tracey was so fond. It was the case, he wrote,

> that men might delude themselves so far as to commit crimes under the persuasion that their actions were meritorious and agreeable to the Divinity. In Spain it was for a long time the custom to burn Heretics, and the tragedy received the name of 'an Act of Faith.' In Ireland the Protestants thought they deserved well of their country, and that they were performing a sort of *act of religion*, and one of utility to the State, in massacreing Catholics; that it was for the [pur]pose of avoiding the dangers which might arise from the prejudices of a portion of the community, that Jurors ought to be taken from the mass and body of those whom the law called to act as such, in order that as far as was possible the danger of having picked Jurors, actuated by feelings and interests favorable or unfavorable to the accused, might be avoided.

Goderich replied that he had not been informed of much of what Viger had told him but said that he felt there must be a statement of facts and indeed an investigation. Viger assured him there would be one and that the Assembly would take charge of it since it was the only tribunal where matters would be conducted in the open and without mystery, unlike what happened when Crown Officers took charge of matters.

After all he had heard, Goderich was still reluctant to voice any direct criticism of the situation in the province other than to say how extraordinary it all appeared. He did, however, allow himself to admit to having read something on the subject in a London newspaper. The piece that Goderich was referring to was a letter signed "A volunteer" that had appeared in the *Morning Chronicle,* London's reformist newspaper, on October 25, 1832. It had contained much of the same information that Viger had already sent to the minister and it had laid great stress on the loyalty that French Canadians had shown during the war of 1812. Goderich's reference to the paper was the nearest a British minister could come to openly supporting the Patriotes' grievance concerning May 21. Viger also interpreted it as sanctioning an inquiry by the Lower Canada Assembly into the action of British troops in the colony. He lost no time in communicating the information to Papineau.[39]

The new parliamentary session

Despite their triumphant bluster, Montreal's conservative press knew that the May 21 affair was unlikely to go away. The military and the magistrates may have been exonerated by both the grand jury and the courts, but the Patriotes still dominated the Chamber and *La Minerve* was still being published, two good reasons why the matter looked likely to remain alive for the foreseeable future. For Montreal's merchant community, the prospect of the new parliamentary session now only weeks away being distracted by the affair to the exclusion of more important commercial matters filled it with alarm. The problem had preoccupied the English party since the end of the election but early attempts to win over public support had not been successful.

The one piece of encouraging news for the party came from an unexpected quarter during the summer. Michel Bibaud's call for a French-language newspaper to defend the province's constitutional status-quo found a sympathetic ear in the person of Joseph-Vincent Quiblier, superior of the Séminaire de Saint-Sulpice. It was in the interests of the Sulpicians to demonstrate their loyalist credentials as negotiations with the British authorities over property rights were reaching a critical stage. They found in Pierre-Édouard Leclère and his nephew, John Jones, the former head printer of the *Courrier des États-Unis*, two men willing to take charge of the new paper while remaining under Quiblier's control. The first issue of *L'Ami du peuple, de l'ordre et des lois* appeared on July 22, 1832, just days after the *Vindicator* had ceased publication. Despite the new editor's assurances that he intended to put all personal animosity aside, the paper demonstrated its true *raison d'être* by attacking *La Minerve* with the same ferocity as its English-language counterparts.

Attempts by the English party to build up support for the military were only partially successful. As early as May 23, the *Montreal Herald* had announced that "addresses of thanks to the Magistrates and to Colonel Macintosh for the energetic measures pursued on Monday to maintain the public peace and to preserve the lives and property of the citizens" would be available in the offices of the newspaper awaiting the signatures of a grateful public.[40] Nothing more was heard of the appeal until, early in September, the *Montreal Gazette* wrote that the addresses had been transferred to the Montreal Exchange. Readers were encouraged to come forward and add their signatures.[41]

The disruption to normal life caused by the cholera epidemic in Montreal may have accounted for the five months it had taken the organisers of the signature campaign to announce the results of their efforts. By mid-October three hundred people had added their names. Unfortunately for them, Macintosh had already left Montreal for New York and it was Captain Temple who turned up instead on October 19 to accept on the regiment's behalf the citizens' thanks. In a short ceremony, Samuel Gerrard, George Auldjo and two other businessmen spoke of their gratitude to the officers and men of the 15th for having saved the lives and property of Montreal's inhabitants. The *Montreal Gazette* printed a half sheet supplement to announce the news.[42] *La Minerve* was not impressed. It reminded its readers that the list of three hundred names had not been published, and for good reason, since the vast majority of people on the list did not live in the West Ward and were either Bagg supporters or friends of *L'Ami du peuple*.[43]

The Patriotes proved more effective in garnering public support. In anticipation of the new parliamentary session, they began a new campaign to highlight their grievances as they had done in 1830. Their most successful meeting occurred on September 28 when Pierre-Dominique Debartzch, a Patriote member of the Legislative Council, and Louis Bourdages organised a meeting at Saint-Charles-sur-Richelieu of leading inhabitants of Richelieu, Verchères, Saint-Hyacinthe, Rouville, and Chambly counties. Among the many resolutions passed that day, the forerunners of the 92 Resolutions, one specifically called for an enquiry to be set up to investigate the events of May 21 and the composition of the grand jury.

At the beginning of November a similar meeting was held in L'Assomption just north-east of Montreal on the initiative of Édouard-Étienne Rodier, the town's recently elected member of the House of Assembly. The meeting coincided with the reappearance of the *Vindicator*. Over the three and half months since the paper had last appeared, its new proprietor, Édouard-Raymond Fabre, the Montreal bookseller, had discussed the future direction of the newspaper with other concerned Patriotes. For some, the Irish connection needed to be maintained. For others, the paper needed to reach out to a wider readership. The 106 American votes that Bagg had received as against just seven for Tracey decided the matter. The new launch of the *Vindicator* came on Friday, November 2 under the editorship of John Thomas, an American.

The intense political activity of the Patriotes during September and October finally spurred the English party into action. A public meeting at the British American Hotel in Montreal was organised for Saturday, November 3, aimed at attracting "those who disapprove of the late assemblies and who wish to declare to His Majesty their attachment to the Constitution under which they live, and which they would preserve unaltered from the threatened changes of the *party*."[44] There was a large turnout, as many as five hundred people according to the *Montreal Gazette*. Many of the people present were those who had actively supported the Bagg campaign: Campbell Sweeny, Joseph Shuter, John Molson Jr, Jules Quesnel, Jean-Baptiste Castonguay, Samuel Gerrard, Horatio Gates, Daniel Arnoldi, George Auldjo, Abner Bagg and William Caldwell among many others. Stanley Bagg was conspicuous by his absence. Michel Bibaud's brother, Pierre, one of the three Bagg supporters who had called for the adjournment of the poll on May 19, reflected the tone of the meeting when he argued that any change in the way the Legislative Council was selected, especially if the people at large were allowed a say, would be dangerous and a reversal of the first principles of government: "It would be erecting a pure democracy which would become absolute and universal," he told a receptive audience, "—and would eventually give rise to cabals and jealousies and to every evil that can possibly await a people."[45]

The Patriotes responded by calling their own public meeting on Wednesday, November 7 at the lumber yard of Louis Roy Portelance. Tracey's former close circle of supporters and advisers turned out in force: Cherrier, Rodier, Robert Nelson, Joseph Roy, Louis Perrault, Dr Pierre Beaubien, Dr Vallée, John and Joseph Donegani, André Jobin, Jacques Viger and Pierre-Louis Letourneux. Two other notable Patriotes present at the meeting were Chevalier de Lorimier and Thomas Storrow Brown. The aim of the meeting was to approve the text of a petition to be presented to the House of Assembly. The document aired the Patriotes' main grievances, both long-running and more recent ones, concerning the state of the province. Some of Tracey's favourite themes—the Legislative Council, the fate of the township lands and the freedom of the press—figured prominently but so too did references to the recent cholera epidemic which was blamed on the increase in immigration, and to the proposed annexation of Montreal to Upper Canada.

Such grievances, however, were a mere preamble to what clearly was the major grievance: the events of May 21. The petition called on the House to set up an investigation to discover and punish those guilty of wrongdoing during the election. A coordinating committee of fifteen was chosen to liaise with committees elsewhere in the district of Montreal and to oversee the collection of signatures in time for the new parliamentary session scheduled to open on November 15.[46]

A week later, La Minerve published the first part of the text on the day the new session opened. A further instalment followed in the next issue and the third and final part appeared on November 23, the day that James Leslie, the Scottish-born Assembly member for Montreal's East Ward, presented the petition before the House. It was the first move in what turned out to be the biggest inquiry the House of Assembly had ever launched in its short history.

The most controversial aspect of the document was the long account of the events that had led up to the shooting of May 21. It was the strongest indictment of the magistrates and the military that the Patriotes had produced since the events themselves. The main targets were those magistrates who belonged to the Legislative Council:

> certain Legislative Councillors residing in Montreal interfered unduly in the Election in question, by shewing themselves the vindictive opponents of Mr Tracey and the Partizans of Mr Bagg, the opposing Candidate: they abused their power for the purpose of adopting (in concert with the majority of the other Justices of the Peace in the said city, and in behalf of their favorite Candidate Mr Bagg) a regular system of intimidation and violence, until then unheard of, and which, if allowed to pass with impunity, would snatch the right of electing the Representatives of Montreal out of the hands of the Electors, and place it in those of the Magistrates.[47]

The petition was equally scathing of the returning officer, the judges of the Court of King's Bench and the sheriff of Montreal all of whom were accused in some way of contributing to the scandal associated with the events of May 21. The document ended on a typically defiant note:

> The blood of our brethren and countrymen has been shed. Men who were exercising a right common to all citizens, (that of being partizans of one Candidate rather than of another) a right which we think we may all exercise, without thereby incurring the risk of being shot, have been killed. We recognise no tribunal on earth, except a Petty Jury, the right of declaring that man innocent of the crime of murder who has taken away the life of his fellow creature.[48]

Setting up the inquiry

The Assembly delegated Leslie, Bourdages and two other members to convey to the governor a request for all official documents in his possession concerning the magistrates' activity during the election, Macintosh's arrest, the coroner's inquest, the application of Macintosh and Temple for a writ of *habeas corpus* before the judges of the Court of the King's Bench, the indictments against Macintosh, Temple, Robertson and Lukin at the Court of King's Bench, the reports of the solicitor general and other Crown Officers, and any other written information which may have been received by the governor. The intention of the Assembly was to go way beyond the narrow confines of the coroner's inquest in its investigation. In less than twenty-four hours, Aylmer had agreed to the Assembly's request. Lt Col Craig delivered a first batch of documents on November 28. More arrived on December 3, the day that the Assembly voted in favour of setting up a committee of the whole House to examine by evidence the events of May 21.

Papineau was surprised at Aylmer's apparent willingness to cooperate and to provide the Assembly with sensitive military documents. In a letter to his wife on December 6, Papineau had an explanation for the governor's change of heart: "He is beginning to see what a very difficult situation he is in. He will raise no difficulty in turning over what he has in his possession, which would not have been the case one month ago. This confirms in a way what I wrote: that a surfeit of evil will perhaps provide its own remedy".[49]

For the first time, Papineau told his wife, the authorities had recognised the right of the Assembly to question and to receive a copy of the orders given to the military, something that would have been unthinkable in Governor Craig's time.

Since he had arrived in Quebec City for the opening of the new parliamentary session, Papineau had sensed a change of attitude towards him even in the most unexpected quarters. Large numbers of people had called on him. Many of them were friends, he wrote in another letter to his wife, but it was another group of people whose visits struck him as both curious and encouraging: "I find it peculiar that more of the military than ever have been visiting me. There are any number of others in the garrison still waiting to do so. It is possible to interpret their behaviour in good part and to see it as evidence of the regret they feel at the military involvement on 21 May"[50] It also demonstrated, Papineau suspected, that the army and its commander-in-chief were apprehensive about the outcome of the Assembly's forthcoming inquiry.

Papineau's optimism received an added boost in late December when he eventually received Viger's letter detailing the conversation he had had with Goderich on October 25. It was an almost certain guarantee, he told his wife, that the governor was powerless to hinder the work of the inquiry: "Next, Lord Aylmer finds himself attacked and warned that the government in England must be expecting the inquiry that we have started, and that if he tries to stop it, he who is one of the accused, the responsibility will be his alone and the determination to do so will be perceived as coming from him and not from overseas."[51]

The prospect of a long inquiry into the events of May 21 whetted the appetite of other groups in Montreal who were keen to air their own grievances about the electoral process. Two petitions were presented in the House on Wednesday, November 28. One came from Raymond Plessis and other electors of Montreal's East Ward accusing Olivier Berthelet, the successful candidate, of having paid for people to be transported from different parts of the city to vote for him, offering them presents, benefits and rewards for doing so, opening and supporting "houses of public entertainment" and employing the services of bullies to ensure his return. They asked for Berthelet's election to be declared null and void.[52]

The other petition was presented by Ebenezer Peck, the American-born member for Stanstead, where he practised law. Normally voting with the Patriotes in the Assembly, Peck surprised many when he presented a petition from Stanley Bagg complaining of Tracey's election and naming a number of electors who he claimed had voted twice. The real victor, Bagg stated, was himself. The Assembly decided to investigate the claims of the East Ward voters but hesitated over Bagg's petition. A short debate followed which offered a foretaste of the debates that were to surround the inquiry. Sensing there was little support for Bagg, Peck decided to withdraw his petition.[53] As the petition was not accepted, the list of those who had supposedly voted twice was never published. Prudently Bagg did not see fit to publish it elsewhere. Once the poll book was handed over to the inquiry, Bagg knew it would have been impossible to continue claiming that fraud had taken place.

The inquiry finally got under way on Tuesday, December 11, 1832. At first two sittings a week were held, but gradually the pace increased to four, five and often six sittings a week. A small number of members conducted the cross-examination: James Leslie, Louis-Hyppolyte La Fontaine, Augustin-Norbert Morin and George Vanfelson for the Patriotes, and Austin Cuvillier, Thomas Ainslie Young, William Power and George Robinson Hamilton for the English party. Most of the work, however, was to fall on the shoulders of Leslie and Cuvillier.

Over in England, Macintosh followed developments in Lower Canada with increasing frustration. Learning of the existence of the inquiry via the pages of the *Quebec Gazette*, he reacted angrily to what he saw as inaction on the part of the authorities in the province: "No opposition had been offered to the Enquiry, but a debate had preceded the examination of witnesses, chiefly remarkable for a vituperative harangue by Mr Speaker Papineau, the obvious tendency of which was, by an attempt, in this stage of the investigation, to attach blame to the Military and Magistrates to induce the house to prejudge the question."[54] The lieutenant colonel was only too well aware that the scene was set for major revelations over which he no longer had any control.

8

The Questionable Conduct of Public Officials

The 1832 statute incorporating Montreal had come too late to affect the policing of Montreal during the West Ward by-election. The magistrates had remained in charge of policing the city but it was the returning officer who had overall responsibility for the election, at least in theory. Evidence now coming to light suggested that the magistrates had superseded their powers by their involvement in the event. The deliberate recruitment of special constables known to favour Bagg combined with the use of well-known bullies to control the crowds at a closely fought election called into question the neutrality that the magistrates were supposed to exercise. The reluctance of the returning officer to impose his authority on them also cast doubt on his neutrality. Similar doubts existed about other officials such as the coroner, the solicitor general, the Montreal sheriff, the high constable and the judges of the Court of King's Bench. The inquiry investigated the role of all these individuals and thereby exposed the workings of the state in Lower Canada as never before.

The bullies in action

The presence of Étienne Benêche Lavictoire, François Dragon, Amable Hintz, Jean-Baptiste Joannette and François Beauchamp, all bullies, before the investigating committee of the House was a coup for the Patriote members though there were risks attached to relying too much on their testimonies. Bullies hired themselves out to the highest bidder. The Patriotes were open to the accusation that they had bought the evidence that they wanted to hear. It was a risk, however, that the party was prepared to take. The petition from certain East Ward electors accusing Olivier Berthelet of having employed the services of bullies to ensure his victory in April 1832 played into the hands of the Patriotes. The pressure was on the House to investigate a practice that both the *Vindicator* and *La Minerve* had condemned in the early days of the West Ward election. The evidence presented at the inquiry suggested that in the most recent elections in Montreal two candidates had employed known criminal elements to intimidate their opponents' supporters.

Three of the bullies each spent three days being questioned at the inquiry: Lavictoire in December 1832, Joannette in February 1833, and Beauchamp in January 1834. Hintz and Dragon were considered less important but their testimony confirmed that of the other three. The evidence of all five implicated several of those whom the *Montreal Gazette* normally described as the "respectable" members of Montreal society.

The inquiry clearly regarded Lavictoire, whose brother Eustache had played a significant role in fomenting the 1812 Lachine riot, as the most important of the five. It was he who had assumed the leadership of the bullies when it came time to discuss money with the Bagg recruiters. He told the inquiry that he was a carpenter by training but said that it was not a trade that he ever practised. He preferred instead to dabble in whatever he found profitable and for the time being, he said, that meant owning a boarding house on Notre-Dame St. He had become involved in the West Ward election after he had attended a meeting at Hamelin's tavern a few days before election day at the request of a constable, Antoine Lafrenière. Lavictoire had recognised few of the people he had seen there except for Mr Laframboise, the merchant, Mr Rottot, captain of the night watch, Pierre Moreau, Joseph Timothée Gaudette, a clerk in the commissariat department, and Xavier d'Aubreville. All were Bagg supporters. They told Lavictoire they had a job for him: "I was requested to engage as many strong young men as I knew to take part in Mr Bagg's election." He was promised that all would be paid generously.

It took Lavictoire a couple of days to round up some forty young men, all of them tough fighters, he said. They included three of his own brothers, the Joannettes, two of the d'Aubreville brothers, François Beauchamp and his two brothers, Louis Montferrand (Joseph's younger brother), William Flynn, Bill Collins, Alfred Collins, Amable Hinz, Édouard Hogg and a man by the name of Gervais. Joannette, a carter, provided some of the other names in his testimony. He had been recruited by one of the d'Aubreville brothers to join the group among whom he recognised Johnny Vincent, François Dragon, George Rolland, Francis Préveneau, Léon Gaudette and Michel Robitaille. Lavictoire took them all off to Lavoy's tavern situated at the entrance to the St Lawrence suburb and one of the regular haunts of Bagg's supporters. There they met Bagg's principal organisers: Rottot, Gaudette, Moreau, Abner Bagg, Alexis Laframboise and Jean-Baptiste Castonguay. Lavictoire acted as spokesman and said that he and his men all expected to be well paid this time for their services. They had been recruited by Olivier Berthelet for the East Ward election and had never been paid. Rottot told them that each man would receive ten shillings a day payable each night. If their clothes were torn or lost, the men would be compensated. In return, their job was to pack the entrance to the polling station and to allow only Bagg supporters access to the poll.

The next day Lavictoire and his men gathered in the Hay Market and went into action shortly after 11 am, shouting down Tracey's address to the crowd. It was a noisy, bad tempered affair. One of Cuvillier's sons had joined in the barracking, shouting as loud as the bullies.[1] Joannette remembered one particular Irishman, Benjamin Workman, who had once worked for Tracey but who frequently interrupted and insulted him. Before voting got under way, Joannette and the others placed themselves on both sides of the poll door. At first, voters were allowed to pass without hindrance but a disturbance arose when Antoine Lafrenière began pushing people about and even striking them. Lafrenière was one of Montreal's fulltime constables attached to the Police Office and was in the employ of Benjamin Delisle. There was surprise when he had turned up and joined the bullies, but as he explained to Lavictoire who questioned him, he was simply following the orders he had received from Rottot, Laframboise, Moreau and the others at Hamelin's. Lavictoire said that he saw Joannette strike Mr Fournier and another individual had assaulted Mr Campbell. Joannette for his part preferred to present himself in a better light. He remembered seeing Louis Malo and a certain Louis Picard exchanging blows with each other: "When we saw them striking each other several persons came forward, and Alfred Collins, Antoine Lafrenière, Minet Lafrenière, and several others set about pursuing and beating Picard. I happened to be before him; I shielded him and said to the others, 'let him alone, he is hurt enough, and there is no occasion to give him more.'"[2] It was at this point that the bullies were told by de Chantal, Moreau and several others to prevent Tracey's supporters from voting.

Leslie asked Lavictoire whether he thought that Dupré had been able to see what the bullies were up to on that first day. "The returning officer could certainly see that we obstructed the entrance to the hustings," replied Lavictoire; "he desired us repeatedly to withdraw but we did not listen to him and we almost became masters of the poll." Had Dupré been able see the assault on William Campbell and Joseph Fournier? Lavictoire said that he could not be certain in the case of Campbell but he was certain that Dupré had seen the attack on Fournier since it had happened right in front of the door where the returning officer had been positioned for some time.[3]

At 5:30 pm the poll closed with Bagg in the lead for which Lavictoire took the credit. Lavictoire then took his men back to Lavoy's to collect their pay. Rottot handed the money to Lavictoire to distribute: ten dollars for himself and three pounds for the others. There was also plenty of alcohol for the men, all paid for by Rottot and Moreau.

The next day however was very different, admitted both Lavictoire and Joannette. They had assembled first at Boulet's tavern on the corner of McGill St and the Hay Market between 9 o'clock and 10 o'clock where they were treated to more alcohol. Stanley Bagg then arrived to take them off to the American church. He was accompanied by a number of people including a young man by the name of Mr Penner from Lachine. "[Penner] said to us, if there is any mischief to be done, I will be the one, and he stirred us up violently against Mr Tracey's people," said Joannette.[4]

As Bagg and his hired men approached the polling station, they were confronted by a group of electors. The bullies advanced with Bill Collins at their head. He began pushing people out of the way, a little too roughly for Joseph Fournier who confronted Bill Collins and pushed him back in turn. The two men came to blows and soon there was a general scuffle between the bullies and their opponents. One of Tracey's supporters, Antoine Voyer, dealt Collins a blow that knocked the man to the ground. Several other people joined in attacking Collins who was left lying unconscious on the ground and covered in blood. There were shouts of "he is dead, he is dead." Joannette and the other bullies raced back to the shelter of Boulet's tavern. From there they watched Collins slowly regain consciousness. Several men ran out and helped him into Boulet's. Outside, the scuffling continued and another of the bullies, Baptiste Latour, suffered a similar fate to Collins. Joannette and some of his men went outside and brought him inside too.

This was not what Bagg's close circle of advisers had planned. De Chantal, Moreau, McKenzie and several others attempted to instill some courage in the men and to get them to take control of the entrance to the polling station, but the bullies were in no mood to listen. If Bagg's friends wanted to get themselves killed, then they should go and try it themselves, Joannette had told them. Inside Boulet's, Christophe Brazeau, "a dark complexioned young man who was there in the quality of surgeon to attend those who might be hurt at the election," as Joannette described him, attempted to put pressure on the bullies to return to the action.[5] But Tracey's men had control of the area around the polling station. When they spotted Brazeau, they chased after him and beat him. John Fisher was another to receive some rough treatment from Tracey's supporters. He was pushed to the ground when standing at the door of Boulet's. Joannette and the others responded to his cries for help and brought him inside the tavern. When Joannette went outside again to fetch Fisher's umbrella, it was snatched from him by a man standing nearby who struck him a blow with it. Lavictoire too came off worse in his confrontation with the crowd. First he was threatened by a man named Cassidy who was wielding a stick and then he was struck by another man named Little. The bullies made their way back to Lavoy's to receive their pay. Lavictoire handed out eight pounds from his own pocket and Rottot a similar amount from his. It was not enough. Rottot went off to see Abner Bagg to receive a further ten pounds and that too was distributed to the men.

Money eventually led to disagreements between Lavictoire and the Baggs. At the end of the election, Lavictoire said, he presented his account to Stanley Bagg's clerk and had received just ten dollars, a fraction of what he had paid out. The clerk told him that Bagg had already handed over some sixty pounds to Rottot and that the balance of Lavictoire's account would not be paid until Rottot had sent in a detailed account of his expenses. Lavictoire later persuaded Rottot to provide him with a breakdown of his payments and he took it back to the clerk and then to Abner Bagg. Both refused to pay Lavictoire any more money. He angrily stormed off threatening to expose the Baggs by writing to the newspapers about them.[6]

The inquiry also had at its disposal the criminal record of several of the individuals named by the bullies as taking part in the violence of the first day. Louis Malo had been convicted of assault and battery in the past and had served three months in jail on one charge. In 1826 Bill Collins and a companion had been charged with murder and had eventually been convicted of manslaughter. They were sentenced to six months in jail and were both branded on the hand. In 1827 E.-X. d'Aubreville and William Flynn were indicted on charges of riot, breaking and entry, assaulting the owner, a certain Charlotte Bélanger, and damaging her furniture. Both were fined five pounds and d'Aubreville in addition was sentenced to one month in jail.[7]

The special constables

Leslie probed the connection between the bullies and the special constables for the period of the election. He first read out a list of names to Lavictoire: Édouard Léon Gaudette, Xavier Brunelle, François Préveneau, Antoine Delaunais, John Vincent, Jean-Baptiste Larochelle, Georges Rolland, Jean-Baptiste Latour and François Mailloux. All had served as special constables, he told Lavictoire. Did he recognise any of the names? Yes, replied Lavictoire, all except Gaudette had been among those he had recruited. Did he know Amable Ainze or Hinze from Laprairie? Lavictoire replied that the man he knew as Hintz had been recruited for the duration of the election. He was strong, a good fighter and had been paid fifteen pounds for his services. Did Lavictoire know how many of his men had been sworn in as special constables after April 26? Only two as far as he knew, he answered, his brother, Barnabé Benêche, and François Dragon. He could not speak for the others. "Perhaps they did like me," he suggested, "I was not sworn and I had a stave like the others." Asked whether the presence of a number of bullies at the courthouse on the third day of the election had attracted any attention, Lavictoire replied that between fifteen and twenty of them had gathered at the courthouse and occupied a prominent position. They were all in possession of their short constable staves. It was impossible not to notice them, said Lavictoire, and he was convinced that the magistrates on duty at the courthouse must have seen them.[8]

Amable Hintz's testimony before the inquiry illustrated part of the problems the Patriotes experienced in relying on the bullies in their search for the truth. Hintz, a master blacksmith from La Prairie, explained that he had been recruited by Louis Malo "and his friends" to help Bagg just as he had done in the past for Olivier Berthelet and Dominique Mondelet. He said that no pay was promised for his services but he did admit that Bagg had taken care of part of his board for a week after the election. He claimed to have arrived in Montreal on the tenth day of the election and only towards the end of the election had Malo asked him to be a special constable. He said he had agreed and had been sworn in. However, the records that had been deposited with the inquiry showed clearly that Hintz's swearing in had taken place on April 27.[9]

François Dragon, a hair-dresser from the St Lawrence suburb, said that Bagg had sent Malo and Captain Rottot to see him a few days before the election to recruit him. On the first day of the election, Rottot went to see him again and promised him he would be paid for his services. His instructions as relayed to him by Robert Armour were to prevent Tracey's voters from getting to the poll and to facilitate access to the poll for Bagg's voters. Dragon said that he received one pound from Malo at the courthouse during the election and two pounds from Abner Bagg at the end of the election. He also claimed that Rottot and Malo asked him to serve as a special constable. Though he had acted as such on several occasions, he said, he had never been sworn in as a special.[10] However, in the list of special constables produced for the inquiry by John Delisle, eighteen are designated as bullies including Dragon and all are said to have been sworn in on either April 26 or 27.

The magistrates

Leslie broadened his questions to enquire about the magistrates' attitude to the two candidates. Lavictoire said he had seen several magistrates in the various taverns frequented by Bagg's supporters. He remembered seeing Fisher, McNider and Cuvillier in either Lavoy's, Boulet's or Luckin's though he agreed that it might have been when public meetings were held there. He had often seen Laframboise in conversation with Fisher and Robertson and he knew that Jules Quesnel was an associate of Laframboise. As regards Cuvillier, Lavictoire knew him well. On one occasion towards the end of the election he had gone to see him to arrange for a voter to be brought from Lachine. It was Cuvillier who agreed to pay for the transport.

Asked whether he had been arrested and bailed during the election, Lavictoire said it had happened perhaps two or three times. He had also gone before the magistrates to post bail for his own men. He could not recall how often but he remembered having appeared before Cuvillier and Holmes and several times before Fisher. A final question from Leslie was designed to bolster Lavictoire's credibility. Had threats been made against him? Lavictoire said that since arriving in Quebec City attempts had been made to prevent him from testifying. The two Delisle brothers had warned him to keep quiet about his role in recruiting men for Bagg. Benjamin Delisle had added that if Lavictoire ever spoke about it, certain people back in Montreal were prepared to harm him.[11]

Not all was plain sailing for the bullies, however. Austin Cuvillier, Jean-François-Joseph Duval and Thomas Young, three members of the House whose sympathies lay with the English party, subjected Lavictoire and Joannette to tough questioning. Cuvillier pressed Joannette on the fighting that broke out on the second day of the election, suggesting that Tracey had brought in his own bullies. Joannette replied that Tracey certainly had a number of supporters who were very strong but they did not fall into the category of bullies. People like Voyer, Restaire, François Lavigne and many others whose names he did not know were not the sort of people who became involved in quarrels on one side or the other. Rather, he said, they were people of a quiet disposition who preferred to restore the peace, not to upset it.[12]

Lavictoire's money-making schemes were apparently well known to certain members of the Assembly who used that knowledge in an attempt to discredit his testimony. Young, member for Quebec City's Lower Town, was privy to detailed information that he was sure would discredit Lavictoire's earlier testimony. Did Lavictoire know a man by the name of Dégré? Lavictoire said he had heard of a François Dégré. Was Lavictoire in the habit of keeping a gaming table either in partnership with Dégré or as an employed assistant? Lavictoire said he had a slight acquaintance with the man but no partnership existed between them and he categorically denied that he had ever kept a gaming table, roulette table, or had superintended any game of chance during his residence in Quebec City. It was possible that Young was confusing him with his brother Éloi Lavictoire, Lavictoire suggested. Unimpressed, Young became more specific. How much did Lavictoire pay the police to tip him off whenever a complaint was made at the Police Office about the roulette table and gambling room kept in the garret of a building situated in the back yard of a house at the corner of St John St and St Stanislas St in Quebec City's upper town? Lavictoire answered, "I do not pay them anything since I do not know them."[13]

When the House committee resumed its inquiry during the next parliamentary session a year later, there was just one bully called to testify: François Beauchamp, a joiner and brother-in-law of Lavictoire. The evidence he had to offer was as suspect as that offered by Amable Hinz. The main culprit in his eyes was Benjamin Delisle. It was Delisle who asked him to attend Lavoy's where he was hired by Moreau and Rottot and was promised ten shillings a day to support Bagg during the election. A few days into the election, Beauchamp claimed that Delisle distributed staves to a small group of special constables including himself, one of the d'Aubrevilles and Éloi Victoire. They were told to watch out for the Irish and even to kill them, for an Irishman could be killed like a dog, he was told. Beauchamp said that he was reluctant to do what Delisle was asking. Lafrenière, the constable, intervened to say that there would be repercussions if they did not do so since large sums of money were involved. Cuvillier had subscribed one hundred pounds for Dominique Mondelet's election and three hundred pounds for Bagg's election.

Beauchamp's testimony concerning Delisle was not credible. Several witnesses who had appeared a year earlier had pointed out that Delisle had a good relationship with the Irish and was well respected in that community. Furthermore, just a week before Beauchamp testified, Patrick Brennan, a tavern keeper, city constable and friend of Tracey, had described to the committee the close working relationship he had always enjoyed with the high constable even to the point of taking charge of the other constables whenever Delisle was absent. In his cross-examination of Beauchamp, Cuvillier had little difficulty in getting him to admit that he had been arrested several times by Delisle for attempting to intimidate witnesses in a case involving Lavictoire.[14]

Other witnesses

Much of the evidence produced by the bullies concerning their violent behaviour on the opening day of the election was substantiated by many of the people who had been present on the Hay Market on April 25. Cherrier was at Tracey's shoulder when the returning officer declared the poll open and had translated Tracey's opening remarks into French. Tracey's words, he said, had been lost in the din created by a group of drunken hecklers led by a bully by the name of Montferrand. Dr Robert Nelson also remembered the scene well. The bullies were very vociferous and very violent, he said, and Tracey's pleas to the bullies, to Bagg and to the returning officer to be heard in silence had no effect. Silence was eventually restored when Cherrier prevailed upon Bagg to control the hecklers. Cherrier maintained that the returning officer had clearly seen what was happening but had made no effort to intervene. His reluctance to become involved at the outset, Cherrier said, merely encouraged the trouble makers and suggested that there existed an official bias in favour of Bagg.[15]

As Tracey's principal legal adviser, Cherrier spent the whole election inside the polling room where his role was to challenge those people he suspected of being ineligible to vote. His first inkling that something was amiss came early in the afternoon of the opening day. Having earlier estimated that Tracey's supporters were in the majority, he watched mystified as Bagg built up an early lead. He went outside to investigate and saw that very few of Tracey's supporters were coming forward to vote. The explanation was clear to see: next to the entrance Minet Lafrenière, a constable from the police office, was actually stopping them from entering the polling station. In a later testimony, Dr Vallée said he remembered the constable well. He had seen him strike an Irishman and the doctor had gone over to remonstrate with him. Lafrenière reacted violently, hitting him on his jaw. Dr Vallée reported the matter to constable Deegan who had been assigned to Dupré but not before an attempt was made to block his way. Dupré was obliged to have Lafrenière arrested and taken to jail.[16]

Later in the afternoon, the situation was no better for Tracey's supporters. Joshua Bell, a leather dealer and shoemaker, spoke of seeing a number of hired bullies stationed on both sides of the door leading into the polling station ready to assault those they suspected were for Tracey. Bell himself made several attempts to register his vote but withdrew each time because of the intimidation. On the final occasion he was chased away by a furious Bill Collins, the most notorious of all the bullies. Several other eyewitnesses spoke of the brutality of that first day. Dr Robert Nelson testified that he had tended some of Tracey's supporters after they had been assaulted by the likes of Bill Collins, the d'Aubrevilles and others. However, the one person who might have provided important evidence was a disappointment to the committee. The returning officer, Dupré, said he had little first-hand knowledge of what had happened outside the American church. In general, he had relied on what people reported to him. He knew that fighting had been started by several of the bullies but he had never been officially informed that Malo had assaulted people. In the case of Lafrenière, he took some credit for having him sent to jail.[17]

Dupré's testimony was contradicted by that of Rodier, who had witnessed many assaults carried out by the bullies, especially one case where Montferrand and Joannette had inflicted a severe beating on a humpbacked Irishman. He had also seen Louis Malo collar another Irishman by the name of John Greece and say to him, "You have nothing to do here, you damned Irishman." Rodier said he complained to Dupré who told him to make out a complaint. Rodier took Greece's affidavit and gave it to Dupré, asking him to do something about it. Dupré declined to act claiming that having Malo arrested would just cause even more of a disturbance.[18]

Patrick Brennan, a city constable, had taken Tracey to the Hay Market on the morning of April 25 and had been caught up in the violence in the afternoon. The Tracey camp had organised a committee of twenty-four English and Irish people who were to ensure that six of their number would be in attendance on each polling day. Any Irishman found to be intoxicated or causing a disturbance would be taken in charge and escorted home. Brennan and William Campbell, a close friend of Tracey, were part of the team on the opening day. After polling opened, they witnessed numerous assaults on Irish voters. Patrick Hanaran, Michael Tongher and William Campbell all suffered at the hands of the bullies. At one point, Brennan saw a Mr Caroll being beaten by a dozen or so men and went to his defence. Brennan received a severe beating and was confined to bed for several days afterwards. He had recognised one of his attackers as being Pat Cuvillier, one of Austin Cuvillier's sons.[19]

Tracey's advisers knew that the bullies were a serious threat to his prospects and that immediate counter-measures were needed. Two meetings were organised for that same evening. One was held in the St Joseph suburb, the other in the St Lawrence suburb. Cherrier had attended the St Lawrence meeting where the discussion concentrated on the violence of the bullies. Cherrier took the floor and recommended that voters arrive as early as possible next morning and give Tracey a commanding lead: "If there are enough of us, no one will dare attack us," he told the meeting. "This is the only proper way to prevent further violence and assaults on individuals." La Fontaine also spoke and supported Cherrier's recommendations. He also stressed the importance of allowing the electors of both sides free access to the poll. There was to be no violence, he said, but if they were attacked they were to repel force with force.

Next morning, Cherrier arrived early at the American church and told the electors already present to keep together on one side of the door leading into the vestibule. The other side was to be left for Bagg's supporters. Cherrier said that he had felt confident that there was safety in numbers and that the bullies would not dare attack, but he was wrong. The bullies waited until Cherrier had left the vicinity of the church before attacking. Tracey's voters began to scatter in all directions and it was with considerable difficulty that Cherrier succeeded in persuading the frightened voters to regroup outside the church. In the end, order was restored and voters were allowed to vote unhindered.[20]

Dupré's only reference to the fighting on the second day was to say that he had heard a rumour that Bill Collins had been beaten up and even killed. He had also received a complaint from some twenty Bagg supporters (among whom he remembered the names of Abner Bagg and Horatio Gates) who said they had been assaulted but the promised affidavits were never produced. As far as Cherrier was concerned, after the second morning, access to the poll was free for the supporters of both candidates, as demonstrated, he said, by the fact that on four of the first eight days of voting, Bagg received more votes than Tracey. La Fontaine was of the same opinion. "It appeared to me," he said, "that every person voted freely and a proof of it, is that a great number of ladies, old men, of infirm persons, of lame persons and sick persons came to vote, and I believe that if there had been any danger, many persons (namely some of the magistrates who had sent Constables to the Poll) would not have sent their ladies."[21]

The Delisle brothers and the special constables

The Patriotes were certain that there was more behind the recruitment of the special constables than the fact that a small number of notorious bullies had joined them. By the time the House committee began its inquiry, Jacques Viger had painstakingly assembled a list of almost all of the special constables who had served between April 28 and May 21. Comparing the 479 names on his list with those in the poll book and drawing on privately gathered information, he was also able to produce a breakdown of the political affiliations of over half of the specials. The result came as no surprise to the Patriote members of the inquiry. The overwhelming majority of the special constables were active supporters of Bagg. The numbers were 216 for Bagg and 48 for Tracey. Viger said he had been unable to discover where the sympathies of the remaining 215 men lay, though as a possible indication, he added, 54 had French Canadian names and 161 had names of people born outside of the country. Viger's investigations also showed that of the 246 who had been sworn in as constables, 142 had voted in the election, of whom 122 were sworn in after they had voted or on the day they had voted. The majority had voted for Bagg and just thirty-one for Tracey.[22]

The people best qualified to explain the strong bias in favour of Bagg in the recruitment of the special constables were brothers Benjamin and John Delisle, the high constable and the clerk of the peace, the two officials who had provided Viger with the names. Both men were subjected to close questioning from members of the inquiry. No other witnesses appeared as often before the committee: John Delisle appeared on fourteen days between December 21, 1832 and March 20, 1833, Benjamin on twelve days between December 19, 1832 and March 4, 1833. Part of their evidence dealt with the presence of so many bullies at the election.

Jacques Viger, highway surveyor of Montreal and joint census
commissioner for Montreal County. No one knew his fellow citizens better
than he. He remained with the soldiers and special constables on the
afternoon of May 21. He produced a wealth of detailed material for the
Assembly enquiry. Jacques Viger was the first mayor of Montreal.
(McCord Museum – II-94237)

Asked about Bill Collins, John Delisle said the man had recently been prosecuted. "The indictment was for murder," he explained, "and he was convicted of manslaughter; in consequence of which, he was branded and imprisoned for several months." Did Delisle have any other dealings with the bullies during the election? He replied that he had sworn in five of them as special constables at the close of the magistrates' meeting on April 26 in the presence of Moffatt. Their names were E.-X. d'Aubreville, William Flynn, Ferdinand d'Aubreville, William Thompson and Amable Loiselle. He was unable to say, however, who had summoned them to the courthouse. During his questioning of the witness, Cuvillier suggested that the bullies were there by chance having remained behind after the close of the Court of Quarter Sessions but Leslie had a different suggestion for Delisle. Were not the bullies day labourers and all very aggressive by nature? Delisle agreed that the two d'Aubreville brothers and William Flynn were but said that he was unsure about the others. Were not most of the specials eligible to vote in the West Ward election and were not most of them Bagg supporters? It was true, Delisle replied, that most were West Ward electors but he could not say how they voted. Finally, was it not true that several of the specials sworn were not qualified to serve as ordinary constables? Delisle agreed that that too was true.[23]

At the beginning of his testimony, Benjamin Delisle told the committee that he had been appointed to the office of high constable in 1831 on the recommendation of the magistrates. It was then put to him that he had reportedly said that the presence of the specials at the election had done more harm than good. Was this true? Delisle said he could not remember having used those words. Why was it then that he wanted to keep Malo away from the vicinity of the polling station?

Because he had been involved in trouble at other elections, Delisle answered, and because some of his enemies might have been present. As regards the five bullies sworn in as special constables on the evening of April 26, Delisle could not account for their presence at such a late hour at the courthouse. Was it not odd that Amable Hintz who lived at Laprairie was summoned as a special? Had someone pointed him out to Delisle? No one in particular, he replied. What had induced Delisle to summon him then as a special? Nothing induced me to summon him rather than any other person, came the reply. Where did Delisle meet him? In the office of the clerk of the peace or possibly in the corridor of the courthouse, said Delisle. Did someone else summon him? I do not know who it might have been, answered Delisle. Were any of the twenty-five bullies summoned by him on or before April 27? Not to my knowledge, said Delisle. Would he have been inclined to summon them as specials? None except Loiselle, he replied, because they were all known to be bullies.

What information did Delisle have about the bullies? Delisle answered that he himself and some of the ordinary constables had arrested a number of individuals for assault and battery during the election. Their names were E.-X. d'Aubreville, William Flynn, Antoine Lafreniere, Eustache Benêche Lavictoire, Eloi Lavictoire, Louis Malo, Etienne Benêche Lavictoire, Alfred Collins, Jean-Baptiste Joannette, Louis Montferrand and Barnabé Lavictoire. Antoine Lafreniere and Louis Malo were ordinary constables, said Delisle, but none of the others were constables, whether ordinary or special. In answer to a question from Cuvillier about the morning of April 27, he stated that he was in the office of the clerk of the peace but he had heard no proposal from any magistrate to send the specials to the polling station. None of the specials were drunk and in any case they were always kept within the church enclosure, out of sight of the people who were voting. He said that he had no recollection of specials ever leaving the church porch to go out among the people brandishing their staves.[24]

Parts of Benjamin Delisle's evidence were contradicted by numerous witnesses. Patrick Brennan had been left in charge of the constables on May 21 between 10:30 am and 2 o'clock during Delisle's absence. All was quiet when Delisle returned to the Place d'Armes and a clearly delighted high constable told Brennan, "You and I can do more to keep the peace than a thousand such constables." It was something that Delisle told him on several occasions during the election, said Brennan.[25] The most damaging contradictory evidence, however, was provided by his own brother. Benjamin Delisle's claim that none of the bullies arrested during the election were special constables was undermined when John Delisle produced a list of fifty-eight special constables sworn in between April 26 and May 22 and whose names had not appeared on his brother's list. Eighteen of the names were those of bullies sworn in on April 26 and 27. They included the now familiar names of E.-X. d'Aubreville, William Flynn, Alfred Collins, Jean-Baptiste Joannette and Barnabé Lavictoire.[26] Benjamin Delisle's evidence was further discredited when on February 23, 1833 Viger produced a definitive list of special constables "sworn to maintain the peace in the vicinity of and near the hustings." The list showed that three bullies had taken the oath before Moffatt on April 26 and twenty-one the following day before C.W. Grant(1), William Hall(3), John Fisher(10), John McKenzie(2), and Austin Cuvillier(5).[27]

The magistrates and the specials

Nine of the magistrates had voted for Bagg during the election. They were John McKenzie, Adam McNider, Dr Robertson, Joseph Shuter, Benjamin Holmes, Jean Bouthillier, Jules Quesnel, Austin Cuvillier and John Fisher. The last five in this list served as part of Bagg's reserve as each voted only after the returning officer had made his proclamation. Three magistrates, André Jobin, Pierre Lukin and Joseph Roy, had voted for Tracey. Evidence was produced before the inquiry that several of the magistrates who actively supported Bagg had few qualms about associating with a band of men whose criminal records were well known to them. Joshua Bell was one the special constables who served without having been sworn in. He was asked to turn up on May 7, a day he remembered well. Benjamin Holmes had given orders for the constables' long blue staves to be cut in half. When it was put to Bell that Holmes had no choice since there were not enough long staves to go round, Bell came up with a different theory. It was, he said, to provide the specials with bludgeons so that they could accomplish their work in extra fast time. All that day he had been stationed behind the church perimeter wall and had been horrified by the attitude of the magistrates and other special constables. They all behaved in a violent manner, swinging their short staves as if preparing for battle. There was absolutely no call, Bell added, for sending groups of specials out into the Place d'Armes. The whole practice struck him as ominous of something worse to come. No arrests were made. In fact, the only people who deserved to be arrested that day were the specials themselves and indeed several of them should have suffered that fate, stated Bell. He had never served again as a special. "I would have paid a fine or gone to jail rather than to go and serve on another day," he said.[28]

Rodier was asked whether during the election he had seen any of the magistrates on very familiar and friendly terms with any of the bullies or specials. Yes, he remembered the morning of May 21 when he had seen Cuvillier arrive surrounded by a group of bullies to whom he was speaking. In particular, Cuvillier and Lafrenière appeared to know each other very well. In fact, Rodier said, it was common knowledge at the time that Cuvillier was privy to everything the bullies did in as much as he had allowed them to become special constables despite their bad reputation as fighters. It was also widely supposed that from the beginning to the end of the election Cuvillier actively supported Mr Bagg—it was he who had called the meeting of the magistrates to arm the special constables and it was he who solicited votes in favour of Mr Bagg. Another circumstance that made Rodier believe that Cuvillier was playing an active part in Bagg's campaign was not just that he voted for Bagg but that his wife did so too on the very day that the magistrates had increased the number of specials claiming that people's lives were in danger. "If Mr Cuvillier was of the opinion that there was danger," Rodier said, "I must naturally conclude that he must have taken an extremely active part in favour of Mr Bagg to allow his lady to come and vote at that time."[29]

Jacques Viger's evidence was of immense importance to the inquiry. Questioned by Leslie about his past experience as a returning officer, he said that on the five occasions between 1820 and 1832 when he had served as returning officer for East Ward elections the magistrates had never once offered him the services of special constables and he had never asked for any. He had always had at his command the high constable or the public crier who was an ordinary constable. How had he managed in the past to impose his authority when there were cases of disorder or fighting? By threatening individuals with punishment or by having them arrested and put in jail, he replied. On one occasion when there had been considerable disorder, Viger had simply adjourned voting to the following day. In an answer to a question from Cuvillier, Viger said that if he had been unable to maintain law and order, he would have adjourned the poll on a daily basis just to tire the protestors out. If he had ever needed to call in the magistrates and constables he would have assumed complete control of them and not surrendered the independence of his court. If there had been a complete breakdown of his authority, Viger would simply have closed the poll and reported back to the House in the hope of establishing a precedent for the future.

Viger was next asked what he thought of the attitude of the magistrates during the West Ward election. Viger replied that on April 27 he had been passing in front of the courthouse between 11 and 12 o'clock and had noticed a large number of people standing on the steps and in the courtyard. Those on steps were holding constable staves in their hands. Mr Lamb, one of Bagg's supporters, told him that the magistrates were preparing to send some special constables to the polling station. Viger asked him whether they were needed. No, I do not think so, he said, since I have just returned from there and all is quiet and peaceful. Viger went inside. A huge crowd had gathered among whom he remembered seeing Rottot, at the time Second Officer of the Watch, Gates, Charles Try and John Jones, the auctioneer. Viger went into the police office and saw Cuvillier sitting in a back room.

— Is it true, he asked Cuvillier, you have decided to send specials to the poll?

— Yes, he answered.

— But why? I said. Is it really necessary?

— Yes, because people are killing each other, he answered, and because law and order has broken down.

— Who gave you this information?

— People have been arriving non-stop from the polling station and complaining of the violence done to them.

— Well, Mr Cuvillier, I said, I can assure you that it is not true. If people have been caught up in violence, it is entirely of their own making or it is because of the strong language they have been using. I have just spoken to a Bagg supporter who told me that all was quiet there. Did the returning officer ask you to send him the specials?

— No, said Cuvillier, we don't need a request from him.

Viger said he suddenly became very annoyed because he considered Cuvillier and the magistrates were interfering in the election and were guilty of encroaching upon the returning officer's authority. He then said to Cuviller with anger in his voice:

— You obviously know the sort of man you are dealing with; you would certainly not act in this way at an election where I was the returning officer.

— What would you do then in such a case? said he with a kind of sneer, raising his spectacles.

— What would I do, sir? I would first say to you and to all your confrères, to the high constable and to all his constables, in as a temperate a manner as I could, go back home, gentlemen, and be quick about it. If you did not leave immediately, I would set the whole mob after you and it would have been the fastest imprisonment under a returning officer's warrant they had ever experienced in their lives. You surely are aware that there is only one magistrate at an election and that is the returning officer. Everyone from the chief justice down to the lowest bailiff, from the colonel to the last drummer, every person in the presence of the returning officer has no other duty except to receive his orders.

Cuvillier replied that irrespective of what Viger had just said, the magistrates would do what they thought necessary.[30]

The evidence presented at the inquiry concerning the bullies, special constables and the magistrates was damning, though it might not have convinced a jury in a court of law. It was damning for Austin Cuvillier who appeared to be able to call on the services of both officials and special constables, the night watch and any number of bullies whenever a candidate he favoured fought an election. It was damning for Robert Armour, editor of the *Montreal Gazette*, whom François Dragon accused of instructing him on what to do outside the polling station. And it was especially damning for Stanley and Abner Bagg whose heavy financial outlay to foment violence at the polling station made a mockery of their indignant protests to the returning officer on May 20. If more were known about the Mr Penner from Lachine who Joannette claimed arrived with Stanley Bagg at the polling station on the second day of the election, the testimony might also have been damning for the grand jury whose foreman was Charles Penner from Lachine. However, in the absence of corroborative evidence, the accusations made by the five bullies against Tracey's opponents remained open to doubt.

The May 19 adjournment

The returning officer's controversial adjournment of the poll on Saturday, May 19 came under close scrutiny from the inquiry. For Tracey and his inner circle of advisers, it had been clear proof that Dupré was under the sway of the Bagg camp. However, after the inquiry had heard from the few witnesses who had been present at the polling station at the time, no clear picture emerged.

Austin Cuvillier, Montreal businessman and city magistrate. The former star of the Patriote party had by 1832 become a committed Tory. He played an active part in attempting to fix the West Ward by-election in favour of Bagg. (McCord Museum – M5205)

Dupré was of course the central figure in the affair. Six months after the event, he was still aggrieved over the treatment he claimed to have received at the hands of Tracey and was keen to have his grievance placed on record. Questioned by Leslie, he admitted that he had refused to allow two of Tracey's supporters to record their votes on the Saturday afternoon in question but that was because he had already granted an adjournment as allowed by the law when three electors requested one. Tracey had accused him of being partial and ill-mannered and had then gone outside and told the crowd that Dupré was responsible for a murder that had taken place a few days earlier. Tracey had then called on the Irish to unite and to bring their friends from the country to demand justice from Dupré and to use force if necessary.

Pressed by Leslie to return to the subject of the adjournment, Dupré said he did not express any surprise when the three electors had asked him to adjourn voting for the day. Did he consult any law books before making his decision? No, he replied, the law appeared to him to be very clear on the subject. Certain people had attempted to give a different interpretation of the relevant clause of the act but he had had the opportunity to study the act on several occasions in the past at other elections and he was certain that he had made the right decision.[31]

The poll book, which Dupré had been forced to hand over at the beginning of the inquiry, shed new light on what had happened that day. When polling opened at 10 o'clock Tracey was trailing by one vote and Bagg was nowhere to be seen. He eventually turned up seven minutes late. The first three votes of the day were for Tracey and Bagg objected to all three. At 10:50 am, Dupré made his proclamation. At 11:17 am, John McDonald's wife, Susanna Holmes, turned up and voted for Bagg following an objection from Tracey. At 11:30 am, Dupré read the proclamation again. Seven minutes later, two women turned up to vote for Bagg: Marguerite Viger, a widow, and Marie Claire Perrault, Austin Cuvillier's wife. Dupré read his proclamation again at 11:42 am. Bagg was again in the lead but Tracey had his reserve of electors waiting to react. One minute later, Thomas Horne voted for Tracey and Bagg objected. Almost an hour later, Tracey received another vote and again Bagg objected. The proclamation was read again at 12:40 pm. With just thirteen minutes to spare before the expiry of the hour, Pierre Bibaud arrived to vote for Bagg. The two candidates were level once more. The poll book then shows that Dupré read his proclamation at 1:32 pm. This must have been at Bagg's request since there was no advantage for Tracey to request it. The reason for his doing so came two minutes later when Bagg's three supporters requested and obtained an adjournment. Dupré said he granted the request at 1:45 pm. The poll book states that the six-minute delay was caused by a disruption in the polling station but there may well have been another reason.[32]

The possible background to the controversy came to light early in 1834 when Dr René-Joseph Kimber, the Assembly member for Trois-Rivières, testified before the inquiry. After voting for Tracey on May 14, he had been approached a short while later by Jules Quesnel, John Fisher and Alexis Laframboise. Quesnel asked Kimber whether he thought that three electors had the right to ask for an adjournment of the poll. Kimber replied that he thought it was possible provided the two candidates were in agreement. Quesnel told him that the candidates' consent was not necessary and that they were going to try and apply for an adjournment. Kimber replied that it would demonstrate how weak Bagg really was and it would most likely cause trouble.[33] Kimber's evidence was circumstantial but it did explain why Bagg's supporters were so well prepared when it was time to use the strategy to keep Bagg's chances alive.

John Jordan had been present on May 19 and had been closely involved in the events that day. At 12:40 pm, immediately after the returning officer had read his proclamation, Jordan, Dr Nelson and John Donegani were delegated to go to Pierre Auger's house to request his vote. The journey there and back took almost an hour. When they returned with Auger, Bagg's three supporters had already requested an adjournment but Dupré had still not inscribed the request in the poll book. According to Jordan's recollection, Dupré appeared uncertain and had had to consult several law books before coming to his decision. Auger also testified that Dupré seemed to have no idea how to proceed and looked at various law books after telling him and Donegani that the law was quite explicit and left him no discretion in the matter.[34] Jordan and Auger's version of events would account for the unexplained six minutes between the request for the adjournment and Dupré granting it.

The law that proved so contentious had been promulgated in March 1825. The particular clause (XII) that dealt with adjournments and that Dupré considered so explicit was anything but explicit. The first part dealt with setting the election in motion. The second part dealt with the modalities of closing and adjourning the election:

> Provided also, that nothing in this Act contained shall extend or be construed to extend, to prevent any Returning Officer from closing any Election to be held in virtue of this Act, at any period of such Election, if all the Candidates and the Representative or Representatives of any Candidate or Candidates consent thereto, or if no vote shall have been given during one hour, the Returning Officer having first made Proclamation of his intention to close the Poll at the expiration of one hour from

the time of such Proclamation. Provided always, that after such Proclamation, an adjournment of the Poll, until the ensuing day, shall be granted, if so required by any three Electors, at which time the Election shall be finally closed, if no vote shall be given in the course of one hour, the Returning Officer having made Proclamation of his intention to that effect, previous to the commencement of such hour. And provided also, and the Returning Officer is hereby required to keep the poll at every Election open eight hours at least in each day subsequently to the first day of Election, between eight of the clock in the morning and five of the clock in the afternoon, unless otherwise determined by the unanimous consent of the Candidates, or their Representatives, or by the final close of the Poll.[35]

Bagg's three representatives called for an adjournment two minutes after the proclamation had been made, as the law allowed, and Dupré acquiesced. But by doing so less than four hours after the poll had opened he ignored the requirement to keep the poll open until 5 pm. He did not have the agreement of the two candidates to curtail voting prematurely nor was it the end of the election. Did the request for an adjournment take precedence over the requirement for the poll to remain open for at least eight hours? Dupré thought so but only after a certain amount of research and despite Tracey's protests and those of several electors who were prevented from voting.

The coroner's court

The conduct of the coroner's inquest had been controversial from the outset. Papineau had been persuaded to attend by friends who feared that the coroner would be incapable or unwilling to exert his authority in a case with so many political ramifications. Papineau's mere presence at the inquest had been enough to draw down on his head the wrath of the

Tory press and the accusation that he had attempted to influence its outcome. In ordering the coroner and the lawyer William Walker to appear before it, the House considered it had a good chance of clarifying what had gone on.

Jean-Marie Mondelet was a formidable witness as might be expected of a man whose knowledge of the legal structures of the province had been gained over a period of thirty-four years of public service. He first appeared before the inquiry on Christmas eve 1832. Initially at least, he was questioned with deference and even respect yet he appeared in his early answers to be wary of being drawn too far. The opening questions all centred on his experience of conducting elections in Montreal. Were past elections in Montreal peaceful or hotly contested? he was asked. As a returning officer, he replied, he had witnessed cases of disorder but he had always taken steps to clamp down severely. At a previous election in Montreal at which Papineau had been a candidate, there had been some disorder at the beginning of the poll, but decisive action on his own part, in the form of an arrest, Mondelet said, had quickly restored order. No, he said in answer to another question, he had never thought of calling for the assistance of special constables, or even asking the magistrates to provide help. All the time he had been at the Quarter Sessions he had never once heard of a returning officer asking for special constables to assist him in carrying out his duties. When he had learned that the magistrates had had recourse to such people in the recent election in Montreal West, he had stated at the time that such a measure was not legal unless it could be justified as a case of real urgency.

When the questions shifted to his actions as coroner and became more pointed, Mondelet suddenly lost some of his bravura. He had personally inspected the bodies of the three dead men, he explained, and had them examined by four doctors before instructing the high constable to summon twelve jurors.

— Regarding those jurors, didn't C.-S. Cherrier tell you that there were well-founded objections to some of them, especially to Dubois?

Mondelet said he could only remember Papineau mentioning it to him in the hall of the Fabrique just before the jurors were sworn in and pointing out Dubois as objectionable as a juror.

— Didn't Papineau tell you that several respectable citizens had sworn on oath that after the troops had killed the three men, Dubois had expressed his approval and regretted that many more of them had not been killed?

— I cannot remember.

— Wasn't there an objection to Mr Dewar since he was the business partner of John Fisher, the magistrate, who was directly involved in the events?

— Maybe.

— What did you say in reply?

— I cannot remember.

— Didn't you say that the objections were immaterial since all that was needed for a verdict was a majority of the jurors, seven out of the twelve?

— I cannot remember saying that seven would be enough. If I did, then I was mistaken. I do remember telling the jury that they had to be unanimous in their verdict because there were only twelve of them, and for a verdict to be legal all twelve had to be unanimous.

— Wasn't it when the jurors were about to be sworn in that the objections were made?

— I cannot remember.

— Didn't you say at the time that you doubted whether you had the right to challenge a juror?

— I cannot remember.

Have you ever as a coroner summoned more than twelve jurors?

— I cannot remember.

— Didn't the largest part of the evidence intended to show that the military were innocent come from people who had not been summoned as witnesses but came on a voluntary basis with depositions made out of court?

That question was tantamount to suggesting that Mondelet had mismanaged the collection of evidence at the inquest and he refused to give a direct answer. Instead he defended the approach he had adopted by stating that all the witnesses had been thoroughly cross-examined. On May 24, he pointed out, nine witnesses were heard in support of the charge against the military and fourteen for the defence. The jury had then stated that it had no wish to hear any more.

— But what about Joseph Constantineau, the witness who had begun to give evidence about the violence committed by the special constables?

— I do not remember him.

Did anyone object to your ruling that all the jurors had to be unanimous?

— I cannot remember.

Mondelet told the inquiry that the jury had deliberated from May 24 to 26 and had come into court each day to say that they could not agree on a unanimous verdict, but he could not remember the nature of the complaint the majority members of the jury had made about the minority.[36]

Three days later, Mondelet was back before the inquiry. His memory had made a remarkable recovery. He offered some written submissions to replace the oral answers he had given previously. Yes, he did remember Constantineau. It was when the witness began to speak about the violent behaviour of the special constables in the Place d'Armes that Mondelet had interrupted him and told him to confine his answer to how the three dead men had died and to who had killed them. When Constantineau said that he could not, Mondelet had asked him to withdraw. He also remembered telling the jury that a majority verdict would be sufficient—what he failed to tell them was that they needed to be unanimous since there were only twelve of them.

There was one final question on his conduct of the inquest. When the jury delivered its double verdict, why did he not just withdraw one of the jurors *pro forma* and call a fresh jury, one larger in size than the previous one? He answered that he doubted whether he could have proceeded in that manner.[37]

Walker was among the last witnesses to appear before the inquiry in March 1833. He said he remembered the coroner's inquest well. He had been present each day from May 22 until the coroner had adjourned matters to August 27. He had attended, he told James Leslie, from a professional interest and to satisfy himself that the proceedings were conducted in a proper and orderly fashion. When he realised that the jury of just twelve men was unlikely to reach a unanimous verdict, he viewed what unfolded before him with indifference. However he was prepared to comment on the coroner's inconsistency in dealing with some of the witnesses.

The first nine witnesses, Walker explained, were investigated *viva voce* (with the exception of perhaps one or two of them who had submitted written depositions) and were questioned by the coroner and the jurors. At first, the coroner was interested only in the circumstances that had immediately preceded the death of the three victims. Certain people in court then pointed out to him that there were witnesses willing to appear who wished to present evidence in rebuttal of the charges or at the very least in extenuation or mitigation.

The coroner had acquiesced, Walker said, and some thirteen or fourteen witnesses had then came forward with, for the most part, previously written depositions. Their evidence referred to events that had occurred earlier in the afternoon and even on the previous day. The coroner's ruling had elicited fresh criticism from some of those present in court who accused him of appearing to favour those who were strongly implicated in the deaths under investigation. His inconsistency was blatant, suggested Walker, since he had prevented the earlier witnesses from showing that a riot provoked and prolonged by a group of special constables and other persons had led to the military intervention and the subsequent deaths of the three men.[38]

The grand jury

The inquiry approached the subject of the grand jury from various angles. Their prize witness was Louis Gugy himself, the sheriff of the District of Montreal, a member of the Legislative Council, and the man with overall responsibility for the selection of grand and petty jurors. Also present were Frederick Goedicke, who had been employed by the sheriff to draw up a list of jurors from the city and parish of Montreal, and Charles Richard Ogden, the recently appointed attorney general, who had questions to answer about the manner in which witnesses had been selected to face the grand jury.

Gugy was called before the inquiry on December 19, 1832. He was first asked whether he could supply the list of special jurors and the local lists of each parish that were used to produce the lists of grand and petty jurors for the Court of King's Bench. He replied that it would take him at least a month to do so. What rules and principles had he followed in drawing up such lists? He had followed the rule set down in section 12, chapter 22 of the act passed in the previous session of Parliament, he answered.

Members of the House were fully aware of the new regulations and were certain that that they had not been adhered to in the most recent selection of grand jurors. Cherrier had attempted to bring the fact to the attention of the judges while the grand jury was considering the case but he had been ruled out of order. Denis-Benjamin Viger had had more success when he had broached the subject with Lord Goderich. The law provided the sheriff with strict guidelines in the selection of a petty and grand jury. The area from which he was to choose both sets of jurors covered more than fifty parishes. Each parish had to draw up a list of persons qualified to act as jurors. The sheriff was then obliged to compose a general list of grand and petty jurors by taking the first name— occasionally the first two names—from each individual parish list until all the names had been used up. From these general lists he had to constitute both juries by working his way successively down each list as every new jury was summoned. On August 3, 1832, John Delisle had written to Gugy requesting him to produce two lists. The breakdown of names on the petty jury list showed that Gugy correctly applied the new regulations: the jurors were evenly drawn from twenty-one parishes. Eleven had English names, forty-nine had French Canadian names. Lachine and Pointe Claire were each represented by just one juror, both French Canadian. In comparison, the composition of the grand jury list was very different.

Twelve of the twenty-four grand jurors came from Lachine, one of the smallest of the participating parishes. The other twelve were drawn from the city of Montreal (8), Côte-des-Neiges (1) and Pointe-Claire (3). More information about the grand jurors of Lachine became available when Gugy provided the inquiry with a copy of a letter he had received on May 12, 1832 from James Sommerville, an inhabitant of Lachine and a future grand juror. It was short and to the point. "I have drawn up a list of the Protestant owners of farms in this parish and I find that they all belong to your first class," it read. There followed a list of twenty names, none of them French. Twelve of them were later selected as grand jurors. Asked to explain the presence of so many Protestant farmers from Lachine, Gugy replied that as there were several Protestant congregations there he had asked a militia officer of the parish called James Somerville to obtain a list of those inhabitants who were qualified by law to act as jurors and who were Protestant. Gugy said he had intended to intermix them with other names from the parish but the church warden, Mr Venat Roi La Pensée, had objected and said it would be better if they were to remain as they were. Could he say, he was asked, whether the grand jurors favoured Bagg or Tracey. Gugy said he could not. "I never meddle with elections," he added by way of explanation.

James Leslie was obviously convinced that the opposite was true but Gugy refused to accept that he was guilty of any wrongdoing. How did he explain, Leslie asked, the omission of François Perrin's name from the list of grand jurors and the substitution of that of a James Millar who had gone to England? It was all the clerk's fault, answered Gugy. Exasperated by Gugy's arrogant tone, Leslie tried a different approach. Was it not Gugy who nine months earlier had provided the magistrates with copies of two anonymous letters claiming that plans were afoot to set fire to the city? The question irked Gugy. He complained that the inquiry had no business bringing up the subject but he was prepared to answer. The letters purportedly written by an Irishman had been addressed to Major Grierson who had then given them to Gugy. As they were written in different hands, Gugy explained, the magistrates had decided to take no action and he had returned the letters the same day to the Major.[39] Leslie did not pursue the questioning as he might well have done. It was enough that the inquiry had been reminded that before the election the magistrates had dismissed as worthless rumours that the Irish were planning to set fire to the city. Why they were prepared to believe the same rumours on May 20, 1832 was what the inquiry hoped to discover.

Gugy's convoluted explanation as to why twelve of the twenty-four grand jurors had been taken from the parish of Lachine became even more unacceptable when William Smith Sewell, sheriff of the District of Quebec City, appeared before the inquiry two months later. He was asked how he went about drawing up his list of grand and petty jurors for the Court of King's Bench. He explained that his practice was never to take more than two or three grand jurors from any one parish in the country and never more than six or seven from the city and banlieue of Quebec City.[40] Gugy appeared even more isolated when Frederick Goedike was asked to explain the composition of the grand jury list. The Sheriff's mistakes no longer appeared purely accidental.

Goedike had drawn up his list of jurors from the 1831 assessment books. He had begun work on April 20 and had completed the task around May 1. There were four assessment books, he said, one for the town and three for the suburbs. He had begun with the book for the town. First on the list were those living in St Paul St on the opposite side to the barracks and going as far as McGill St. He had then listed those on the opposite side of the street and worked his way back to the barracks. Leslie handed him the 1831 assessment book and asked him to read out the first eight names of those who should have been on the list of grand jurors. Goedike read out

the following names: 1. TOUSSAINT DUMAS. 2. WILLIAM
WRAGG. 3. JACQUES VIGER. 4. LOUIS BEAUDRY.
5. LOUIS ARDOUIN. 6. BENJAMIN STARNES.
7. RODERICK MCKENZIE. 8. FRANÇOIS PERRIN. Goedike
said that after McKenzie should have come Desmarteaux and
Chicoine, partners, but as he did not know their Christian
names he may have left them off the original list. Leslie then
put it to him that if the grand jury panel summoned the previous August and September had been selected in the order in
which their names stood in Goedike's list, then Beaudry,
Ardouin and Starnes would have been on the jury instead of
Olivier Berthelet, William Peddie, Francis Rasco and James
Millar. Goedike answered that Leslie was correct. Where, he
was then asked, should Olivier Berthelet's name have appeared
on the list? Immediately after Joseph Shuter's, came the reply.
And Pierre Cajetan's? After that of Starnes. What about
Charles Perry? Should not his name have appeared before
those of Rasco and Millar. Yes, agreed Goedike. For his final
question, Leslie referred to the complete list for St Paul St that
Goedike had drawn up for the Sheriff. There were almost one
hundred names on it. Was not Olivier Berthelet's the very last
name on the list? Yes, Goedike had to admit. Not once had
he been able to explain adequately why so many discrepancies
had crept into his list.[41]

Taken together with Gugy's answers, Goedike's evidence
pointed to either incompetence on the part of the sheriff or a
deliberate manœuvre to pack the grand jury with jurors who
were known to be favourable to an acquittal of the British
officers and the magistrates.

The question of the new bills of indictment prepared by
Ogden against the four accused was raised by Leslie at the
beginning of the former solicitor general's cross-examination.
Leslie reminded him that at the time of the *habeas corpus*

hearing on behalf of Macintosh and Temple, Ogden had stated on behalf of the Crown that there was no charge against them. When had he changed his mind? Ogden replied that it had been on the opening day of the new term when the coroner informed the court that one of his jurors had died over the summer. "I deemed it to be my duty to bring the matter under the consideration of the jury then sworn to enquire into all matters of a criminal or supposed criminal nature." He had prepared the bills in order to have a full enquiry, he said. That prompted Leslie to question Ogden about his understanding of a grand jury enquiry. At the time of the acquittal, the *Quebec Gazette* had complained that witnesses had been called who were convinced ahead of time that the action of the army on May 21 had been justified. Was Ogden responsible for inscribing the names of the witnesses on the back of the indictments? Yes, he was, he replied. Why was John Delisle's name included on the list? Ogden had no adequate explanation. Leslie then read out the names of eleven other witnesses, all but one of whom had originally given testimony at the coroner's inquest. Eight of the ten coroner's witnesses were considered to have given evidence in defence of the two officers. The one other witness, James Carswell, a special constable who had been on duty on the afternoon of May 21, had sworn an affidavit that had been used by Macintosh and Temple in support of their *habeas corpus* application. Leslie wanted to know what inference Ogden had drawn from their depositions that allowed him to think that they could support the indictments he had prepared before the grand jury. Ogden's reply was as elaborate as it was vague, as were many of his other answers:

> What interference (sic) I may have drawn from the perusal of these depositions so far back as the month of August last, I am

not now prepared to say, but if I inscribed their names on the back of the indictments, it must have been under the conviction that their testimony would throw some light upon the transaction of the 21st May, and the better subject matter submitted to them.

Leslie was no more successful in getting Ogden to explain why he had summoned Adjutant James Hay of the 15th. How on earth was he able to support the indictments? All Ogden was prepared to say was that Hay had in his possession the requisitions signed by the two magistrates. Leslie attempted to broaden the questions. Did Ogden know of any other instance in the country where crown officers inscribed on the back of indictments for wilful murder the names of all the witnesses first heard during the coroner's inquest both for and against the alleged killer or killers? Ogden replied that his experience was limited to just two cases of murder, once when he prosecuted and the other when he defended. He was not prepared to say what other crown officers did. In the one case when he prosecuted, he thought he may well have inscribed on the indictment all the names of those heard at the coroner's inquest. Leslie pressed him further. Did he know of any instance where crown officers inscribed the names of witnesses who had made no deposition on oath in support of the charge on the indictment but who were supposed to be in possession of written documents that were likely to weaken that charge? Ogden replied that it was not unusual to inscribe on indictments the names of persons who in the estimation of the crown officer might throw light and afford assistance to the grand jury in its inquiry. Why were only Robertson and Lukin included in the indictment? Was it because they had signed the requisition? Ogden replied, "I did what I considered my duty." Moffatt had played a more active role in directing the movement of the troops yet he was not indicted— why not? Ogden refused to answer. Why did Ogden not order the arrest of Robertson and Lukin? Was it because he was confident they would be acquitted? Ogden prudently left that question unanswered.[42]

On the basis of their testimony, Mondelet and Dupré come across as very different from Gugy and Ogden. The coroner's supposedly faulty memory was probably a deliberate ploy to cover up the embarrassment he felt at having blundered in his original charge to the inquest jury. It was his incompetence rather than a desire to engineer a hung jury that lay behind the failure of the jury to deliver a unanimous verdict. Dupré's decision on May 19 to adjourn voting prematurely was not to the liking of the Tracey camp but there was no evidence that he was in league with Bagg to keep him in the race. Some of the magistrates had exploited the ambiguity of the wording of the law relating to the duty of returning officers and the stratagem had worked. In comparison, Gugy and Ogden had acted deliberately to ensure that the grand jury delivered the verdict that the governor required. The regulations concerning the selection of grand and petty juries stipulated how the process was supposed to be conducted. Other sheriffs had applied them and Gugy too had demonstrated that he was capable of changing his former practice when he drew up the list of petty jurors.

The composition of the grand jury, however, was a blatant example of a packed jury and Gugy could provide no adequate explanation for his action. Ogden also had a hand in influencing the grand jury's deliberations. Inscribing on his indictments the names of the witnesses who had previously testified on behalf of Macintosh and Temple at the coroner's inquest distracted the grand jury from its principal task and encouraged it to perform as if it were a petty jury. As solicitor general, Ogden must have known what the consequences of his action would be. His justification was as naive as it was perverse.

9

The Reading of the Riot Act?

When the inquiry turned its attention to the subject of the military's presence in the Place d'Armes on the afternoon of May 21 and Robertson's decision to read the Riot Act, the Patriote members felt they had solid reasons for questioning the legality of both actions. Papineau had spent hours in the library of the Assembly pouring over some ninety folio volumes of the *House of Commons Journal* in preparation for the opening of the inquiry and had come up with some interesting findings. In a letter to his wife, he gave her a sample of some of the references he had found that supported his contention that the army and the magistrates had no business interfering in an election. The first was dated March 17, 1725: "It was resolved that Ed Marshall having presumed to read the proclamation against riots while the Burgesses... were duly assembled by virtue of his Majestys writ for the election of a Representative is guilty of high infringement of the freedom of electors: ordered in the custody of the Sergeant at Arms."

Another was dated December 1741: "That the presence of a regular body of armed soldiers at an Election is a high infringement of the Liberties of the subject, a manifest violation of the freedom of elections, and an open defiance of the laws and constitution of this kingdom."

Papineau told his wife he was confident he would find other precedents but he was less sure that the House would find enough witnesses to back up his claims.[1]

Until the inquiry opened, most of the eyewitness accounts of what had happened on the afternoon of May 21 had come from the same source: Robertson, Holmes, Macintosh, Temple and the sixty or so Bagg supporters who had provided sworn affidavits. Nevertheless, no clear picture of the incidents that occurred between 2:30 and 3:15 emerged from the different accounts, at least to the satisfaction of the Patriotes. Did the various episodes of fighting and scuffling that took place between 2:30 and 3 pm justify calling out the troops? Did the situation worsen between 3 and 3:15 pm to the point that the Riot Act needed to be read? The tendency of certain special constables in their affidavits to use such terms as "tumult" or "riot" to describe the trouble that broke out merely confused the issue. Did those special constables mean that there was destruction of public and private property and that people's lives were in danger? None of the evidence so far available suggested that either was true. There was even some serious doubt as to whether Robertson had indeed read the act. The affidavits of those who claimed to have witnessed the magistrate making the proclamation provided less than reliable evidence. Yet the grand jury had based its majority verdict on the basis of such evidence. The Patriote members of the House now set themselves the task of proving the illegality of the actions of both the magistrates and the military

Early fighting in the Place d'Armes

There was general agreement that the first trouble of the day occurred immediately following a short altercation between John Jordan and Dieudonné Perrin though not everybody witnessed the incident. Robertson and Holmes had made no mention of it claiming instead that the first sign of trouble occurred near the polling station at 2:45. Henry Mackenzie present in the Place d'Armes spoke only of a "tumult" at 3 pm. Robert Howard, a special constable on duty all day, claimed that there was "great excitement and a tendency to riot and tumult" but gave no other details.[2]

The clearest account the House was given came from Dr Pierre Beaubien, a Tracey supporter, whose testimony was given at the end of 1833. He had been standing in front of the Fabrique at 2:30 pm when he saw a quarrel erupt between Perrin and Jordan close to the tower of the old parish church. A crowd had gathered, he said, and some of the constables had become involved. Fighting then broke out involving fists and staves. After several minutes, it was all over. A few minutes later, a second scuffle developed a short distance away. That too lasted just a few minutes and as people began dispersing Beaubien noticed the arrival of a detachment of the 15th Regiment. It was between 2:45 pm and 3 pm, he said. A third scuffle then took place near the Fabrique and Henderson's store but there too peace was restored after a few minutes. Beaubien suspected that this third incident was due to the presence of a number of special constables who had assembled in front of the Fabrique much to the annoyance of a large section of the crowd. Beaubien had been talking to Benjamin Holmes when the magistrate was suddenly called away to investigate some trouble involving Louis Malo. The problem was resolved, Beaubien stated, when Holmes ordered Malo to join his fellow constables behind the enclosure wall of the parish church.[3]

A different perspective of the trouble in the square was provided by François Dragon, one of the special constables stationed inside the enclosure wall. He had seen Perrin approach and shove another man out of the way with his shoulder. Both men had their umbrellas open and both began to fight. At the same time, opposite the church, Louis Malo was also fighting. Dragon then heard Benjamin Delisle shout, "Murder." Delisle came up to Dragon and ordered him out into the square, saying, "They are killing each other." A short while later, Malo came up to Dragon and held up part of his frock coat. "They have torn my coat, but I gave it well to one of them," he said. Then, brandishing a small piece of brass, seven or eight inches long, and an inch and a half square at the end, he said "I gave it to him with this." Dragon said that he too became caught up in the fighting but after a short while his courage failed and he ran away. Cuvillier asked him whether the piece of brass Malo showed him was in fact a small constable's stave, Dragon said he believed it was.[4]

Other witnesses had a less clear view of what happened. Michel-François Trudeau, a medical student, was near Henderson's store when the first fight broke out. He recognised John Fisher and Dieudonné Perrin among those involved and from what he could see Fisher was not doing much to maintain the peace. "He appeared to me to be engaged in a scuffle with several persons there; and I believe he was doing like many others, that he was fighting. I cannot say whether he was one of the aggressors, or defending himself." Trudeau estimated that the trouble lasted fifteen or twenty minutes but did not specify whether he was referring to the first scuffle or to all three. Louis Lussier, a tavern keeper, grocer and special constable had observed one of the scuffles from Dillon's corner. His recollection was that it had lasted just a couple of minutes. In his account to his fellow magistrates, Robertson had said that the trouble had lasted between fifteen and twenty minutes but he was not well placed to estimate the precise duration since he had left the Place d'Armes some time after 2:45 to consult Holmes at the bank in St James St.[5]

One witness, Joseph-Félix Larocque, a former Hudson's Bay Company chief trader, minimised the original incident, suggesting that alcohol had been responsible, though his evidence was hearsay. Camille Lacombe had told him that he had been with Perrin in the bank earlier in the afternoon. Perrin appeared to be in an inebriated state and had told Lacombe that he was going to kick up a row at the poll. In an earlier affidavit, one of Bagg's supporters, Thomas Baron, a barrister from Trois-Rivières, claimed to have spoken to Jordan (written as Jourdain in the affidavit) at a later stage who told him how much he regretted the whole affair. It had all been a misunderstanding, he had said. He had been a close friend of Perrin's for a number of years, so much so that when Perrin had torn Jordan's umbrella, Jordan had taken it as a joke. However, a few Irishmen had witnessed the incident and wanted to know whether Jordan was a Tracey supporter. When he told them that he was, they had chased Perrin and had assaulted him. This had then led to more fighting, said Baron.[6]

It was not until January 1834 that the House had an opportunity of hearing from Jordan first hand. By then his memory was a little hazy. He confirmed that it was around 2:30 pm that Dieudonné Perrin had struck him with an umbrella but gave no detail of any verbal exchange between the pair or of a conversation with onlookers. Everything had happened so quickly, he said, "I had hardly turned round to ascertain who had thus struck me when I perceived two or three individuals striking him." The affray had become general, he remembered, and John Fisher had gone off to call out the troops. Questioned further on the earlier incident, Jordan admitted that there was probably no real malice behind Perrin's blow.[7]

The reason the troops were called out seems to have been less the intensity of fighting, which was sporadic and short-lived, than the panic experienced by John Fisher when caught up in a scuffle. One of the affidavits submitted by Macintosh and Temple after their arrest described the incident. Lieutenant Jeremiah Wilkes Dewson, quarter-master of the 15th Foot happened to be crossing the Place d'Armes around 3 pm on May 21 when he said he saw "fighting and acts of violence." John Fisher had come running towards him, covered in mud, crying out, "What is to be done to preserve the peace? Murder will be committed." Dewson told him that if he went to the main-guard with a magistrate's order, he would find Captain Temple with a party of men ready to cooperate.[8] Most likely Dewson had arrived on the square at least ten minutes earlier which would have allowed Fisher sufficient time to bring Captain Temple and his men back to the Place d'Armes by 3 pm, the time at which most people agreed the troops had arrived.

By then, calm had returned to the square. Even the scuffle that took place close to the polling station shortly before 3 pm did not attract the attention of those inside. This was one of the points the House raised with Dupré during his three days of interrogation. Mindful that it was the returning officer who had been instrumental in forcing the magistrates to take their precipitate action on May 20, Leslie asked Dupré whether he had noticed any significant difference in the crowd's behaviour on May 21 compared to other days. No, he answered, there was certainly no disposition to violence on the Monday, but he was careful to qualify his answer by stating that he had spent most of the day inside the polling station and knew only what had been reported to him. Why then, he was asked, had he requested several constables to be positioned inside the passageway leading into the polling room. Merely as a precaution, Dupré replied. Pressed to explain the decisions taken that day by the magistrates, Dupré insisted that he had not been consulted—what the magistrates did was their responsibility and theirs alone. They had not informed him that they had called for military assistance and no one had told him that the Riot Act had been read close to the poll.

Asked to confirm that Holmes and Lukin had gone to see him after the troops arrived, Dupré agreed that there had been some contact between the magistrates and himself but there had been no mention of the Riot Act. Holmes had come to him and requested that the poll be adjourned because of all the noise and because the troops had arrived in the square. Dupré admitted that he didn't really understand what Holmes had said to him. He had then turned to Lukin and asked him who had sent for the troops. Lukin said that he had been responsible after he had been assaulted while trying to keep the peace, or words to that effect. Dupré said that he had made no comment but decided to go outside and see for himself what the situation was on the Place d'Armes. There was no noise and there was no sign of any trouble, he said. Tracey or some of his supporters, he could not remember exactly, objected to the poll being adjourned, and without their assent, Dupré said, he had no option but to refuse the magistrates' request.[9]

Dupré's evidence was crucial. As returning officer, his role and powers were paramount during the election, a fact the magistrates appeared to have recognised if not always respected over the previous three weeks of voting. On the evening of Sunday, May 20, Dupré had specifically asked for more constables to be on duty inside the polling station to guarantee his own protection but he had not asked for military assistance nor had he expressed any alarm about the contents of the Bagg letter that he had included with his own.

On the Monday afternoon, Robertson had sent Holmes and Lukin to speak to Dupré at some time between 3 and 3:15 pm. The reasons the two magistrates gave for adjourning the poll—noise and the presence of the army—suggests that no riot was in progress at the time, a fact confirmed by Dupré when he ventured outside to see for himself. Holmes knew that Robertson was intending to read the Riot Act but decided to keep the returning officer in the dark. It is difficult to understand why Holmes did not at least hint that the situation might necessitate the reading of the Riot Act unless he knew that Dupré would never have agreed to it in view of the calm that then existed around the polling station. Lukin's reason for calling out the military was a feeble one (if he really did accept responsibility for doing so) and the two magistrates would have appeared ridiculous had they suggested to Dupré that a riot was under way on his very doorstep.

The reading of the Riot Act

Within minutes of reporting to Robertson that Dupré had refused to adjourn the poll, Holmes and Lukin accompanied the senior magistrate back to the place from where they had just come and watched as he read the Riot Act. This at least was what both Robertson and Holmes claimed—other evidence suggested that Lukin had neither seen it or heard it read.[10]

Had a riot suddenly broken out in a spot where the returning officer claimed all was calm and peaceful only minutes earlier? Who exactly were the rioters that Robertson addressed and ordered to disperse within the hour? Neither Robertson nor Holmes felt the need to give these details in their accounts. At the time news that the Riot Act had been read close to the polling station was received with a great deal of scepticism. *La Minerve* and the *Vindicator* were both convinced that the proclamation had never been made. Even the Tory press had some misgivings. Knowing that the military had opened fire some two hours after Robertson was supposed to have read the act and at some distance from the Place d'Armes, the *Canadian Courant* conjectured that the act had been read a second time. It reported that it had occurred thirty minutes before the shooting.[11] That version restored the legality of the army's action but posed the problem of why the act needed to be read at a time when everyone, magistrates and military included, agreed that all was peaceful. The grand jury had decided that the Riot Act had conferred immunity on the military against the charge of homicide. The Patriote members of the House were equally convinced that a crime had been committed.

As a witness, Benjamin Delisle, the high constable, inspired little confidence. His answers were evasive and at times implausible given the role he played throughout the election. When the *Canadian Courant* reported that the Riot Act had been read a second time, it did so only a matter of days after the event when the situation was still confused. When Delisle stated that the act had been read opposite Robertson's house on St James St some thirty minutes before the troops opened fire, more than six months had gone by during which time he had almost daily contact with Robertson and the other magistrates. If he had hoped to protect Robertson, the plan backfired. Three weeks later, a clearly embarrassed Delisle appeared again before the House to apologise for various inaccurate statements he had made on January 9, 1833. He now stated that Robertson had not read the Riot Act a second time when the troops were in St James St. He had seen Robertson carrying a book in his hand and had merely presumed that the magistrate had read the act.[12] Delisle was not required to

explain his error but the implication was clear: he had presumed that the troops would only open fire if they had been
covered by the Riot Act.

Other witnesses, all Tracey supporters, had not heard the
first reading. Dr Robert Nelson said he had not heard it read.
Joseph-Félix Larocque had been standing at Dillon's corner
just a few yards from the polling station, yet he did not hear
Robertson read the act. John Donegani and Stephen Field,
both merchants and present in the Place d'Armes for most of
the day, both testified that they heard nothing. Joshua Bell, a
leather dealer and shoe maker, was adamant that he heard no
proclamation of the act and he added for good measure that
"to the present time, after all that has appeared in the public
prints, I am not convinced that it was read on that day." Jean-
Michel François Trudeau was equally convinced that no
proclamation was read that afternoon. "I think it would have
been difficult to read without my hearing it read," he said, in
reply to a question, and added, "It might possibly have been
read in some retired corner, but it was not read on the Place
d'Armes." Jacques Viger, who had spent two hours under the
church portico with the troops and had spoken to Captain
Smith, Lukin and Robertson, said that none of them told him
the act had been read.[13]

John Flaherty, a butcher, was another witness who had not
heard the act despite being in the square from 1:30 pm
onwards. He was questioned closely by Cuvillier on the matter. "Did Robertson tell you that he was going to read the Riot
Act?" asked Cuvillier. "I heard him say so," replied Flaherty,
"but I did not see him read it. He went towards the poll, and
the persons who came from there, said to me that he had not
read it." He noticed that Dr Robertson carried his book under
his arm for some considerable time when he was out in the
square.[14]

The most striking testimony to throw doubt on Robertson's veracity came from Louis-Hyppolite La Fontaine who had arrived in the Place d'Armes shortly after 3 pm. He had met Robertson opposite the office door of the Fabrique, very close to the polling station, at around 3:20 pm. Robertson told him that he was carrying a copy of the Riot Act and that he was going to read it. La Fontaine said that by then there was no longer any disturbance and that all was quiet. There was absolutely no need to read the Riot Act, he told Robertson. He himself had restored order by restraining Louis Malo on two separate occasions. The first time by stopping him and another constable from assaulting two of Tracey's supporters, and then again, five or ten minutes later, by dragging him off an Irishman whom he was assaulting. La Fontaine told Robertson that if he went ahead with his plan, it would cause deep offence and might even trigger a more serious disturbance. He had the impression that he had said enough to convince Robertson to drop his plan because the magistrate then withdrew without reading the act. There was no further mention of the Riot Act that afternoon, said La Fontaine.[15]

John Jordan's evidence supported La Fontaine's. Jordan said that he had been inside the Fabrique office about 4 pm as far as he could remember when he had seen Dr Robertson with one of his friends who was holding an umbrella over him. Robertson opened a book as if to read something but found it impossible to do so. There was a huge crowd present but no disorder. Jordan said that he was later told that the act had been read inside the church enclosure but he had no first-hand knowledge of the fact.[16]

None of the affidavits from those special constables who claimed to have witnessed Robertson reading the act was conclusive enough to disprove what La Fontaine and Jordan stated. Henry Mackenzie had stated that Robertson had come forward at 3 pm to read his declaration following a disturbance near Henderson's store but that it had then needed Mackenzie to go about informing the crowd (the special constables consistently used the term "mob" in place of "crowd") that the act was in force and that all should disperse. If true, it was an impossible task and one that had no more effect on the crowd than Robertson's own proclamation. Robert Howard thought it was at 3:30 that the act was read but all he saw was Robertson advancing into a crowd with his book. William Boston saw Robertson and Holmes go forward but had to admit that he had heard and seen nothing. Only two special constables were adamant that they had accompanied Robertson into the crowd and stood nearby while he read his proclamation—the problem was that for Isaac Aaron it had taken place at 3:30 pm and for James Carswell it had been between 2 and 3 pm. Aaron also provided the extra detail that immediately after the proclamation Robertson had handed over the book containing the Riot Act to someone inside Henderson's for safekeeping. If true, this would have invalidated the action the magistrate had just taken.[17]

James Leslie turned to the legal aspects of the Riot Act when he questioned Charles Richard Ogden, the new attorney general for Lower Canada. Ogden proved to be a very difficult witness. The first questions dealt with the aftermath of May 21. If the authorities really believed that a riot had taken place, what steps, wondered Leslie, had been taken to apprehend the guilty?

— Had there been any indictments for riot, tumultuous assembly or affray in relation to the events of the 21st?

— No, replied Ogden.

— Had he received any depositions on which to ground an indictment, for a felony, for example, committed on the Place d'Armes on the 21st, or the destruction of a public building before the troops arrived?

— No, came the reply.

— Had any Crown Officer or private prosecutor brought an indictment of a similar nature?

— Not to my knowledge, said Ogden.

Leslie then turned to the second arrest of Macintosh and Temple and to the arguments Ogden presented in court on their behalf. Did he not say that since the Riot Act had been read and the order to disperse given, the two officers could not be indicted or tried for the death of citizens killed as a result of their orders? Ogden admitted that he had referred to the act and had even quoted a clause or two in support of his argument but he had given other reasons, he said, why the officers should be freed.

Leslie pressed him on some of the finer points of the act.

— Did the obligation to disperse after the reading of the proclamation oblige the returning officer to close or adjourn the poll?

— That question involves a legal opinion—I have none to give, answered Ogden.

— Did it deprive the electors of the right to vote at the poll?

— That is also a legal question and I beg to decline answering it.

— Did it apply to all those who were present in the Place d'Armes, without exception?

— That is also a legal question and I decline giving any opinion.

— Do you believe that the act is in force in this province?

— That again is a matter of legal opinion which I must also decline to offer one.

— Has the disposition of the statute been complied with, which directs it to be read at the opening of each quarter session?

— It may or may not have been read.

— Have you ever heard it read during the whole of your practice, or learned that it had been so?

Ogden said he had no recollection of ever having heard it read, but then he had practised very little in the court of quarter sessions and that had been many years previous.

— During an election, has a justice of the peace the right to read the Riot Act in the vicinity of the poll without consulting the returning officer?

— That too requires a legal opinion and I have none to give.

— Was he not aware that the House of Commons had declared that it would be a high infringement of the freedom of an election if a magistrate were to do so?

Ogden replied that he was unaware that such was the case.

Leslie made several other attempts to press Ogden on the application of the act in Lower Canada but each time he came up against the same obstinate refusal to provide an acceptable answer.[18]

In the absence of any comment on the matter by the magistrates and army officers, the House sought to discover what reaction there was at 4:15 pm, the time by which the crowd should have dispersed. Only Jacques Viger was able to describe the atmosphere behind the enclosure wall. He detected, he said, a certain nervousness among the military and the magistrates, having been in conversation with them from time to time during the course of the afternoon. At one point, Captain Smith asked him whether he thought that people in the Place d'Armes were armed. Viger told him that he did not think such a thing possible. At 4:45 pm Robertson asked him when the poll would close and Viger had replied that it would be at the usual time of 5 o'clock. Lt-Col Macintosh also showed signs of impatience, as if he could not wait to return to barracks. Cuvillier wanted to know why. "I thought I could see that in his countenance," replied Viger, "and drew that inference from the manner in which I was asked when the poll would close. The troops were fatigued with standing such a long time, and Captain Temple had made them twice counter march under the portico to relax them." The special constables too were in combative mood. Viger saw two acts of violence on an Irishman named Keogh whom Lukin had been keeping close to him in order to take his affidavit in relation to Robert Cooke's attempt on the life of Charles Curran on May 18. "He was twice collared, and threatened with ill-treatment by two or three constables who had their staves in their hands, on the steps of the Piazza of the Church, and he was twice extricated from the hands of the Constables by Messrs Lukin and Robertson severally, in my presence."[19]

None of the evidence presented before or during the inquiry suggests that Robertson read the Riot Act. History has only his word that he did so. None of the evidence suggests that the fighting and scuffling that took place between 2:30 and 3 pm constituted a riot and indeed there is evidence that some of the worst violence was committed by Louis Malo and the special constables and only the rapid intervention of the magistrates prevented them from inflicting more serious harm. The various disturbances, as some of the special constables called them, hardly justified military intervention.

Had John Fisher not lost his nerve during one bout of fighting, there would have been no need of the army. Robertson too lost his nerve. By the time the troops arrived in the Place d'Armes, the disturbances were over. Robertson could have

ordered the military detachment to return to barracks but the
temptation to influence the election then at a critical stage by
a show of strength was too strong.

Having signed the requisition form as required by army
regulations, Robertson needed the support of the returning
officer but for once Dupré had stood his ground. Had a riot
been in progress, it is inconceivable that the two magistrates
sent to persuade Dupré to adjourn the vote would not have
been successful. Robertson was in danger of losing face in the
presence of the garrison commander. As an act of bravado he
announced he was going to read the Riot Act. His problem
was where to read it. The square had been calm for more than
fifteen minutes, as even Dupré had testified. Robertson therefore made a show of heading over to where the crowd was
most dense—in front of the polling station. If he had really
intended to read the act, his chance meeting with La Fontaine
would have given him the opportunity to enlist the moral
support he needed to persuade Tracey's supporters to disperse. Instead he squandered the chance. Unable or unwilling
to read the act, he resorted to subterfuge. He returned to
where Macintosh was waiting and told him the act was in
force. Significantly, he made no attempt to order the troops
to disperse the crowd. Instead, he preferred to keep the troops
out of sight for the rest of afternoon until polling had finished
for the day. The troops could then have returned to barracks
and none would have been the wiser. Unfortunately, the special constables were still in combative mood and little was
needed to provoke them.

Military Guidelines

Two months into the inquiry the Chamber became aware that
certain documents in Governor Aylmer's possession and rel-

evant to its investigations had been deliberately withheld despite his promise of complete cooperation the previous November. The House wrote to him on February 21, 1833 requesting to see copies of the missing documents. In his reply two days later, Governor Aylmer refused the House's request on the grounds that the documents in question related to "the details of the Military Service, and to prospective and contingent arrangements, with a view to the preservation of public tranquility in the City of Montreal."[20] The House immediately ordered the governor's answer to be referred to the standing committee of privileges and elections.

Aylmer backed down and decided it would be more prudent to cooperate. Copies of the documents were prepared and handed over in time for the next session of the House inquiry. It was a significant victory for Papineau.[21] The documents requested included parts of the correspondence between Macintosh and the governor's military secretary, the rules for issuing ball cartridges to the troops and, most importantly, a military document that had been sent to William Robertson more than three months earlier. It was this document that excited the curiosity of the inquiry. As soon as its contents became known, it was easy to understand the governor's embarrassment.

The document implicitly blamed Macintosh and the magistrates for their lack of judgment at a critical point on May 21. To make matters worse, the author of the document was none other than Lieutenant Colonel Duncan McDougall of the 79th Highlanders, the man who had replaced Macintosh as commander of the Montreal garrison.

The document was dated November 8, 1832 and had been written shortly after McDougall's arrival from Kingston. In a covering letter addressed to William Robertson in his capacity as senior magistrate, McDougall said he wished to bring to the notice of the city's magistrates the procedure that British officers were expected to follow when called out by the civil power to put down a riot. That procedure was contained in a series of instructions that was attached to the letter and was similar to the one that troops under his command in Great Britain had always followed to protect lives and property at times of riot. Pointedly, he added that the same procedure had always received the approval of local magistrates. They could well have been used during the recent Bristol riots, he suggested. There the mob was made up of a hard nucleus of no more than one hundred people. Had there been a proper understanding between the military and civil authorities, twenty soldiers would have been enough to regain control of a situation that had caused so much devastation in that city. He could have added that the events of May 21 in Montreal were in no way comparable to the wide-spread rioting that had taken place in Bristol one year earlier.

McDougall began by reminding the magistrates of the wording that they had to use when requisitioning troops in cases of civil disorder:

> The Officer commanding the troops and those under his command are hereby required and ordered to restore and preserve the peace of the city, by dispersing all mobs, and by acting against all who are, or may be, engaged in attacking persons or property, either by firing on them, or in any other manner that he, or they detached under his orders, may consider necessary to protect the lives and properties of the inhabitants and to re-establish and maintain the peace as well as the safety of the City which is now in danger.

A magistrate then had to read the following proclamation: "Our sovereign Lord the King charges and commandeth all persons being assembled immediately to disperse themselves and peaceably to depart to their habitations, or to their lawful business, upon the pains contained in the Act."

Before the troops could be called into action, however, a number of safeguards needed to be respected. The first concerned the duties of the magistrate in charge:

> 1. Troops must be accompanied by a magistrate who must be in possession of the Riot Act and the magistrate must not be allowed to quit the party until he states that there is no further need of their services or he gives orders to the troops to act.
>
> 2. The Riot Act must be read before the soldiers approach the mob and he must be prepared to give the promptest and most decisive orders for their putting an end to disorder and tumult. If he quits the party, the troops must be withdrawn.

Even then, there was a moral obligation on the part of the officers to adopt a cautious approach before engaging with a mob:

> 3. Officers are enjoined to make a marked difference in their proceedings towards mobs arising from any popular excitement, unattended by attacks on property, or during outrages, and those tumultuary assemblages, evidently congregated for the purpose of the attack and destruction of public buildings or private property.
>
> 4. Officers are ordered to treat persons composing mobs of the first mentioned character, more as children than as men and to use in the first instance, every kind of persuasion and advice, as well as to shew as much forbearance towards them as the circumstances of the case can possibly justify.
>
> 5. The second category are 'Tumultuary assemblages with the purpose of the attack and destruction of public buildings and private property, or being assembled (no matter for what purpose) to attack or destroy public or private property.'

Only in the case of the second category was the officer in charge permitted to use force:

> 6. When troops arrive near where mob is destroying property, he must caution in a loud voice all well-disposed people to disperse, and that all who remain after such caution, must be considered, if not actually guilty, yet passively, and most culpably so, in adding to the confusion, and the number of the mob by their presence.
>
> 7. After the caution, the Officer must proceed against the rioters as against the worst description of the enemies of his country, bearing in mind that an energetic and vigorous performance of his duties in the first instance is likely to prove in the end the most merciful course that can be adopted in respect to the mob itself, and decidedly the most conducive to the best interests of the place where the particular riot occurs, as well as of that of the whole of His Majesty's subjects.[22]

The repeated references in the instructions to attacks on public and private property are important in that they show clearly what the British understood to be a riot. A riot was not some disturbance of the sort that occurred sporadically on the afternoon of May 21 or on the opening day of the election when Bagg's bullies were guilty of numerous assaults on voters attempting to vote for Tracey. English law distinguished between a riot and a mere affray, as Jacques Crémazie explained ten years later in his book *Les lois criminelles anglaises*. A riot referred to a situation where the commotion and violence were the result of a certain level of premeditation. Where there was no premeditation, the law preferred to use the word "affray." In explaining the term, Crémazie seemed to have had the events of May 21 in mind, "Thus people who suddenly quarrel with each other in the market place or elsewhere are not guilty of a riot but merely of affray."[23] A riot, on the other hand, was what had happened in Bristol a year earlier.

McDougall's reference to Bristol was significant. It was a subject that was on every British officer's mind and Lt Col Macintosh was no exception. News of riots in various English cities in support of parliamentary reform had reached Montreal in early December 1831 and newspapers there had given them wide coverage. But it was the Bristol riots that had shocked most people. They began on Saturday October 29, 1831 and lasted for three days during which more than fifty buildings were destroyed. At the height of the trouble, the authorities summoned a troop of Light Dragoons and Dragoon Guards under the command of Lieutenant Colonel Brereton and the Riot Act was read. Brereton, however, refused to fire on the mob since the mayor was unwilling to give him a written signed order to that effect. Eventually the officer ordered the Dragoons to draw their swords and to go into action against a mob carrying out the destruction of Queen Square. Deaths were in the hundreds. Afterwards the military authorities were accused of failing to prevent widespread looting and destruction of property. The trial of a number of rioters began on January 2, 1832. A week later, it was the turn of Brereton to face a court martial for dereliction of duty in his handling of the riots. On January 12, five rioters were sentenced to death. The following day Brereton committed suicide.[24]

The subject must have crossed Macintosh's mind more than once when the two magistrates spoke to him late on Sunday, May 20. It must still have played on his mind the following afternoon as he waited under the portico of the parish church, anxious to return to the garrison. If at the time of taking up the command of the Montreal garrison Macintosh had instructed local magistrates in the correct procedure for dealing with urban unrest, it is unlikely that troops would have been present in the vicinity of an election on that same afternoon. At 5 pm, as Dupré declared voting ended for the day, it was Macintosh's misfortune to be surrounded by magistrates who had a vested interest in seeing to it that Tracey lost the election.

10

The Shooting

The Patriotes felt they had a mountain to climb when it came to investigating what had happened over the fifteen short minutes that followed the close of the poll on May 21. The amount of evidence that had accumulated since the time of the coroner's inquest was considerable. However, the vast majority of eyewitness accounts, presented in the form of affidavits, had come from people directly implicated in some official capacity in the events under investigation: army officers, rank and file soldiers, magistrates and special constables. As most of the affidavits were sworn with a view to defending the military against an accusation of homicide, it was inevitable that Tracey and his supporters were presented in the worst possible light. Nevertheless, when certain affidavits dealing with the period immediately before the troops opened fire were scrutinized, a number of discrepancies had come to light. The Patriotes hoped that other discrepancies would appear as eyewitnesses were cross-examined before the House. The inquiry therefore concentrated on three distinct phases of those final fifteen minutes: firstly, the departure of Tracey from the polling station and the attack on his supporters; secondly, the stone fight between the special constables and Tracey's supporters; and finally, the military intervention and the shooting.

The end of polling

There was a marked difference between the evidence heard at the coroner's inquest and the evidence contained in the affidavits produced later in defence of Macintosh and Temple in relation to Tracey's departure from the polling station. All were agreed that Tracey had left first and instead of following his usual practice of exiting via a gap in the fence in front of the polling station and then turning right, he and his close advisers had turned left inside the fence and had followed the path towards Henderson's store where the special constables and other Bagg supporters were lined up. Once he had cleared the fence Tracey had then headed back in the direction of St James St. For some of the special constables, this was sheer provocation. Isaac Aaron said that after Tracey came outside, the "mob" following him had pushed and knocked down all before them. William Fisher claimed that Tracey and his "adherents" had then advanced into the middle of the Place d'Armes. For Joseph Bowron the provocation was both deliberate and threatening: Tracey and supporters walked into the centre of the square and had immediately formed a line in front of the church putting themselves "in an attitude of defiance with hurras and shouting." According to these affidavits, Tracey's action was just the prelude to further acts of violence and a concerted attack on Henderson's store by his supporters. In Robert Howard's opinion, it was the prelude to a full-scale riot.[1]

Why the jubilant supporters of the candidate who was leading by three votes and whose victory was likely to be confirmed the next morning should suddenly decide to riot was not examined in any of the affidavits. No affidavit referred to the assault by the special constables on the few Tracey supporters who had remained behind in the Place d'Armes after the main body had departed along St James St. Those details had been revealed during the coroner's inquest and in Théophile Bruneau's affidavit sent to Joseph Roy. Michel Jacques had told the inquest that he had seen first one constable then several attack one of the Tracey stragglers; then they had attacked a companion of the man when he had called for assistance. The attack was so violent, Jacques said, that Delisle had intervened in an attempt to restrain the first constable. Bruneau had named the three of the constables involved as Try, Farquar and Malo and had said the victim was Irish. Further corroboration during the inquest had come from Alexander Robertson, a witness who had defended the army's action. He had witnessed the assault on the stragglers, about six in number and mainly boys or young men, he said, by one of the constables and had tried to give assistance to the victim who had been beaten unconscious.

During his cross-examination, Benjamin Delisle was asked what had occurred after voting ended. For someone who had been directly involved in the incidents—he said he had been standing at the door of the polling station—his reply was astonishing:

> After the poll was closed, about five o'clock, there were a number of Irish, two or three hundred at least, who were throwing stones, and shouting. In a very short time after, I saw a few special constables amongst them with blue sticks, and who were defending themselves, at least, as I thought. It was impossible for me to go amongst them to re-establish peace, as the quantity of stones which were thrown, rendered it dangerous to approach.[2]

He then claimed that Bagg had left the polling station first with his supporters and that Tracey and his party had chased after them and had eventually caught up with them. A fight had then developed between the two groups with Tracey at the head of his supporters throwing stones.

Three weeks later, Delisle returned to face the inquiry. He apologized for misleading the House on a number of significant points concerning the events of May 21 thereby casting doubt on much of his previous evidence before the inquiry. He appeared one last time on March 4, 1833 to petition the House for a leave of absence to attend the King's Bench where he was required as a material witness in a trial. Papineau seized the opportunity to express the frustration members had felt at the answers Delisle had given them: "It cannot fail to strike observation, that whenever he was interrogated by the Hon. Member for East Ward, he recollected nothing, his want of memory was incredible—but on the contrary, when the defence of the magistrates is being upon (sic), he has a fresh remembrance of particulars [...] He appeared to have composed a romance to serve the occasion, and had the hardihood to recite it here."[3]

Delisle was told he had "wilfully and maliciously given false evidence" and was therefore guilty of a high misdemeanour and a breach of the privileges of the House. A warrant was issued for his arrest and the following day he was committed to jail.[4]

If Delisle really had been standing at the door of the polling station as he claimed, then it was likely he found himself standing shoulder to shoulder with the returning officer a few minutes after 5 pm. But what Dupré saw was very different from what Delisle and his special constables had described. Dupré had as usual positioned himself at the entrance to the polling station to watch the two candidates depart. Tracey had left shortly after 5 o'clock and was joined by a group of his supporters who had been waiting inside the railings. Dupré had watched them walk the full length of the railings as far as the exit close to Henderson's house where Bagg's supporters were always congregated. This time a number of special constables were also present: a few minutes earlier, Delisle had ordered his men to leave the precincts of the polling station and to line up in front of Henderson's facing the parish church.

Tracey had then headed off along St James St, as usual, surrounded by his supporters except for a small group, between ten and fifteen, estimated Dupré, that went back to the corner of Henderson's house. By this time, Bagg had also left the polling station with three or four of his followers and had joined up with the rest of his supporters. There was a noisy confrontation between both groups, with Tracey's small group chanting victory slogans and Bagg's replying with insults. Dupré said that he was not unduly alarmed and went back inside the polling station to collect his papers. He had not seen any trouble.[5]

The witnesses who recounted what next happened had either voted for Tracey or would be considered as sympathetic to his cause. Very few discrepancies exist between their various accounts.

Etienne-Alexis Dubois had been watching from the window of the Fabrique where he worked as a clerk. Tracey left shortly after 5 o'clock, he said, and seven or eight of his supporters remained behind, shouting, "hurrah for Tracey." Tracey had gone a good hundred yards along St James St when a number of constables who had been positioned in the centre of the Place d'Armes ran forward and used their staves to attack the people who were chanting Tracey's name. Dubois saw Charles Try knock an Irishman to the ground with his

The old and new Bank of Montreal buildings on St. James. The new building stands on the site of the Fabrique and the fire station where voting took place from May 5 to 22. Benjamin Holmes observed the trouble between Tracey's supporters and special constables from the upper floor of the old building to the left. (McCord Museum – MP-0000.364)

stave. Louis Malo then ran forward and struck another Irishman who was shouting "hurrah" just twenty feet from the window where Dubois was standing. Malo had used a small club or life preserver against the man who appeared to Dubois to be dead. A moment later somebody tried to lift the man but there were no signs of life. The body remained there until some time later a group of people approached and carried it off.[6]

Dr Pierre Beaubien had observed the same scene from almost the same angle as Dubois. He had been standing on the pavement between the polling station and the bank and had watched as first Tracey and then Bagg departed with their friends. As Bagg reached the corner of Henderson's, his supporters began shouting "hurrah." At the same time, four or five individuals who had remained behind after Tracey had departed and were standing opposite the Fabrique began shouting, "hurrah for Tracey." "Then commenced the scene of 21 May," said Beaubien. Two individuals rushed from the midst of the constables and Bagg supporters and headed straight for the people who were shouting in favour of Tracey. The first to arrive began to strike as many as he could with his fists. The second was armed with a short constable's stave and used it repeatedly against one person in particular. His victim fell to the ground and lay there motionless and was still there when Beaubien moved away from his position some time later.[7]

Hosea B. Smith, a Montreal merchant, had been standing at Dillon's corner since 4:30 pm. Tracey and his supporters had already passed the bank in St James St when Bagg and his friends left the polling station and headed in the direction of his home in the company of his supporters. When they reached Henderson's, Smith heard someone cry out from amongst them, "stand your ground, drive them off." He then saw a number of constables (he recognised Charles Try as one of them) emerge from the group and begin beating several individuals "in a most violent and brutal and murderous manner." Two individuals were knocked to the ground and one appeared to be dead.

Cuvillier asked Smith whether he had noticed anything unusual when the candidates had left the polling station. Smith said he remembered that Tracey and his friends had walked farther along the pavement than usual because of a puddle of water opposite the opening by which they usually left.

"Can you state positively there was a puddle of water preventing them coming out at their usual place?" Cuvillier asked.

"I can state positively that it was a puddle of water and mud I should not like to have gone through if I could have gone by any other way," replied Smith.[8]

John Flaherty, a butcher by trade, was present on the Place d'Armes from 1:30 pm onwards, sheltering under the porch of Mr Dubois's house, next door to Henderson's store. His testimony was particularly interesting since he found himself in close proximity to the special constables as Bagg and his friends emerged from the polling station. John Fisher was standing with the constables. Another magistrate, Joseph Shuter, then came up and led them in cheering Bagg as the candidate went by. Shuter then turned his attention to the stragglers from Tracey's party. "Come, my boys," he shouted to the special constables, "let's have a rally into them now, and give them a damned drilling." A man who was standing next to the magistrate remonstrated with him saying that it was not right to maltreat people who were dispersing. Their lives should not be put in danger simply for shouting and cheering at the end of polling, he told Shuter, adding that it was usual for people to act this way on such occasions. Shuter became angry and had wagged his finger at him, saying, "You damned rascal, I will have you brought to order." As they quarrelled, a cry went up, "Come, my boys, we must not be cowards." With that, some nine or ten constables ran towards the stragglers and began assaulting them. Louis Malo delivered three or four blows with his fist to the head of a man who was lying on the ground. Flaherty then heard Delisle cry out, "Murder!"[9]

Cuvillier then took up the cross-examination of Flaherty. Was there a scuffle at Henderson's corner when Tracey's party had left the polling station? No, said Flaherty, there was only shouting and a waving of hats, and the same after he departed. There was no scuffling until the magistrates and the constables reacted. Most people were going home and dispersing in all directions. What about the stragglers who remained behind after Tracey's party had set off along St James St? asked Cuvillier. A good many remained behind, shouting and cheering, agreed Flaherty, but there was no violence. They were all scattered about near the poll and were going off home, some towards St Lawrence suburb and some elsewhere. Flaherty said he saw no one make use of offensive language or make any gestures.[10]

A few other witnesses added some minor details. Louis Lussier, a tavern keeper and grocer, had been sworn in as a special constable on May 15. He estimated that some ten or twelve of Tracey's supporters had stayed behind in the Place d'Armes. They attempted to pass through a group of special constables who blocked their way and who told them that they had no business there. When the supporters tried to push their way through, the constables assaulted them. Stephen Field, a merchant, was inside Andrew Galt's shoe store on the corner of Notre Dame St and St Joseph St. From the second storey Field had watched the scuffle between some of the constables and certain individuals. The first constable to strike a blow with his stave was a man by the name of McKenzie. Field knew him as a clerk who had been for some time with Moffatt, Gillespie and Co of Montreal. Other constables had joined in, shouting, "we will drive them off." Field lost sight of them when they finally disappeared down by the bank. Finally, Pierre Lebert, a butcher, named three of the constables who had knocked the unnamed Irishman unconscious as Malo, Try and a certain Duncan Curry, a grocer and tavern keeper of Notre-Dame St.[11]

Édouard-Étienne Rodier did not refer to any particular incidents but he did name Louis Malo and William Farquar as two of the more violent constables on duty that afternoon and he specifically singled out François Dragon as a bully who had assaulted many people with his shortened stave. Rodier admitted that at one point in the afternoon he had became so incensed at the treatment the constables were meting out to Tracey's supporters that he had collected some people together with the intention of driving the constables back. It was only the swift intervention of La Fontaine, who took him by the collar, that prevented him going ahead with his plan.[12]

On the strength of this evidence, it is clear that a terrible sequence of events had been set in motion. Louis Malo's violent conduct and that of certain other special constables shortly after 5 pm was entirely consistent with what had been happening all afternoon. It was a violence that the magistrates were unwilling or incapable of controlling. Cuvillier had attempted to demonstrate that Tracey had been at fault by walking in front of Henderson's store and that his supporters had provoked the special constables by bustling them as they went by. It was a poor attempt to justify the unjustifiable. The small group of Tracey supporters who remained behind on the Place d'Armes may have been foolhardy to celebrate their candidate's expected victory so close to where the special constables were massed but their conduct was not illegal. The magistrates should have regarded it as high spirits or "popular excitement," as Lieutenant Colonel McDougall phrased it, and not as anything more serious. Instead, they had waited until the returning officer had gone back into his office before they exacted their revenge on their opponent's supporters. If they had intended to provoke a riot, the first stage was now complete.

The stone fight

Dr Pierre Beaubien was the best placed of the witnesses to see what next occurred. The young men being assaulted close to Henderson's store managed to attract the attention of the main group of Tracey supporters who by now had advanced almost a hundred yards along St James St. As support began to arrive, a stone fight began in the Place d'Armes between the two groups of supporters. Bagg's group, however, had the support of the special constables and gradually the Tracey group was pushed back close to where Beaubien was standing. Reinforcements eventually arrived to lend assistance to the smaller group and the tables were turned on the special constables and Bagg supporters who were then forced to retreat. A fierce stone fight began between both sides. Bagg's side was eventually forced to seek refuge inside Henderson's or behind the perimeter wall of the parish church. Some of Tracey's supporters threw stones at Henderson's store and broke several panes of glass before they were persuaded to rejoin the main group in St James St.[13]

The same scene from a different perspective was given by Joshua Bell who was part of the main body of supporters accompanying Tracey along St James St. He said they were somewhere between the Methodist Chapel and Captain Piper's house when they heard men running after them and yelling, "for God's sake, come back, your friends are a-murthering." (Bell explained that this was an Irish expression meaning "your friends are getting cruelly beaten"). The majority of the people with Tracey returned to the square and saw that a confrontation was in progress between two groups of stone throwers. As Bell was making his way back, Dupré re-emerged from the polling station. In front of Henderson's, Dupré said, a number of constables, some armed with their batons, were engaged in scuffles with other individuals. Over by the bank, a small group of some fifteen people had appeared and were throwing stones in the direction of the constables who were using their batons. Dupré said that he had not regarded the incident as serious enough to prevent him from departing. He had even managed to pass unscathed through the group of stone throwers as he made his way home.[14]

Some of the witnesses spoke of seeing certain magistrates taking an active part in the stone throwing. John Flaherty said that he saw Shuter, Fisher and Quesnel all throwing stones. Pierre Lebert said he had seen Moffatt and Fisher pick up stones and throw them at Tracey's supporters. Augustin Lognion, a wheelright, was equally adamant that he had seen Fisher and Moffatt throw stones. Toussaint-Hubert Goddu, a farmer from Sainte-Marie-de-Monnoir, said he had seen Joseph Shuter, whom he described as a crockery-ware merchant, throwing stones. Goddu added that he knew Shuter well having served with him in the war of 1812 as an officer in the incorporated militia.[15]

During the coroner's inquest certain witnesses had claimed that a deliberate attack had been made on Henderson's store with the intention of murdering all those who had found refuge there. Similar accusations were made in the affidavits that Macintosh and Temple had presented in court. George Fowler had claimed that only the intervention of the troops had prevented the destruction of the store. Moffatt stated that the attack on the store meant that loss of life and further destruction of property was inevitable. Similar sentiments were expressed by those who were inside the building when stones began to fly. However, several of the witnesses who appeared before the inquiry had a very different perception of the incident.

Stephen Field had seen some special constables retreat as far as Henderson's while still under attack from Tracey's people. Some of the stones that were aimed at the constables missed their target and hit the store instead. Hosea Smith had a similar tale. He had also seen some of Tracey's supporters throwing stones at the special constables and at those who were standing opposite Henderson's house. Asked about the damage to Henderson's store, Smith said that he had returned to the Place d'Armes the following day and had counted between fifteen and twenty broken panes of glass, but there was no other damage. What time had elapsed between Tracey leaving the poll and the end of the affray? About five or six minutes, he answered. Jean Michel François Trudeau had taken refuge inside Henderson's store along with many of the special constables. His perception from inside the store, however, was that the stones were not being aimed at the building but rather at the people who were running away. Order was restored in a very short time, he said, and certainly before the troops came on the scene.[16]

There was no unanimity about the number of people involved in throwing stones. No estimate of the figures had been given at the coroner's inquest and the affidavits had merely referred to a "mob" being involved. A few witnesses at the inquiry minimised the incident. André Jobin had arrived in the Place d'Armes a few minutes after 5 o'clock as the first stone fight began. As more and more people became involved, he ran for protection to the doorway of Mr Doucet's house. From there he could see a man stretched out on the ground, as if dead. A crowd made up as far as he could tell of special and ordinary constables suddenly ran off towards the church enclosure. A small number of people who had stood their ground continued to throw stones at the group running away. They then took aim at Henderson's store. Louis Lussier also said that no more than five or six of Tracey's supporters threw stones at Henderson's house, breaking three or four panes of glass, At most, he said, the incident lasted about three or four minutes.[17]

John Flaherty remembered it differently. Questioned by Cuvillier about the number of people who threw stones at Henderson's store, Flaherty said he thought that about sixteen or eighteen people had been involved, more or less. He had heard glass break and the window shutters rattle as stones were thrown. How many people were gathered around the house? A great many, Flaherty said. How long did the stone throwing last? It was a volley of stones, as if they were firing together with muskets, he answered. Some of the crowd called out "shame" and told them to stop, which they did immediately. They then noticed that the troops were leaving the front of the church so they turned around and departed along St James St.[18]

What Flaherty had failed to notice or did not remember was the involvement of La Fontaine. Several witnesses told the inquiry that the trouble in front of Henderson's was brought to a speedy end when La Fontaine exerted his authority over the stone throwers. Jobin had watched him go up to one individual and force him to hand over the stone he had been holding. La Fontaine then took him by the arm and sent him off in the direction of St James St. The individual offered no resistance and went off along the street.[19]

Joshua Bell witnessed the same scene from the steps of Mr Dillon's house where he had sought safety from the stones. He saw about four or five men throwing stones at Mr Henderson's house. All but one of them quickly retreated and La Fontaine who had suddenly appeared had little difficulty in getting him to depart too. Bell said that it appeared that all the trouble was then over but almost immediately some four of five special constables came running forward, "and in the most barbarous and savage looking manner, they attacked with the greatest appearance of fury and vengeance a man of the name of Michael Deegan, a man whom I have known for years as a peaceable and respectable citizen. He was attacked in such an awful manner, as it appeared to me, that I very much doubted if they would spare his life."

Asked by Cuvillier to name the constables involved, Bell said that Charles Try, the cabinet-maker, William Farquar, the grocer and Louis Malo, the constable, were three of them but he could not remember the others. Cuvillier then wanted to know what Deegan was doing when he was attacked. "He was standing as still as I am now, without offending any person at the time," replied Bell.[20]

The accuracy of Jobin and Bell's testimony was confirmed when La Fontaine himself was questioned about the incident. He said that he had left the polling station in the company of Tracey and Donegani and when all three had gone as far as Dr Robertson's house in St James St they heard someone shout that Tracey's supporters were under attack from the constables. La Fontaine turned round and saw stones flying in all directions. He left Tracey and returned to the Place d'Armes, all the time stopping people from throwing stones and sending them back towards the Hay Market. Most did as they were directed, La Fontaine stated. When he reached the Place d'Armes, he saw that there were just three of Tracey's supporters still standing close to Henderson's, two Irishmen and a French Canadian. La Fontaine told them to leave and two of them did so immediately. The third man, an Irishman, was farther away and appeared to be preparing to throw a stone at Henderson's house. La Fontaine went over and knocked the stone from the man's hand with his umbrella. Taking him by the arm, La Fontaine made him walk in front as they walked back in the direction of St James St.[21]

From the evidence presented at the inquiry, the sudden escalation in the fighting close to Henderson's store arose from the legitimate desire of Tracey's friends to rescue the few stragglers of their party from the hands of a group of baton-wielding special constables. The sight of one of the victims lying on the ground unconscious or even dead added to the anger of those who suddenly had to confront the combined forces of special constables and Bagg supporters, all acting with apparent impunity in the presence of several magistrates. The only means at their disposal were the stones left lying about as a result of the work being done to macadamise St James St. Both sides were equally guilty of the fighting that then ensued. Even the magistrates were reported to have taken an active part in the stone throwing. Only the determination of the Tracey supporters to stand their ground succeeded in driving off the larger group. As the fighting ended certain individuals took their revenge on Henderson's store where some of the special constables had taken refuge. To those caught inside, the noise of breaking glass and of stones hitting iron shutters was a frightening experience but this in itself was not proof that the attackers were intent on gaining entrance and killing the occupants. The whole of the fighting had lasted a few minutes at most, mainly because the Tracey side quickly brought the situation under control. La Fontaine's swift action prevented the confrontation between the two camps escalating into anything more serious. However, for certain constables— in particular those who had viciously attacked Michael Deegan—the fight was not yet over.

The decision to open fire

The two most important officials present in the Place d'Armes, Macintosh and Robertson, had not witnessed the fighting in front of Henderson's. Robertson said that he had first become aware of the trouble when he had heard noise, wild yelling and the sound of stones striking windows and iron shutters coming from somewhere between Henderson's and the bank. When he looked, he had seen the body of a man lying on the ground close to the store apparently dead. It was at this point that he saw Joseph Shuter running across the square in his direction and shouting that the troops were needed as the mob was murdering people and destroying property. Robertson then saw Moffatt running towards him gesticulating in a manner that Robertson interpreted as meaning that he should advance with the military.

Macintosh gave two slightly different versions of the same scene. In his first affidavit he had said that a violent affray took place in the Place d'Armes and that the constables were driven back into the church enclosure and were followed by some of the "rioters." He had then ordered the soldiers to load with ball cartridge and to advance into the square in a column of two divisions. Informed that the mob was murdering a man close to St James St he said he had then headed in that direction. In his second affidavit, Macintosh stated that both magistrates and constables came rushing back through the gates of the church enclosure followed by many other persons "the last of whom were furiously assaulting the constables and others with bludgeons, stones, etc." Afraid that his men might be rushed, he said, he ordered ball cartridges to be primed and loaded. It was then that he claimed that several magistrates called on him to bring out the troops on the grounds that the "rioters" were murdering people and attacking houses. Macintosh never explained what happened to the many attackers armed with bludgeons and stones who supposedly now found themselves inside the narrow space between the enclosure wall and the portico and faced by a contingent of armed British soldiers and irate special constables. The fact that no other eyewitness made mention of an armed intrusion inside the church precinct throws real doubt on Macintosh's version of events.

When the army filed out into the Place d'Armes, it is not clear what the Colonel's intention was. It was clearly not to protect Henderson's store. Both Moffatt and Shuter had been involved in the stone fight and both had sought safety behind the precinct wall but only Joseph Shuter had called for military intervention using terms that suggested a riot was in progress. Moffatt made no reference to his gesticulating to Robertson as he ran across the square and seemingly had not thought of using the army until he heard Shuter say that one man was already dead and that others might be killed unless the army acted to prevent it. If several magistrates called on Macintosh to intervene, as he claimed, it was because Shuter had convinced them that a death had taken place. And it was supposedly to prevent a murder that Macintosh claimed to have advanced towards St James St unaware that he was heading to the very spot where constables under Shuter's command had just left one man for dead and another badly injured. However, as eventually came out at the inquiry, Macintosh had been in no hurry to rescue the man who the magistrates had said was being murdered.

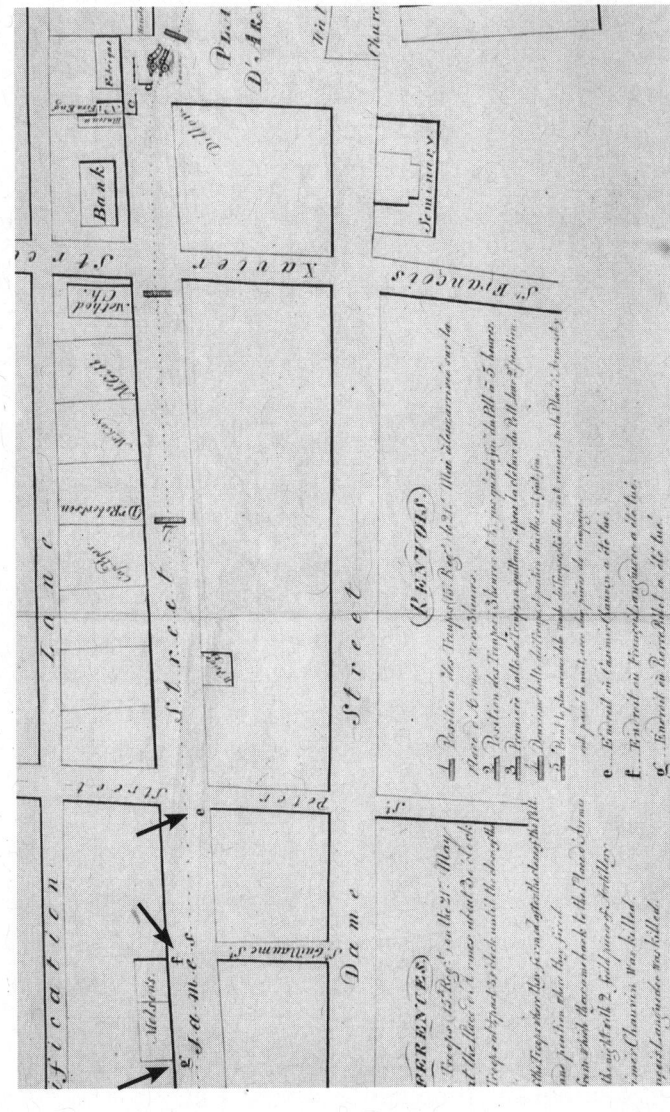

Detail of Jacques Viger's map. The solid vertical lines show the different positions taken by the troops. The line in front of Dr Robertson's house is the point where the troops stopped and opened fire killing the three bystanders. Points E, F and G indicate where the three men fell. (McCord Museum — M2291-P1)

After La Fontaine had escorted the last of the stone throwers back towards St James St, said Beaubien, the square was then clear of people. On the opposite side of the square he could see the troops leaving the precinct of the parish church via an exit in the perimeter wall opposite Notre Dame St and heading towards Dr Arnoldi's house. There they made a temporary stop before finally heading towards St James St. At almost the same time, he saw those special constables and Bagg supporters who had earlier sought safety behind the enclosure wall running in a more direct route towards St James St. At their head was Joseph Shuter who was gesturing to them and urging them on, shouting, "Come, my boys." The Shuter group arrived at Dillon's corner ahead of the troops and chased after Tracey's supporters along the street. A new confrontation began as both sides threw stones at each other until the arrival of the troops sent the Tracey followers running off in the direction of the Hay Market.[22]

André Jobin had also felt that La Fontaine's speedy intervention in front of Henderson's had put an end to the disorder. All was now quiet around Henderson's store. However, his attention was suddenly drawn to a crowd of special and ordinary constables running towards the bank brandishing their short staves in the air and shouting very loudly. They headed across the Place d'Armes towards St James St while the troops followed immediately behind them advancing at double-quick time. Louis Lussier could recall only what the army had done. After leaving the portico the troops had first formed a line about 40 feet in front of houses to the north west of the square (where Dr Arnoldi's house was situated). They had remained there for some five or six minutes, Lussier estimated, while fighting broke out on the other side of the square.[23]

La Fontaine told the inquiry that he felt that his action had succeeded in averting all further trouble. He had been the last person to leave the Place d'Armes and all was quiet—no stones were being thrown and no one was fighting. He remembered seeing the constables and Bagg's supporters assembled near the perimeter wall of the church at the corner of Notre-Dame St. As he and the Irishman approached St James St, Bagg's supporters led by several constables, among whom he recognised Louis Malo and Charles Try, began chasing after them. La Fontaine and his companion had just passed the bank when their pursuers turned into the street behind·them. Ahead of La Fontaine were several of Tracey's supporters scattered here and there, "but comparatively speaking," he said, "they were few in number."

Suddenly behind him, he heard the sound of stones being thrown. He looked back and saw that both sets of supporters were throwing stones at each other but he could not say who had started it. Once more he set about persuading Tracey's supporters not to retaliate, an easy enough task, he added, as they were so few in number. He had set off again towards the Hay Market and had just passed Mr Gibb's house when he saw the troops turn into St James St. They were close to the polling station and were marching in La Fontaine's direction.[24]

What happened next had been fully documented both in the depositions at the coroner's court and in the many affidavits collected by the magistrates. Stones were thrown, only by Tracey's supporters, according to some eyewitnesses, by both sides, according to others. The officers repeatedly warned the crowd to disperse, according to their own testimony and that of others, or the order to open fire came without any verbal warning being given, according to several other testimonies. Few of the witnesses called before the inquiry had been near enough to the troops when they had opened fire, but the few that had provided strong testimony.

South-west view of Notre-Dame St looking eastward showing the façade of the old church of Notre-Dame shortly before its destruction in 1830. On the right is the entrance to seminary of St Sulpice.

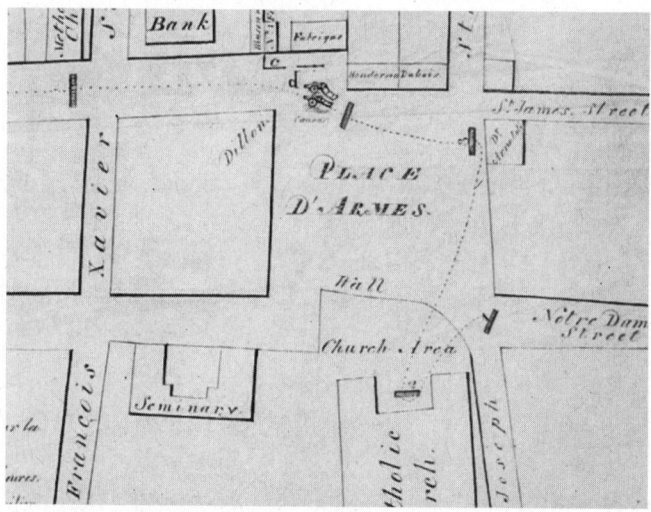

Close-up of Jacques Viger's plan showing the Place d'Armes and the route followed by the troops.

When the troops headed into St James St, Joshua Bell said, the special constables "were pretty much round them, like bees round a hive, both in front and rear of them." The constables who were in the rear and on both sides of the troops were throwing stones. The other people who crowded around the military were mainly Bagg supporters. Jean Michel François Trudeau was also present in the street when the military arrived. Trudeau saw that the special constables and many of Bagg's supporters were at the rear and on both flanks of the troops and were engaged in throwing stones at Tracey's supporters who were at some distance down the street. When the troops halted level with Dr Robertson's house, Trudeau said, he did not see any disturbance in front of them, "I believe that Dr Tracey's party was at too great a distance to reach the troops, if any stones were thrown at them, for I did not see any thrown." Two or three minutes after halting, the troops opened fire, Trudeau said, when the vast majority of Tracey's supporters appeared to be at some considerable distance from them. Both Trudeau and Bell were asked what amount of time had elapsed from the time the poll closed to the time the first shots were fired. Both answered that the time could not have exceeded fifteen minutes. Louis Lussier added that he heard no military commands or warnings. Asked by Cuvillier whether people had thrown stones at the troops, Lussier replied that eight or ten at most had done so. How near were they to the troops? About three quarters of an acre (156 ft), was Lussier's reply.[25]

When the troops had started to advance along the street, La Fontaine said he had begun walking more slowly, intent on keeping the few Tracey supporters ahead of him. They had reached a point between Mr Wragg's house and St Peter St when La Fontaine heard the sound of firing. He turned round and saw that troops were shooting at them. A musket ball struck the fence a foot above his head. What was the size of the crowd between St Peter St and the place from where the troops had fired? asked Leslie. Fifteen people at most, he answered, and he and Rodier had been two of the people nearest to the troops. "If there had been more, it is very probable that there would have been more victims." When La Fontaine reached the Hay Market, he turned and saw that there was scarcely any one left in the street. From the time he had left the poll to the time the troops fired, he estimated that less than fifteen minutes had elapsed.

La Fontaine went immediately to Tracey's house in St Antoine Suburb and returned to the scene of the shooting with Cherrier. The troops were close to the American church together with three of the magistrates, Moffatt, Quesnel and Lukin. La Fontaine spoke to Lukin and asked for an explanation for the shooting of unarmed men. "Mr Lukin appeared to be in tears," said La Fontaine, "and very much affected at the result of that firing; he told me that it was not his fault."[26]

Côme-Séraphin Cherrier told the inquiry that he had spent the entire day inside the polling station, as he had done on all other days, and had not left it until just after 5 o'clock in the company of Tracey and his friends. Somewhere along St James St he had lost contact with Tracey. He was nearly opposite the American Presbyterian Church when he heard the sound of gun fire. "I thought they were firing with blank cartridge," he said, "for so short a time had elapsed since I had left the hustings that I could not imagine any occurrences of so serious a nature had taken place as to call for such cruel means, as firing with ball on the people." In his estimation, some ten to fifteen minutes had elapsed between his leaving the polling station and the shooting.[27]

Dr Pierre Beaubien was not on the street when the shots were fired. He had gone to his house in St François-Xavier St before the troops had reached St James St. His only view therefore was of the space between the bank and the Methodist church. He had seen a first detachment pass along St James St and then heard a discharge of fire that sounded at first like a volley and then a running fire. Shortly after he saw a second detachment pass opposite his street marching at double-quick time and that was soon followed by a third detachment. Beaubien left his house and went to investigate. He came across three bodies stretched out on the ground. Learning that the troops had opened fire when level with Dr Robertson's house, Beaubien measured the distance from there to where the bodies had fallen. Chauvin was 378 feet away, Billet was at 558 feet and Languedoc at 768 feet.[28]

Rodier had left the polling station with Tracey at 5 pm and had drawn level with Dr Robertson's house when they heard people calling on them to return, that the constables were murdering one of their men. Rodier rushed back and had reached the bank when he saw La Fontaine advancing with an agitated Irishman. He turned back and was heading towards the Hay Market when the troops suddenly appeared in the street. "What was the reaction of people to the arrival of the soldiers in the street?" he was asked. Rodier was adamant that there had been no attack on the soldiers:

> From St François-Xavier St as far as the south west corner of Dr Robertson's house, according to my knowledge and the position in which I stood at the time, it was almost impossible that the military or the party about them, could have been struck by the stones which might have been thrown by Dr Tracey's partisans, and had they thrown any in that space of time, I believe it would have been impossible for me not to have noticed it, for I was the nearest person to the troops, in the middle of the street, I was perfectly cool; for it could not enter my head that the Troops would fire, and thus I could observe all that was going on.

Rodier kept walking while keeping the soldiers in view. He was close to Mr Wragg's house when he saw the soldiers stop opposite Dr Robertson's house. Rodier stopped too. An Irishman by the name of Creed was a short distance from the troops, shouting and gesturing at them.[29] Suddenly Malo rushed out from behind the troops and began assaulting him. The Irishman fell to the ground under the blows. Malo then calmly returned to his position to the rear of the troops. There had been no reaction from any of the magistrates or officers. To Rodier it seemed as if they had waited for Malo to get back in position before their next move: "I instantly saw a Military man on the right of his Troops advance two or three steps in front of the front rank, with his sword drawn, return again to his place, immediately make a sign with his sword and the discharge of Musketry followed immediately. The troops to the left fired several shots at once and the others fired one after the other."

Rodier's first reaction was to think that they had fired blank cartridges since between where he was and St Peter St there were, he said, no more than fifteen people. He even began shouting "blank, blank" to reassure the people around him. Then he came across the body of Chauvin. Rodier attempted to apply first-aid but the young man was already dead. The troops began to advance as Rodier remained bent over the body. He sprang up and confronted the first officer he saw. "See what you have done—here is a dead man," he said to Lt Dewson. Without stopping Dewson stepped over Rodier and the dead body saying "so much the better" and continued along the street with his soldiers marching in closed ranks. Rodier could not understand why they had opened fire. "In the position the Troops were in when they fired," said Rodier, "I am persuaded they could not be injured by Mr Tracey's partisans that had remained behind. They committed a cold and premeditated murder."

The matter seemed clear in Rodier's mind:

> If they were struck by any stones, it can only have been in the general scuffle, and having given time to the partisans of Mr Bagg to get away from those with whom they were engaged, and having waited until they had nobody before them but the partisans of Mr Tracey I must believe that those who ordered them to fire, were determined to carry Mr Bagg's Election, even at the expense of the lives of Mr Tracey's partisans. I am certain that had the Troops waited five minutes longer, before firing, there would not have been one of Mr Tracey's partisans in St James St in front of them.[30]

André Jobin had been as astonished as La Fontaine and Rodier at the sudden intervention of the troops:

> I could not think where they could then be going, for the crowd having withdrawn into St James St, I saw no tumult, nor anything that could attract them. When the troops had filed off through St James St, I followed them at some distance, and stopped at the corner of St François Xavier and St James Sts. A moment after arriving there, I heard a discharge of musquetry from the troops which I had seen enter St James St, and which were then a little further than Dr Robertson's; I thought they had fired with blank cartridges, but I was very much surprised on learning that they fired with ball cartridges, and had caused the death of several individuals.

Jobin estimated that about ten minutes had elapsed between the troops leaving the portico and their firing on the crowd.

In answer to a question from Cuvillier, Jobin said he had seen Fisher at the time of the shooting since he had been standing close to him. Fisher appeared extremely agitated and somebody was holding him by the arm preventing him from going forward towards the troops, saying "Don't, Mr Fisher." He also saw Mr Emery Cushing, a tavern keeper, who as the soldiers fired, clapped his hands several times, saying repeatedly "That's right." When Cuvillier asked him why he had not tried to intervene as a magistrate during the trouble that occurred after 5 o'clock, Jobin answered:

> That did not occur to me, and I do not think that a sensible man, possessing the least prudence, would have interposed with people who were fighting in that manner, to stop them; for people who are fighting cannot distinguish the magistrates from any other individual, neither did it occur to me to go and meet the special constables when I saw them advancing on the Place d'Armes to go into St James St. I am satisfied that if I had attempted it, they would have walked over me without knowing me.

Leslie asked him why Fisher acted in the way he had. Jobin said that Fisher felt he had lost the election and was experiencing a combination of anger and disappointment: "He could not overcome his anger."

Augustin-Norbert Morin asked Jobin what he thought in general of the conduct of the magistrates and of the special constables in the period immediately after 5 o'clock. His answer was the harshest indictment made by any of the witnesses before the inquiry:

> I sincerely believe that if the constables had only advanced as far as the middle of the Place d'Armes and remained there, everything would have ended there, and that nothing more would have taken place, because the crowd had already withdrawn into St James St and there was not the least tumult on the Place d'Armes [...] From the moment, or during the whole time that I saw what was going on the Place d'Armes (after five o'clock) I do not think that their intention was to keep the peace; I considered them at the time, as acting, and taking an active part in favor of Mr Bagg's friends, because it was in pursuit of Mr Tracey's partizans that they directed their steps; and obstin-

ately bent against those whom they were pursuing, to make me believe that they wished to maintain the peace.

Who in his opinion were the real aggressors in St James St on that Monday afternoon? His answer was unequivocal. The special constables were the guilty ones, he said: "I then considered them as the aggressors. I saw none pursuing them, I only saw the troops that accompanied them, and whose presence made me believe that they then thought themselves strong enough to beat those who had beaten them; for they had been beaten in the first scuffle, and had withdrawn. That was the first and only idea which I had at the time."[31]

From the evidence presented, it is possible to conclude that the desperate rush to reach the safety of the perimeter wall had been a public humiliation for the special constables and in particular for Joseph Shuter, the man who only five minutes earlier had led his special constables in an attack on a small group of Tracey supporters. His claim that people were being murdered and that houses were being attacked, as if the Bristol riots had suddenly come to Montreal, was a lie and a desperate ploy to cover up his own humiliation. None of the other magistrates had seen what Shuter claimed to have witnessed. Moffatt had been along side Shuter outside Henderson's and had been involved in the stone fight yet his affidavit did not speak of lives being lost or of property being destroyed. Nor had he called for the army to intervene as Robertson had imagined. Shuter wanted revenge and he found in Robertson a compliant colleague.

Macintosh had responded promptly to Robertson's request for military assistance. The magistrate claimed to have told him that a riot was in progress and to have formulated the request using the phraseology of the requisition form he had signed two hours earlier. Sergeant William Gleeson, however, said that Robertson had merely requested Macintosh to march his men out into the Place d'Armes as they were needed there. As the troops emerged into the square, the evidence of Macintosh's own eyes and ears would have told him that there was no riot in progress. The crowd had dispersed and all was quiet. In retrospect, he had to concoct a reason for having ordered the troops to load their rifles inside the perimeter wall. The pretence that rioters armed with bludgeons had invaded the church precinct and had posed a danger to the troops was far-fetched. Once in the empty Place d'Armes, Macintosh was uncertain what he was supposed to do. It could not have been, as he later claimed, to prevent someone being murdered close to St James St because he marched his men in the opposite direction and brought them to a halt outside Dr Arnoldi's house. That should have been the limit of the army's action but Shuter had decided to take matters into his own hands. He led his second illegal attack of the afternoon against Tracey's men but knowing this time that he could count on the support of the army.

The evidence heard during the inquiry concerning the shooting in St James St was not very different from what had been disclosed during the coroner's inquest. Eyewitnesses said that the special constables had thrown stones at Tracey's people. Certain affidavits in support of the army had denied it, others had said it was true. Even witnesses for the defence at the coroner's inquest had seen the constables throw stones. The army affidavits had claimed that ample warning had been given to the crowd to disperse or be fired upon, a claim that received little confirmation even from those eyewitnesses who felt that the shooting was justified. Even Lieutenant Dewson failed to confirm the fact.

The crux of the matter was the size of the crowd confronting the troops. Macintosh's claim that he faced a dense crowd of many hundreds of people throwing quantities of large stones at the military and civil authorities was as fanciful as his claim that the church precinct had earlier been invaded by Tracey supporters. A crowd of that size rioting and throwing stones should normally have inflicted serious injury on those on the receiving end. Yet only a few soldiers reported receiving minor bumps and scratches. The only damage that interested the army was to Private Thomas Allcock's fire-lock which was struck by a stone. It is also inconceivable that Malo would have been able to advance alone in front of the troops, beat an Irishman to the ground and then leisurely return to his position behind the line of troops unscathed if a crowd of several hundred was throwing heavy stones against him and the army. The only reasonable explanation for the lack of any injury to the troops and magistrates and for the ability of Malo to continue to assail individual Tracey supporters was that no crowd actually confronted the troops and that the small number of people who attempted to throw stones in their direction were generally too far away to cause any real harm. It was for this reason that when the troops opened fire the only victims were not scores of "rioters" supposedly massed in front of them but three innocent men who happened to be standing at the other end of St James St unaware that it had suddenly become the most dangerous street in all of Montreal.

The aftermath

The inquiry sat for a total of ninety-nine days spread over two parliamentary sessions during which fifty witnesses had been heard. It had taken almost fifteen months for the inquiry to complete its work. No final report was ever produced. The inquiry had opened in December 1832 when emotions were still running high and the Patriotes were still angry after the grand jury's dismissal of all charges against the two officers and the two magistrates. When the final witness had finished his testimony on Monday, March 3, 1834, the Patriotes were totally preoccupied by the 92 Resolutions. That document had been written as the events of May 21 were on the minds of the authors. It is no surprise therefore to find a reference to them in the section concerned with the abuses for which the House demanded reparation. Two subsections of Resolution 84 deal specifically with the West Ward by-election:

> 5thly. The intermeddling of members of the Legislative Councils in the election of the representatives of the people, for the purpose of influencing and controlling them by force, and the selection frequently made of returning officers for the purpose of securing the same partial and corrupt ends; the interference of the present Governor-in-chief himself in the said elections; his approval of the intermeddling of the said legislative councillors in the said elections; the partiality with which he intervened in the judicial proceedings connected with the said elections, for the purpose of influencing the said proceedings, in a manner favourable to the military power and contrary to the independence of the judicial power; and the applause which, as commander of the forces, he bestowed upon the sanguinary execution of the citizens by the soldiery.

> 6thly. The interference of the armed military force at such elections, through which three peaceable citizens, whose exertions were necessary to the support of their families, and who were strangers to the agitation of the election, were shot dead in the streets; the applause bestowed by the Governor-in-chief and Commander of the Forces on the authors of this sanguinary military execution (who had not been acquitted by a petty jury) for the firmness and discipline displayed by them on that occasion.[32]

The end of the inquiry prompted no public pronouncement from the governor as the grand jury's verdict had done. Despite the determined efforts of Cuvillier, Young and others to discredit the evidence of the bullies and special constables, Aylmer could derive no satisfaction from any of the findings. In an act of spite, he exacted revenge on the Patriotes by striking Roy and Jobin from the list of magistrates in 1833. The House, for its part, did succeed just once in eliciting a response from him in relation to the events of May 21. It came on March 18, 1833, two days before the inquiry was suspended after seventy-seven sittings. A few days earlier, the House had decided to mark the occasion by presenting an address to him in which it drew his attention to certain statements Macintosh had made nine months earlier. The House sought clarification from his Lordship in a series of questions.

The first was in reference to Macintosh's affidavit of June 1, 1832 in which he had said that "before the Troops moved against the Rioters, William Robertson, Esquire, aforesaid, repeatedly stated that the Civil Authorities had had information of the most positive kind, that there was a plan arranged for firing the Town and Suburbs in various places, so as to draw the military away in different and opposite directions, and in small bodies, that they might be more easily overpowered." The House wanted to know whether the governor had instituted an inquiry to ascertain whether such a plan had ever existed. "Was it an act of levity," it asked with all mock seriousness, "or wicked contrivance on the part of one who is in the Commission of the Peace for the District of Montreal, and on half-pay of His Majesty's Forces?"

The second question related to something that Macintosh had written in his letter to the governor on May 22, 1832. Was it correct, as Macintosh had claimed, "that he was informed by Dr Robertson and Captain Temple that many acts of violence had been committed, and that many of them (the crowd) were in possession of fire-arms?" Was Macintosh also correct in adding, "At the same moment I was informed that the Rioters were in the act of murdering a man on the side of the Place opposite St James St."? Was there an enquiry? The final question asked whether Statute 1 Geo.1 c 5 (the Riot Act) was in force in the Province.

Craig brought the governor's reply to the House in person. No enquiry had been instituted, Aylmer had written, nor did he regard the magistrate in question as guilty of any act of levity or wicked contrivance to irritate or mislead the officer. No enquiry either had been instituted to investigate the other matters raised by the House. Indeed, the governor was not aware of the existence of any grounds for supposing that Lt Col Macintosh had been irritated or misled by any individual whatever upon the occasion in question. "On the contrary," he wrote, "the Governor in Chief feels assured, that he, Lt Col Macintosh, in complying with the requisitions and directions of the Magistrates, acted in every particular as became him, and faithfully discharged his duty as a Military Officer, and a good subject of the King." In reference to the Riot Act, the governor stated that the statute was indeed in force and formed part of the criminal law of the land by the 14th of his late Majesty George III. c 83, Section II.[33] No more was said on the matter but the Patriotes must have felt that they had made their point.

Further embarrassment could have been caused to the authorities if someone had sought to exploit one of the many affidavits that had been submitted by Macintosh and Temple in support of their bail request. At the time, it would not have attracted any real interest but as more became known about the activity of certain magistrates on the afternoon of May 21, the affidavit should have drawn attention to itself. It was sworn on May 26, 1832 by Robert Fowler, a cabinet-maker and special constable, who was one of the many special constables standing at Henderson's corner between 3:30 and 5 pm on the afternoon of May 21. After the poll closed, he stated that he had been insulted, struck by umbrellas, and then forced to flee to the safety of the church enclosure when Tracey's party threw stones at him. Inside the enclosure, he said, "he saw there Mr Shuter, a magistrate of this city, and saw him there quiet and with the intention of keeping the peace. Fowler did not see Mr Shuter give any order to trouble the peace, or to excite the people, but on the contrary, all his endeavors were to pacify them."[34] The affidavit had been sworn before Joseph Shuter.

The victims of May 21 became part of the martyrology of the Patriote movement. In March 1833, a certain Louis Pantaléon sent Ludger Duvernay a copy of a song entitled *A la mémoire du 21 mai* and requested him to publish it in *La Minerve*. The first verse set the tone for the rest of the song:

O vingt et un! jour mémorable
Sois imprimé dans tous les cœurs.
Une cohorte méprisable
Vient subjuguer nos défenseurs.
Les enfants du sol s'assemblent
Pour se choisir un candidat
Les bureaucrates se rassemblent
Et sur nous commettent l'intentat (sic) (2).[35]

Duvernay did not publish the song but he found another way of commemorating the day. On June 24, 1834 he organised the first political celebration of the Feast of St John in the garden of Tracey's friend, John McDonnell. Among the solemn toasts made by the sixty people present at the banquet, one was made in silence: to the memory of Jocelyn Waller,

Ludger Duvernay, publisher of La Minerve, was imprisoned with Tracey in January 1832 for "libelling" the Legislative Council. In 1834 he founded (what was later to become) the St-Jean-Baptiste Society and instituted the tradition of celebrating June 24 as Quebec's national day by holding a banquet during which he toasted the memory of Tracey and the three victims of May 21, 1832.

Daniel Tracey and the three victims of May 21. Two of the victims had been married but their wives had received no compensation for the deaths of their husbands. The grand jury's verdict had declared them guilty of riot by association thus absolving the British authorities of any responsibility. In 1838, shortly after arriving in Lower Canada, Lord Durham granted an amnesty to many of the province's political prisoners still languishing in jail. The news gave fresh hope to the two widows and a letter was sent on their behalf to the new governor-in-chief of the British North American colonies:

> The humble petition of Josephte Gagner, widow of François Charpentier *dit* Languedoc, and of Scholastique Labranche, widow of Jean-Baptiste Billet, from the city of Montreal, humbly sheweth: that on 21 May 1832, their husbands returning from their usual place of work were killed by the bullets fired by His Majesty's troops to disperse a turbulent gathering during an election. The two unfortunate victims who were thus shot were at some considerable distance from where the commotion was taking place and at no time had they taken any part in the election. Since then your petitioners have on several occasions been led to hope that the Government would come to their aid, now that they are advanced in years, having lost their sole support when they lost their husbands but to no avail. They entreat Your Excellency to take into his gracious consideration their state and their misfortunes and whatever help your Excellency will be pleased to grant he will receive the prayers and good wishes of his unfortunate petitioners.[36]

It is not known whether the British authorities ever responded to their petition.

Conclusion

The killing of three defenceless French Canadians in Montreal by British troops in May 1832 was the result of the actions of a small number of magistrates whose attempts to control the outcome of a by-election went terribly wrong. The magistrates were aided and abetted in their plan by special constables supposedly recruited to enforce the law and when defeat appeared imminent they were able to call on weak and compliant British officers in a final desperate attempt to secure victory for their candidate. In the aftermath of the killings, the perpetrators were protected by the full panoply of state institutions, from the coroner's court to the Court of King's Bench, before receiving the ultimate accolade in the form of public thanks from a grateful governor.

Nothing highlighted more glaringly the inadequacies of the colonial regime in British North America.

The political and ethnic divisions within Lower Canadian society, exacerbated by the tensions between the different branches of colonial government, played their part in creating a climate of suspicion and loathing in sections of Montreal's English community. The *Montreal Herald* and the *Montreal Gazette*, two of the worst offenders, regularly filled their pages with violent abuse of the French Canadians and their Irish supporters. Politics, however, cut across ethnic and linguistic lines. The Patriote party had its complement of prominent

English-language supporters of the likes of James Leslie, Wolfred and Robert Nelson and Daniel Tracey. The English party could count on such recent French Canadian recruits as Austin Cuvillier, the Mondelets and those connected with *L'Ami du peuple*. Such divisions, however, were not sufficient in themselves to trigger the political agitation that gripped the province in 1832. It needed an event so unexpected yet so evidently unjust to galvanise the province into action. The catalyst was the Legislative Council which had decided to indulge in a deadly game of politics by imprisoning Tracey and Duvernay. The subsequent political protests set in motion a series of events that ultimately culminated in the disaster of May 21.

The decision to imprison the two editors was out of all proportion to the supposed offence. The epithets that so antagonised the Council were mild compared to the insults and slurs that the Tory press regularly directed against Papineau and the Assembly. Criticism of the Legislative Council had long been a staple of Patriote rhetoric and both Patriote newspapers had previously published critical comments without causing alarm among the councillors. The reason for the aggressive riposte this time was the presence on the Council of George Moffatt. Since the death in May 1831 of John Richardson, speaker of the Council and successful businessman, Moffatt had been waiting for the opportunity to establish himself as the new spokesman of Montreal's mercantile élite. Tracey and Duvernay were easy targets and Moffatt had jumped at the chance to prove his credentials. He was also protecting his own financial interests. Moffatt had invested extensively in property and was viewing with interest the prospect of new investment opportunities with the British American Land Company. Tracey was Quebec's most outspoken critic of the company's latest scheme. Moffatt imagined that a spell in jail would discourage the unruly Irishman from interfering further in the activities of Montreal's merchant community.

The plan backfired. Tracey left prison more determined than ever to oppose those he called the London speculators and his newly acquired hero status led to the Patriotes offering him the opportunity to contest Richardson's old seat, one that the English party considered theirs by right. The West Ward election without Tracey would have lasted a few days and would have attracted little attention. In normal circumstances, there would not even have been a Patriote candidate, but the imprisonment of Tracey and Duvernay had transformed the situation in Montreal. The business community knew it too. As the editor of the *Vindicator*, Tracey was a mere inconvenience but as a member of the Assembly he would become a serious danger to their long-term commercial interests. The likes of Cuvillier, Moffatt, Fisher, Holmes and Shuter were first and foremost businessmen. Bagg was their natural candidate and they saw no reason why they should not use all the resources available to them as justices of peace to help him to be elected. After all, it would not be the first time that they had offered a candidate a helping hand.

Bagg's preparations for the election involved recruiting an imposing number of bullies, men whose muscle power had earlier helped Olivier Berthelet to win Montreal's East Ward. Bagg also had the services of Louis Malo, a constable and convicted criminal and the deputy foreman of the night watch. The magistrates' support for Bagg was made plain on the first day of voting when they failed to prevent the bullies from assaulting electors waiting to vote for Tracey. The returning officer's reluctance to move against the bullies convinced the Tracey camp that he secretly supported Bagg. It also persuaded the magistrates that the official was weak-willed and malleable, a situation they were to exploit during the course of the election.

When the bullies were routed, the magistrates simply brought them back as special constables. Their identities were clearly known to Cuvillier, Moffatt, Fisher and other magistrates who swore them in on the first two days of the election. In the case of Cuvillier, it was his son, Pat, who joined the bullies in disrupting the first day of voting. Even when the hard core of bullies operating as special constables were arrested for assault and battery the magistrates saw no reason to dispense with their services. As Lavictoire observed, compliant magistrates were always ready to release the arrested men on bail. The conduct of many of the other special constables was also suspect. The decision to cut their traditional long staves into smaller sizes may have been done to distribute them to as many of the specials as possible but the result was to transform an unwieldy symbol of authority into a more manageable baton that was used to assault people. There was evidence to show that the excessive force used by certain constables was directly linked to the easy availability of these weapons.

The magistrates policed the election irrespective of the wishes of the returning officer and at times in contravention of the law. The instigator was Cuvillier. It was he who first assembled the magistrates on the pretext that armed individuals were planning violence at the poll. With no evidence or sworn affidavit to back up his claims, he had little difficulty in persuading his fellow magistrates to believe him. The returning officer, however, refused the offer of one hundred special constables. That should have been the end of the matter as the returning officer had the final say in policing the election. But Cuvillier, Moffatt, Fisher, Robertson and the other magistrates were determined to influence the election by an excessive show of force under their command. Cuvillier's prediction of planned violence at the poll proved groundless but the returning officer had effectively relinquished his authority to the magistrates.

Hypolite St George Dupré had been the wrong man to take charge of the West Ward election. Indecisive, inexperienced and lacking the ability to stand up to the magistrates, he allowed himself to be manipulated by Cuvillier. Even his request on day four of the election for up to two hundred special constables was a futile attempt to re-establish his authority by attempting to weed out the bullies from their midst. But his referring to the more notorious of them by name was proof that both he and the magistrates knew that the presence of bullies at an election, even when masquerading as special constables, was a recipe for violence.

Dupré's worst decision during the election was to adjourn voting prematurely on May 19 at the request of three Bagg supporters. Bagg was in deep trouble. He had used up his reserve of electors whereas Tracey's was standing by and ready to vote. Bagg was one hour away from losing the election but his supporters had a plan ready and waiting to gain an adjournment. It was a well-coordinated move and it gave their candidate thirty-six valuable hours to find new electors. Other witnesses present in the polling station at the time disputed Dupré's claim that his decision was based on a clear understanding of the law. The ambiguity of the legal text had forced him to consult a number of authorities. In the case of doubt the most sensible course of action would have been to allow those waiting to vote to do so. Bagg knew that this would have handed victory to his opponent. If ever Tracey's supporters needed a reason to riot, they had one and this was the time and place. But heated tempers, strong words and one irate Irishman climbing onto Dupré's table was the nearest

Montreal came to witnessing a riot that Saturday afternoon.

Bagg knew that the adjournment was only a temporary solution. In the absence of new electors, he had to find a way of eliminating Tracey from the race altogether. The bullies had failed in the task and the special constables had been no better. The plan needed to be clear-cut.

What better than to accuse Tracey and his supporters of planning a riot to coincide with the next opening of the poll?

Bagg needed only to inform the returning officer to be sure that the warning reached the magistrates. The plan had the hallmarks of Cuvillier stamped all over it. He had succeeded once before in persuading the magistrates to react to unfounded rumours. He was sure that a letter couched in similar terms and signed by Bagg would have the same effect. Proof was not necessary—it was enough to say that the "respectable" opinion was convinced that the information was correct. Panic would do the rest. Dupré's letter ensured that there would be a strong presence of special constables in the Place d'Armes the next day. Bagg and the magistrates ensured that the army would also be involved.

On the morning of May 21, the supposed violence of Tracey's supporters failed to materialise. The anger they had expressed on the Saturday afternoon had given way to renewed optimism as Tracey took a five-vote lead in the first hour of voting. Over the next five hours, the returning officer read his proclamation six times requiring Bagg to find a voter each time to prevent the election from ending.

Bagg was still trailing by one vote and the proclamation had been read when John Fisher took it upon himself to bring in the army.

The fighting that had broken out was sporadic and confined to one corner of the Place d'Armes. It was not the riot that Bagg had predicted and it did not justify the presence of armed soldiers. The returning officer was not informed nor was his permission sought. A British officer had brought armed soldiers to a by-election in spite of the absence of a signed requisition form and after the fighting was over. The senior magistrate on duty should have ordered them to return to barracks. Instead, he devised a way of keeping the military present in a final attempt to swing the election in favour of Bagg.

If Robertson read the Riot Act at 3:15 pm close to the polling station, as he claimed he did, it was a foolhardy and irresponsible action on his part. There was no trouble in the Place d'Armes at the time and those closest to the magistrate when he spoke would have known that Tracey was in the lead. His action would have been immediately interpreted as sheer provocation and even as an attempt to save Bagg from impending defeat. The risk of provoking rather than suppressing a riot was too great even for a magistrate who openly supported Bagg. It makes more sense in fact to conclude that Robertson changed his mind at the last minute. Certainly the subsequent behaviour of people suggests that this is what happened. The law required the crowd to disperse within an hour of the act being read but no order was given to the constables to enforce the requirement. It would also have been necessary to prevent people from gaining access to the Place d'Armes but this was not done either. Macintosh did not raise the subject when Robertson returned to his side after supposedly reading the act. It is inconceivable that the constables would have allowed Margaret Louisa Hoyle to approach the poll and vote for Bagg if the Riot Act were in force. It is equally hard to believe that Macintosh would have allowed his men to leave the Place d'Armes if he really believed that a riot had just taken place. Military, magistrates and constables all behaved as if the Riot Act had never been read.

William Robertson, professor and head of the medical faculty of McGill College and city magistrate. He was on duty in the Place d'Armes on May 21 for the final two hours. He ordered Macintosh to intervene after the poll closed and urged the officer to open fire. (Photo 2009: James Jackson)

The first real violence of the day came less than five minutes after the poll closed for the day. The perpetrators were a group of special constables led by Joseph Shuter. The victims were a few Tracey supporters whose light-hearted celebrations were too much for the magistrate. If the assault was intended to provoke a confrontation with the larger body of Tracey supporters, it worked. The stone fight that ensued was over in a matter of minutes but it had lasted long enough for the likes of Shuter and Moffatt to call for military backup. Robertson had no need to aggravate the situation by ordering the troops to go into action but he was anxious not to lose face a second time in front of British officers. It is not obvious what Macintosh's perception of the situation was. He had heard shouting and yelling but when he led his troops out into the square from behind the church enclosure wall, the Place d'Armes was practically deserted. He had no real idea where he was supposed to go or what he was expected to do. He did not appear to consider St James St as the trouble spot since he marched his men in the opposite direction. If Shuter and his special constables had not suddenly decided to go charging after Tracey, there would have been no tragic outcome to the day's events. Shuter's one desire was for revenge. Macintosh and Robertson provided him with the means.

The final confrontation of the day was the crucial one and was deliberately created by the civil and military authorities. On one side were armed soldiers, magistrates, special and official constables, and a motley crowd of Bagg supporters. On the other was a scattered crowd of Tracey supporters spaced out along St James St as far as the Hay Market on McGill Street. The sudden appearance of the soldiers had frightened many into running off along adjacent streets. A small group had stood its ground and threw back the stones that had first been aimed at it but the distance between the two groups was too great for any real injury to be done to either side. Macintosh's claim that he was confronted by a well-organised crowd of several hundred men manoeuvering in military fashion and bombarding his troops with huge rocks can be dismissed as mere fantasy. The only injuries reported by a few military men were negligible. The simple fact was that the vast majority of Tracey's supporters had already made their way with Tracey to the Hay Market. The small number who still lingered in the street were vastly outnumbered by their opponents who were free to throw stones despite the presence of several magistrates and the army. There was no riot, the army was in no danger and the soldiers had few targets in front of them. The three men who died were in the wrong street at the wrong time. They were so far away that they probably died unaware that there were troops in the street. In their unjustified use of excessive force against defenceless citizens Robertson and Macintosh were guilty of a crime that deserved the full rigours of the law.

Attempts to ascribe guilt in the killings were frustrated as first the coroner's inquest and then the grand jury failed to deliver justice. In the case of the coroner, incompetence rather than a malicious intent to sabotage the outcome of the inquest was the reason for the double verdict delivered by the jury. The grand jury was a different matter. Gugy, Ogden and the Court of King's Bench each had a role in determining the final outcome. Gugy had seen to it that the jury was packed with jurors who could be guaranteed to find in favour of the two British officers and the two magistrates. Ogden had ensured that the grand jury heard witnesses who were sure to undermine the indictments he had prepared against the accused. Chief Justice James Reid presented his charge to the jurors in such a one-sided fashion that an acquittal was the inevitable result. The odds had been carefully stacked in favour of the accused by office holders who had spent their lives demonstrating their loyalty to the crown. Ogden was rewarded in 1833 when he was appointed attorney general of Lower Canada. Gugy was not so lucky. In 1836 a special committee of the House accused him of fraud, perjury and negligence and recommended that the governor dismiss him. London concurred and in the spring of 1837, Gugy's long service as a servant of the crown came to an abrupt end.

The cover-up that the authorities so carefully engineered in 1832 has had a remarkably long life. For 175 years, historians have faithfully endorsed the grand jury's flawed verdict. The reasons for this situation remain a mystery. The quantity of printed material concerning the killings is immense yet even such an obvious source as the *Journals of the House of Assembly* has failed to interest the majority of historians who have written on the subject. If any thought to wonder why the supporters of the candidate who was only hours away from being declared the victor should suddenly want to jeopardise the outcome by rioting and burning their own houses, none ventured to offer an explanation. All have accepted that only a riot could explain why British troops would open fire on unarmed civilians in Montreal. Some have had personal reasons for believing so. In recent years, a small number of English-language historians in the odd belief that loyalty to the crown was their first duty have done little more than reproduce what was published in the Tory press of the time. In the case of certain French-language historians, dislike of the Patriotes has led them to follow suit. The history of Quebec has not been served by this neglect. Admittedly the event was quickly overshadowed first by the cholera epidemic and then by the publication of the 92 Resolutions, but its importance should not be minimised. It became the defining moment in the history of the Patriotes. For the likes of John

Neilson, it was the end of the road. But for the younger generation of Patriotes, Louis-Hippolyte La Fontaine, Augustin-Norbert Morin, Charles-Ovide Perrault, Édouard-Étienne Rodier, Côme-Séraphin Cherrier and the Nelson brothers, it was the one incident that convinced them of the need for a more radical approach in their dealings with the British authorities. The count-down to the events of 1837 and 1838 had begun.

Abbreviations

BAnQ-M	Bibliothèque et Archives nationales du Québec, centre d'archives de Montréal
BAnQ-Q	Bibliothèque et Archives nationales du Québec, centre d'archives de Québec
CAN	*Le Canadien*
CC	*Canadian Courant and Montreal Advertiser*
CIHM	Canadian Institute for Historical Microreproductions
DCB	*Dictionary of Canadian Biography Online*
JHALC	*Journals of the House of Assembly of Lower Canada*
MG	*The Montreal Gazette*
PRO	Public Record Office, London
MIN	*La Minerve*
QG	*The Quebec Gazette*
QM	*The Quebec Mercury*
RHAF	*Revue d'histoire de l'Amérique française*
VIN	*The Vindicator*

Notes

Introduction

1. Geo. 1 St.2 c.5
2. "The extraordinary effect of the Act was to convert, by mere command, every person who chanced to be in the vicinity of the reading after the expiry of an hour, into a felon. A closer reading of the Act however, reveals that although it creates a new *felony*, its penal sections refer explicitly to *treason*." Vogler, *Reading the Riot Act,* 2 (author's emphasis).
3. Blackstone, *Commentaries*, vol. 2, Bk 4, 108.
4. Keele, *The Provincial Justice,* 349.
5. Wallot, 'Une émeute à Lachine contre la "conscription"' (1812)", 112-137; 202-232; Mills, 'French Canadians and the Beginning of the War of 1812 Revisiting the Lachine Riot,' 37-58; Dessureault, 'L'émeute de Lachine en 1812; la coordination d'une contestation populaire,' 215-251.
6. Pentland, 'The Lachine Strike of 1843,' 255-77; Boily, *Les Irlandais et le canal de Lachine: La grève de 1843*; Way, *Common labour: workers and the digging of North American canals, 1780-1860.*
7. Senior, *British Regulars in Montreal: An Imperial Garrison 1832-1854,* 109-133; Alexander, *Passages in the life of a soldier, or, Military service in the East and West*; See, 'Variations on a borderlands theme,' 128-131. The mayor, Charles Wilson, who had married Daniel Tracey's sister, Ann, in 1835, was blamed by the Protestant press for the disaster.
8. Foster, '"The Montreal riot of 1849,' 61-65. For an account of riots in post-Confederation Quebec, see Pariseau, 'Les mouvements sociaux, la violence et les interventions armées au Québec 1867-1967, 67-79.'
9. Clark, *Movements of Political Protest,* 268-9.
10. *The Revolt of French-Canada, 1800-1835.*
11. Manning, 344, 347.
12. Manning, 348.

13. See in particular *British Regulars in Montreal* and *Redcoats and Patriotes: the rebellions in Lower Canada 1837-38.*

14. 'The influence of the British Garrison on the development of the Montreal Police,' 64.

15. *Redcoats and patriotes*, 7.

16. Morton, *A military history of Canada*, 73.

17. *Histoire des Patriotes*, 2003.

18. *Histoire de Montreal*, 1970-74; *Papineau et son temps*, 1977.

19. *Le Bas-Canada 1791-1840*, 1976.

20. *Le Bas-Canada 1791-1840*, 352.

21. 'L'Élection dans le quartier-ouest de Montéal en 1832; analyse politico-sociale,'1978.

22. 'L'Élection partielle du quartier-ouest de Montréal en 1832: analyse politico-sociale', 565-84.

23. 'Women at the hustings: gender, citizenship and the Montreal by-elections of 1832,' 72-94.

24. Textes colligés et présentés par Gilles Boileau. 1999.

Chapter one

1. The census showed that the population of the Island of Montreal was 43,773, of whom 27,297 lived in the city (12,492 in the East Ward and 14,805 in the West Ward). The figure for Lower Canada was 511,919. Census and statistical returns of the province of Lower Canada 1831, *JHALC*, 41.

2. See J. Bouchette, *The British Dominions in North America*, 1:212-229; Bosworth, *Hochelaga Depicta*, 111-114; Bernard, Linteau and Robert, 'La croissance démographique et spatiale de Montréal dans le 1er quart du 19e siècle,' 3, and Trépanier, *Les rues du vieux Montréal au fil du temps*. For an account of the role of the business community in the transformation of Montreal, see Ste Croix, 'The first incorporation of the city of Montreal 1826-1836.

3. Maurault, *La Paroisse. Histoire de l'Église Notre-Dame de Montréal.*

4. *VIN* 25 March 1832.

5. Ibid.

6. See Monière, *Ludger Duvernay et la révolution intellectuelle au Bas-Canada.*

7. *MIN* 2 January 1832.

8. According to the *DCB* Tracey was born "probably in 1794 in King's (Offaly) County." However, several months after Tracey's death, the *Vindicator* reprinted from the *Irish Republican Shield* a biographical

sketch by Patrick Byrne of New York that stated that Tracey was "born in the opulent and Patriotic town of Roscrea, county of Tipperary, Ireland in May 1795,"(*VIN* 26 February 1833). The monument over Tracey's tomb in the cemetery of Notre-Dame-des-Neiges in Montreal (section C, no.9), erected by his brother John in 1866, clearly states that he was native of Roscrea.

9. France Galarneau, 'Daniel Tracey;' Jackson, 'The radicalization of the Montreal Irish: the role of *The Vindicator*,' 90-97.

10. *VIN* 3 January 1832.

11. Elizabeth Nish, 'Charles-Elzéar Mondelet.' *La Minerve* published the letters on 14 October, 21 November, 15 December 1831 and 9 January 1832.

12. *MIN* 9 January 1832. English translation in *VIN* 17 January 1832.

13. *MIN* 26 January 1832; *Journals of the Legislative Council of the province of Lower-Canada*, Friday, 13 January 1832, 110-113.

14. *MG* 20 January 1832; *VIN* 20 January 1832.

15. *QG* 20 January 1832.

16. *QM* 21 January 1832.

17. *CC* 18 January 1832.

18. *QG* 18 January 1832.

19. *VIN* 24 January 1832.

20. *VIN* 27 January 1832.

21. *VIN* 27 January 1832. The *Vindicator* published Duvernay's letter in translation on 3 February 1832.

22. *VIN* 14 February; 28 February 1832.

23. *VIN* 2 March 1832.

24. *QM* 14 February 1834.

25. *MG* 20 February 1832.

26. *MG* 20 February 1832.

27. *MG* 23 February 1832.

28. *MIN* 12 March 1834.

29. Letter of L. Gosselin to A.N. Morin, 22 February 1832, 'Papiers Duvernay conservés aux Archives de la province de Québec," 155-156. Bibaud's monthly journal, *Le Magasin du Bas-Canada*, was printed on the same presses as *La Minerve*.

30. *CAN* 22 February 1832.

31. *MIN* 23 February 1832.

32. Cannon, *Historical record of the Fifteenth*, 66-74.

33. *MIN* 1 March 1832; *VIN* 2 March 1832.

34. *VIN* 2 March 1832.

35. *MIN* 2 March 1832

36. *VIN* 2 March 1832. Two years later, Sicotte had become an established member of the Patriote party. At a banquet given in Sicotte's honour on 24 June 1834, Duvernay first proposed the idea of setting up a "Société St-Jean-Baptiste." 'Papiers Duvernay,' 145.

37. *VIN* 6 March 1832.

Chapter 2

1. *MG* 22 March 1832.

2. Pouliot, 'Antoine-Olivier Berthelet;' 'Clément-Charles Sabrevois de Bleury.'

3. *MIN* 5 April 1832.

4. *The Quebec Gazette*, Published By Authority, 5 April 1832.

5. See Bilson, *A darkened house: cholera in nineteenth-century Canada* and Morris, *Cholera 1832: the social response to an epidemic.*

6. *MG* 29 March 1832.

7. *VIN* 16 March 1832.

8. The news had originally been reported in the London *Morning Chronicle*, 10 February, 1832.

9. *VIN* 3 April 1832.

10. H. Senior, 'George Perkins Bull,' E.K.Senior, *British regulars in Montreal*, 12.

11. *VIN* 10 April 1832. See Anatole Browde, 'Settling the Canadian colonies: a comparison of two nineteenth-century land companies, 299-335.

12. Tulchinsky, 'George Moffatt.'

13. Monet and Tulchinsky, 'Austin Cuvillier.'

14. *VIN* 13 April 1832; *MIN* 16 April 1832; *MG* 16 April 1832.

15. *CC* 21 April 1832. Gates was, like John Molson Sr, Joseph Shuter, Peter McGill and Stanley Bagg, an officer of the Provincial Grand Lodge for the district of Montreal and William Henry. See F.W. Terrill, *A chronology of Montreal and of Canada from A.D. 1752 to 1893*, 114-115.

16. *MG* 19 April 1832.

17. *VIN* 13 April 1832.

18. Saturday, 9 March 1833 (69th sitting), Proceedings and minutes of evidence taken before a committee of the whole house, appointed to examine by evidence into the events connected with and which led to the interference of an armed military force, at the late election of a representative for the West Ward of Montreal; and on the the Petitions and Documents referred to the said committee, *JHALC* 42 (1832-33), appendix M.

19. *MIN* 16 April 1832; *VIN* 17 April 1832.
20. Cited in *VIN* 17 April, 1832.
21. *VIN* 17 April 1832.
22. *MIN* 26 April 1832. Dupont and Mathieu, *Les Métiers du cuir*, 283.
23. *VIN* 20 April 1832.
24. *MG* 23 April 1832.
25. *VIN* 20 April 1832.
26. Ibid.
27. *VIN* 24 April 1832.
28. *List of the proprietors of the British American Land Company incorporated and established by charter and act of Parliament (1834)*.
29. Langelier, *List of lands granted by the Crown*.
30. *VIN* 24 April 1832.

Chapter 3

1. *VIN* 24 April 1832.
2. *VIN* 24 April 1832.
3. *MIN* 26 April 1832; *VIN* 27 April 1832.
4. *MIN* 26 April 1832; *VIN* 27 April 1832.
5. Cherrier, Thursday, 17 January 1833 (25th sitting).
6. *VIN* 27 April 1834.
7. Poll book for West Ward 1832 (BAnQ-M, TL19, S41). All details concerning voting figures, voters' names and challenges are taken from this document.
8. Cherrier, Thursday, 17 January 1833 (25th sitting).
9. *MG* 26 April 1832.
10. Court of special sessions, 26 April 1832. All details concerning the courts of special sessions of the peace are taken from Copies of official communications, reports and other documents, *JHALC* 42(1832-33), appendix M. For a full discussion of the role of Montreal's justices of the peace, see Fyson, *Magistrates, Police, and People: Everyday Criminal Justice in Quebec and Lower Canada, 1764-1837*.
11. E.H. Bensley, "William Robertson." *DCB*.
12. Court of special sessions, 26 April 1832.
13. *VIN* 27 April 1832.
14. *VIN* 1 May 1832.
15. *VIN* 1 May 1832.
16. Viger, Saturday, 23 February 1833 (56th sitting).
17. Court of special sessions, 28 April 1832.

18. Ibid.

19. *MG* 30 April 1830.

20. *VIN* 4 May 1832.

21. Court of special sessions, 5 May 1832.

22. Ibid.

23. Ibid.

24. Ibid.

25. *VIN* 1 May 1832.

26. *MG* 7 May 1832.

27. *MG* 10 May 1832.

28. *VIN* 11 May 1832.

29. *VIN* 15 May 1832.

30. *MG* 14 May 1832.

31. *VIN* 15 May 1832. In September 1832 the Court of King's Bench dismissed accusations of subornation of perjury against both of Tracey's supporters.

32. *VIN* 18 May 1832.

33. *VIN* 15 May 1832

34. *VIN* 18 May 1832.

35. *VIN* 22 May 1832. The shooting in St Joseph St was the first act of violence recorded by the night watch since the opening of the by-election. Reports of the night watch of Montreal from 29/30 April to 15/16 June, *JHALC* 42 (1832-33), Appendix M 10:26 Report of the night watch from 18 to 19 May 1832.

36. *La Minerve* questioned whether Cuvillier's wife had the right to vote. Several years before, it reported, Cuvillier had attempted to protect her money from his creditors by changing their matrimonial regime from one of community of property to that of separation as to property. After his creditors appealed, Cuvillier's wife was forced to pay her husband's debts. The paper suggested that their marital regime had still not changed and that only Austin Cuvillier was eligible to vote. *MIN* 21 May 1832.

37. *MIN* 21 May 1832; Poll book.

38. *MIN* 21 May 1832.

39. *MG* 21 May 1832.

40. The original document correctly spells the name of Captain Spencer. VM 35, vol 7, Fonds des juges de paix de Montréal, Archives de la ville de Montréal.

41. Court of special sessions, 20 May 1832

42. PRO WO76/317.

Chapter 4

1. Poll book.
2. *MIN* 24 May 1832.
3. Court of special sessions, 20 May 1832, no 2.
4. Macintosh's affidavit, 26 May 1832. Copies of official communications, reports and other documents.
5. Poll book.
6. Ibid.
7. Robertson's affidavit, court of special sessions, 23 May 1832.
8. Robertson's affidavit, court of special sessions, 23 May 1832.
9. *MIN* 22 May 1832.
10. *CC* 23 May 1832.
11. Papineau to John Neilson, 6 June 1832, in Aubin and Blanchet (eds), *Lettres à divers correspondants*, 260-64.
12. Roy, Saturday, 22 December 1832 (8th sitting).
13. *VIN* 22 May 1834.
14. *MG* 24 May 1834.
15. 5 Geo.4.c.33. *The provincial statutes of Lower Canada.*
16. Poll book.
17. *VIN* 22 May 1832. Tracey's linking of Montreal and Manchester was significant. It was a reference to the Peterloo Massacre at St Peter's Field in Manchester, England, on August 16, 1819, where some 60,000 people had gathered to call for parliamentary reform. The rally was a peaceful one but local magistrates sought military assistance. Sixty cavalrymen of the Manchester and Salford Yeomanry charged the crowd with sabres drawn. Eleven people were killed and over 600 were wounded. The government later commended the action of the magistrates and the military.
18. *MIN* 24 May 1832; *VIN* 25 May 1832.
19. *VIN* 25 May 1832.

Chapter 5

1. *CC* 23 May 1832.
2. Abbot-Namphy and MacKinnon, 'Jean-Marie Mondelet.'
3. Cherrier, Friday, 18 January 1833 (26th sitting).
4. Papineau to John Neilson, 6 June 1832, in Aubin and Blanchet (eds), *Lettres à divers*, 262.
5. Report of the coroner's inquest. Divers documents produced before the said committee, and which have not as yet been printed, no. 7, *JHALC* 42 (1832-33), appendix M.

6. Viger, Tuesday, 29 January 1833 (35th sitting).

7. Lists of witnesses delivered by the clerk of the peace to be examined by the coroner. Divers documents produced before the said committee, and which have not as yet been printed, no. 6, *JHALC* 42 (1832-33), appendix M.

8. C.R. Ogden to governor, enclosing a transcript of the depositions taken at the inquest, 2 June, 1832. Copies of official communications, reports and other documents, no. 9, *JHALC* 42 (1832-33), appendix M. All subsequent references to the inquest are taken from the same transcript.

9. Papineau to John Neilson, 6 June, 1832, 261.

10. Viger, Saturday, 26 January 1833 (33rd sitting); Walker, Friday, 15 March 1833 (73rd sitting; Sewell, *A Treatise on the Law of Coroner*, 173.).

11. *VIN* 25 May 1832.

12. *VIN* 29 May 1832.

13. Report of the coroner's inquest.

14. Papineau to John Neilson, 6 June 1832, 262-64.

15. Report of the coroner's inquest.

16. Statute law stipulated that in the vicinity of an election, keeping the peace there fell under the jurisdiction of the returning officer and that he had the power and the authority to maintain and enforce order at the election. The law read that "if any person or persons shall commit violence, or be engaged in any affray or riot, or be armed with clubs, staves, or other offensive weapons …the said Returning Officer shall have power and authority, on view, …to arrest or confine or commit to prison, any such person or persons so offending." (5 Geo. IV, c. 33, xxix).

17. Court of special sessions, 23 May 1832.

18. *CC* 23 May 1832.

19. *MG* 24 May 1832.

20. Cited in *MG* 24 May 1832.

21. "Committee made up of French Canadians, friends of justice and of truth."

22. "citoyen respectable pour son caractère et sa conduite" "de la violence et de la grossièreté de son style et de son langage;" "des Canadiens généralement de classe basse ou ignorante."

23. *VIN* 29 May 1832.

24. John Spencer finally provided an affidavit on 28 May 1832. In it he admitted having had difficulty hearing what Tracey had said on the opposite side of the street. He also made no reference to any "party of persons disposed to commit the most violent outrages." Ogden to gov-

ernor, 4 June, 1832, enclosing a transcript of all the affidavits which accompanied the petitions of Macintosh and Temple to be discharged from arrest. Copies of official communications, reports and other documents, no. 10, *JHALC* 42(1832-33), appendix M.

Chapter 6

1. Buckner, 'Whitworth-Aylmer,'

2. Papineau to governer general, 22 May 1832, Orders, resolutions and references, appendix, no 1, *Appendix to JHALC* 42(1832-33), appendix M.

3. Macintosh to governor, 22 May 1832. Continuation of the copies of official communications, reports and other documents, etc, *JHALC* 42(1832-33), appendix M.

4. Letter of C. Sweeny, Montreal, 13 June 1832, on the conduct of the coroner's enquiry, Macintosh on Canada, 1-4, Stewart Museum library, Montreal, (RB 971.038 M18 1833).

5. Memorandum from governor, 28 May, 1832. Copies of official communications, reports and other documents, no. 7. *JHALC* 42 (1832-33), appendix M.

6. Ste. Croix, 'Charles Richard Ogden.'

7. Ogden to governor, 30 May 1832. Copies of official communications, no. 8.

8. Macintosh to governor, 29 May 1832. Orders, resolutions and references, *JHALC* 42 (1832-33), appendix M. The information was leaked to Cuvillier who accused Papineau in the House of Assembly of a compound felony. However, on 28 February 1833, in a letter to Viger, Charles John Forbes, the army's deputy commissary general in Montreal, agreed that during their conversation the name of Papineau had never once been mentioned. See J. Viger, 'La Saberdache bleue,' 9:167-8. Archives du Séminaire de de Québec, P32- Fonds Viger-Verreau

9. Ogden to governor, 2 June 1832. Copies of official communications, no. 9.

10. Affidavits, Ogden to governor, 4 June, 1832, no. 10.

11. Affidavits, Ogden to governor, 4 June, 1832, no. 10.

12. Ibid.

13. *MG* 31 May 1832.

14. *VIN* 4 June 1832

15. *VIN* 1 June 1832; *MIN* 31 May 1832.

16. *VIN* 8 June 1832.

17. *VIN* 5 June 1832.

18. *GQ* 24 May 1832; *CAN* 26 May 1832.

19. *CAN* 1 June 1832 (English text reproduced from the *Vindicator*, Friday, June 8, 1832).

20. *VIN* 8 June 1832.

21. Ibid.

22. Macintosh to governor, 9 June 1832. Continuation of the copies of official communications, reports and other documents, etc, *JHALC* 42(1832-33), appendix M.

23. J.B. Glegg to A.F. Macintosh, 11 June 1832. Documents having reference to the occurrences which took place in Montreal on the twenty-first May, 1832; transmitted to the House of Assembly in compliance with its address of the 12th December, 1832, *JHALC* 42 (1832-33), appendix M.

24. *VIN* 2 March 1832.

25. *VIN* 18 May 1832.

26. *VIN* 8 June 1832.

27. *VIN* 8 June 1832.

28. *VIN* 12 June 1832.

29. Cited in *VIN*, 15 June 1832.

30. *VIN* 15 June 1832.

31. *VIN* 19 Jun 1832.

32. *VIN* 26 June 1832.

33. *MIN* 19 July 1832.

Chapter 7

1. See Fyson, 'Jurys, participation civique et représentation au Québec et au Bas-Canada,' 85-120.

2. Lessard, 'Louis Gugy.'

3. BAnQ-M, TL.19.S1.SS1. The twelve men from Lachine were Charles Penner, JP, Ashburnham Newman, John Fraser, James Sommerville, John McMartin, Andrew Leishman, Thomas Dawes, William Gordon, Donald Duff, JP, William Reid, John Larmouth and Donald McMartin. In contrast, the grand jury that had sat during the previous criminal term comprised seventeen jurors from the city of Montreal, two from Longue Pointe, one from Rivière des Prairies, one from Pointe Claire, one from St Laurent and two from Lachine. *MIN* 26 July, 1832.

4. *MG* 28 August 1832.

5. Ibid.

6. Report of the coroner's inquest. Divers documents produced before the said committee, and which have not as yet been printed, no 7, *JHALC* 42 (1832-33), Appendix M.

7. *MG* 30 August 1830; *MIN* 30 August 1832.

8. *MIN* 30 August 1832.

9. James Reid to governor, enclosing a copy of the presentment, Copies of official communications, reports and other documents, no. 11, *JHALC 42 (1832-33)*, appendix M.

10. *MIN* 3 September 1832. Various legal authorities of the time support the position defended by *La Minerve*. Chitty, *A practical treatise on the Criminal Law*, wrote that in general the grand jury hear evidence only in support of the charge and not in exculpation of the defendant. (1:317). Keele, *The Provincial Justice, or Magistrates Manual*, wrote: "The grand jury may insist upon the same strictness of proof as is required on the trial, though it is not usual to do so, nor to weigh the evidence with that degree of scrutiny with which it is afterwards sifted by the judge and jury. They are to hear evidence only on behalf of the prosecution; for the finding of an indictment is merely in the nature of an enquiry or accusation, which is afterwards to be tried and determined" (p.235). However, Chitty suggests that occasionally a more merciful approach might be followed in consideration of the ignominy, anxiety of delay and the misery of a prison inflicted on the accused, in which case the grand jury ought "as far as the evidence before them goes, to be convinced of the guilt of the defendant." (1:317).

11. *MG* 4 September, 1832.

12. General Order issued from Headquarters in Quebec on 3 September 1832, Documents having reference to the occurrences which took place in Montreal on the twenty-first May, 1832; transmitted to the House of Assembly in compliance with its address of the 12th December, 1832, *JHALC* 42(1832-33), appendix M.

13. Aylmer to Robertson, 3 September 1832, ibid.

14. FitzRoy Somerset to Lord Aylmer, 23 October 1832. Macintosh on Canada, D, Stewart Museum library, Montreal. (RB 971.038 M18 1833).

15. *MG* 6 September 1832.

16. *MG* 11 September 1832.

17. *QG* 7 September 1832

18. Documents accompanying the governor's letter (29 March 1833), no. 2: François Tavernier's affidavit; no.3: James Magaughran's affidavit; no. 4: Samuel J. Pierce's affidavit. Orders, resolutions and references, *JHALC* 42 (1832-33), appendix M

19. Walker, Saturday, 16 March 1833 (74th sitting).

20. Documents accompanying the governor's letter of 29 March 1833. No. 5: Théophile Bruneau.

21. Joseph Roy's order for the arrest of Macintosh and Temple. Orders, resolutions and references, appendix, no. 2, *JHALC* 42(1832-33), appendix M.

22. Walker, Saturday, 16 March 1833 (74th sitting).

23. Documents accompanying the governor's letter (29 March 1833), no. 7: Joseph Roy to John Delisle 17 September 1832.

24. Macintosh's petition, 15 September 1832. Continuation of the copies of official communications, reports and other documents, etc," *JHALC* 42 (1832-33), appendix M.

25. Walker, Saturday, 16 March 1833 (74th sitting).

26. Macintosh to Craig, 17 September 1832. Continuation of the copies of official communications, reports and other documents, etc.

27. Charles Gore to Sir John Colborne, 6 October and 17 October 1832. Documents having reference to the occurrences.

28. A.F. Macintosh to the Deputy Adjutant General, 6 October 1832. Documents having reference to the occurrences.

29. G.A. Eliot to A.F. Macintosh, 9 October 1832. Ibid. Macintosh received permission to be absent between 10 October 1832 and 9 January 1834 in order to go to Europe.

30. *MG* 27 October 1832; *QM* 10 January 1833. Macintosh never returned to his regiment in Lower Canada. On 8 April 1834 he was placed on the half pay list and later spent two years studying at the senior department of the Royal Military College. PRO WO76/317.

31. Viger to Goderich, 11 July 1832. Correspondence of Mr Viger with the Colonial Minister, from 11th July 1832 to the 11th September 1833. *JHALC* 43 (1834), appendix B. Divers documents addressed to the Honourable Louis Joseph Papineau, Speaker of the House of Assembly, by the honourable Denis B Viger.

32. Ouellet and Fort, 'Denis-Benjamin Viger.'

33. Viger to Goderich, 17 July 1832, appendix B.

34. Lord Howick to Viger, 26 July 1832, appendix B.

35. Viger to Lord Howick, 28 July 1832, appendix B.

36. Viger to Goderich 28 July 1832; Howick to Viger, 31 July 1832; Viger to Goderich 2 August 1832. Appendix B.

37. Viger to Goderich 29 August 1832, appendix B.

38. Howick to Viger 8 September 1832, appendix B.

39. Substance of a conversation with Lord Goderich, relative to the Indictments laid before the Grand Jury at the criminal Court of August

and September, at Montreal, against Messrs Macintosh, etc., 25 October 1832. *JHALC* 42 (1832-33), appendix G. The *Morning Chronicle* article was reprinted in *Le Canadien* (24 December 1832) and in the *Vindicator* (1 January 1833). For Goderich's views on the political situation in Lower Canada, see Buckner, *The transition to responsible government.*

40. *Montreal Herald*, 23 May 1832, cited in *QG* 25 May 1832.

41. *MG* 6 September 1832.

42. *MG* 20 October 1832.

43. *MIN* 28 October 1832.

44. *MG* 1 November 1832.

45. *MG* 5 November 1832

46. *MIN* 8 November 1832.

47. *JHALC* 42 (1833), 74.

48. Idem, 78.

49. "Il commence à s'apercevoir qu'il se roule dans des draps sales. Il ne fera pas de difficultés de communiquer tout ce qu'il a par devant lui, ce qui n'eut pas été le cas il y a un mois. Cela vérifie un peu ce que j'écrivais que l'excès du mal apportera peut être son remède." L.-J. Papineau to his wife, 6 December 1832, in Aubin and Blanchet (eds), *Louis-Joseph Papineau. Lettres à Julie* 256.

50. "C'est une singularité qu'il y ait plus de militaires que jamais qui m'aient fait visite. La garnison est longue à n'en jamais finir. L'on peut interpréter cette circonstance en bonne part et dire qu'ils donnent une preuve de leur regret de l'intervention du militaire au 21 mai." *Lettres à Julie,* (17 November 1832), 252.

51. "Ensuite, milord Aylmer se trouve attaqué & averti que le gouverne-ment en Angleterre doit s'attendre à l'enquête que nous avons com-mencée, et que, s'il veut interrompre, lui qui est inculpé, la responsabilité en sera pour lui seul et la détermination envisagée comme la sienne pro-pre et non comme venant d'outre mer." *Lettres à Julie,* (24 December 1832), 260.

52. *JHALC* 42 (1833).

53. *QG* 30 November 1832.

54. Macintosh on Canada, C.

Chapter 8

1. Lavictoire, Wednesday, 19 December 1832 (5th sitting).

2. Joannette, Tuesday, 12th February 1833 (46th sitting).

3. Lavictoire, Thursday, 20 December 1832 (6th sitting).

4. Joannette, Wednesday, 13 February 1833 (47th sitting)

5. Joannette, (46th sitting).

6. Lavictoire, (5th sitting).

7. Four convictions against Louis Malo, and others: court of general quarter sessions of the peace. Divers documents produced before the said committee, and which have not as yet been printed, no 13, *JHALC* 42 (1832-33), appendix M.

8. Lavictoire, 20 December 1832.

9. Hintz, Monday, 25 February 1833 (57th sitting).

10. Dragon, Monday, 18 March 1833 (75th sitting).

11. Lavictoire, 20 December 1832.

12. Joannette, 13 February 1833.

13. Lavictoire, Friday, 21 December 1832 (7th sitting).

14. Beauchamp, Monday, 27 January 1834 (7th sitting). The twenty-two sittings of 1834 are from Proceedings and minutes of evidence etc, *JHALC* 43 (1834) appendix.

15. Cherrier, Thursday, 17 January 1833 (25th sitting); Nelson, Monday, 14 January 1833 (22nd sitting).

16. Cherrier, (25th sitting); Vallée, Thursday, 14 March 1833 (72nd sitting).

17. Bell, Saturday, 9 February 1833 (44th sitting); Dupré, Tuesday, 11 December 1832 (1st sitting).

18. Rodier, Saturday, 9 March 1833 (69th sitting).

19. Brennan, Monday, 20 January 1834 (4th sitting).

20. Cherrier, (25th sitting).

21. Dupré, Friday, 14 December 1832 (2nd sitting); Cherrier,(25th sitting); Lafontaine, Friday, 17 January 1834 (3rd sitting).

22. Viger, Monday, 28 January 1833 (34th sitting).

23. John Delisle, Tuesday, 8 January 1833 (18th sitting); Friday, 11 January 1833 (20th sitting).

24. Benjamin Delisle, Saturday, 5 January 1833 (16th sitting); Monday, 7 January 1833 (17th sitting); Wednesday, 9 January 1833 (19th sitting).

25. Brennan, Wednesday, 22 January 1834 (5th sitting).

26. Viger, Monday, 28 January 1833 (34th sitting).

27. Viger, Saturday, 23 February 1833 (56th sitting).

28. Bell, Monday, 11 February 1833 (45th sitting); Tuesday, 12 February 1834 (46th sitting).

29. Rodier, Wednesday 20 March, 1833 (77th sitting).

30. Viger, Thursday, 24 January 1833 (31st sittting).

31. Dupré, Monday, 17 December 1832 (3rd sitting); Tuesday, 18 December 1832 (4th sitting).

32. Poll Book.

33. Kimber, Monday, 13 January 1834 (1st sitting).

34. Kimber, Monday, 13 January 1834 (1st sitting).

35. An act to repeal certain acts therein-mentioned, and to consolidate the laws relating to the election of members to serve in the assembly of this province, and to the duty of returning officers, and for other purposes (22 March 1825), 5 Geo.4.C33, XII.

36. Mondelet, Monday, 24 December 1832 (9th sitting).

37. Mondelet, Thursday, 27 December 1832 (10th sitting); Friday, 28 December 1832 (11th sitting).

38. Walker, Friday, 15 March 1833 (73rd sitting).

39. Gugy, Wednesday, 19 December 1832 (5th sitting). Sommerville to Gugy: Divers documents produced before the said committee, and which have not as yet been printed," no 1, *JHALC* 42 (1832-33), appendix M.

40. Sewell, Monday, 25th February 1833 (57th sitting).

41. Goedike, Tuesday, 19 March 1833 (76th sitting); Wednesday, 20 March 1833 (77th sitting).

42. Ogden, Thursday, 14 February 1833 (48th sitting); Friday, 15 February 1833 (49th sitting).

Chapiter 9

1. L.-J. Papineau to his wife, 6 December 1832, in Aubin and Blanchet (eds), *Louis-Joseph Papineau. Lettres à Julie*, 257.

2. Ogden to governor, 4 June, 1832, enclosing a transcript of all the affidavits which accompanied the petitions of Macintosh and Temple to be discharged from arrest. Copies of official communications, reports and other documents, no. 10, *JHALC* 42(1832-33), appendix M.

3. Beaubien, Friday, 7 February 1834 (12th sitting).

4. Dragon, Monday, 18 March 1833 (75th sitting).

5. Trudeau, Saturday, 12 January 1833 (21st sitting); Lussier, Friday, 8 March 1833 (68th sitting).

6. Larocque, Friday, 1 February 1833 (38th sitting); Baron's affidavit, Ogden to governor general, 4 June, 1832.

7. Jordan, Monday, 3 February 1834 (10th sitting).

8. Affidavits, Ogden to governor, 4 June 1832.

9. Dupré, Monday, 17 December 1832 (3rd sitting).

10. Viger, Saturday, 26 January 1833 (33 sitting); Beaubien, Wednesday, 19 February 1834 (17th sitting).

11. *CC* 2 June, 1832.

12. Benjamin Delisle, Wednesday, 9 January 1833 (19th sitting); Wednesday, 30 January 1833 (36th sitting).

13. Nelson, Tuesday, 15 January 1833 (23rd sitting); Larocque, 1 February 1833; Donegani, 1 February 1833; Field, Saturday, 9th February 1833 (44th sitting); Bell, (44th sitting); Trudeau, Saturday, 12 January, 1833; Viger, Saturday, 26 January, 1833 (33rd sitting).

14. Nelson, Tuesday, 15 January 1833 (23rd sitting); Larocque, 1 February 1833; Donegani, 1 February 1833; Field, Saturday, 9th February 1833 (44th sitting); Bell, (44th sitting); Trudeau, Saturday, 12 January, 1833; Viger, Saturday, 26 January, 1833 (33rd sitting).

15. La Fontaine, Saturday, 2nd March (63rd sitting).

16. Jordan, Wednesday, 29 January 1834 (8th sitting).

17. Affidavits, Ogden to governor, 4 June 1832.

18. Ogden, Friday 15th February 1833 (49th sitting).

19. Viger, Friday, 25 January 1833 (32nd sitting). The Irishman whom Viger calls Keogh was in fact Michael Keoan, a shoemaker, who lived and worked with Robert Cook. Keoan was called later to give evidence about the attack on him by the special constables. (Monday, 25 February 1833-57th sitting).

20. Orders, resolutions and references, *JHALC* 42 (1832-33), appendix M.

21. See Papineau's speech of 28 February 1833 on the sovereignty of the House. Louis-Lamonde and Larin (eds), *Joseph Papineau : un demi siècle de combats*, 239-247.

22. Letter from Lt Col McDougall of the 79th Highlanders to William Robertson, JP, and instructions of this officer for the guidance of troops who may be called on to act in aid of the civil power. Divers documents produced before the said committee, and which have not as yet been printed, no 12, *JHALC* 42 (1832-33), appendix M.

23. "Ainsi des personnes qui tout à coup se querellent sur un marché ou autre place ne sont pas coupables d'émeute mais seulement d'un simple tumulte.", *Les lois criminelles anglaises*, 46.

24. See Caple, *The Bristol Riots of 1831 and social reform in Britain*.

Chapter 10

1. Ogden to governor, 4 June, 1832, enclosing a transcript of all the affidavits which accompanied the petitions of Macintosh and Temple to be

discharged from arrest. Copies of official communications, reports and other documents, no. 10, *JHALC* 42(1832-33), appendix M.

2. Benjamin Delisle, Monday, 7 January 1833 (17th sitting).
3. *QG* 13 March 1833.
4. Monday, 4 March 1833 (64th sitting).
5. Dupré, Monday, 17 December 1832 (3rd sitting).
6. Dubois, Monday, 27 January 1834 (7th sitting).
7. Beaubien, Friday, 7 February 1834 (12th sitting).
8. Smith, Wednesday, 16 January 1833 (24th sitting).
9. Flaherty, Tuesday, 12 March 1833 (70th sitting).
10. Flaherty, Wednesday, 13 March 1833 (71st sitting).
11. Lussier, Friday, 8 March 1833 (68th sitting); Field, Saturday, 9th February 1833 (44th sitting); Lebert, Monday, 4 March 1833 (64th sitting).
12. Rodier, Saturday, 9th March 1833 (69th sitting).
13. Beaubien, Friday, 7 February 1834 (12th sitting).
14. Bell, Saturday, 9 February (44th sitting); Dupré. Monday, 17 December 1832 (3rd sitting).
15. Flaherty, Tuesday, 12 March 1833 (70th sitting); Lebert, Monday, 4 March 1833 (64th sitting); Lognion, Thursday 7 March, 1833 (67th sitting); Goddu, Friday, 22 February 1833 (55th sitting).
16. Field, Saturday, 9 February 1833 (44th sitting); Smith, Wednesday, 16 January 1833 (24th sitting); Trudeau, Friday, 11 January 1833 (24th sitting).
17. Jobin, Wednesday, 2 January 1833 (13th sitting); Lussier, Friday, 8 March 1833 (68th sitting).
18. Flaherty, Wednesday, 13 March 1833 (71st sitting).
19. Jobin, Wednesday, 2 January 1833 (13th sitting).
20. Bell, Saturday, 9 February 1833 (44th sitting); Monday, 11 February 1833 (45th sitting).
21. La Fontaine, Saturday, 2nd March (63rd sitting).
22. Beaubien, Friday, 7 February 1834 (12th sitting).
23. Jobin, Wednesday, 2 January 1833 (13th sitting); Lussier, Friday, 8 March 1833 (68th sitting); Trudeau, Friday, 11 January 1833 (24th sitting).
24. La Fontaine, Saturday 2nd March, (63rd sitting).
25. Bell, Saturday, 9 February 1833 (44th sitting); Trudeau, Friday, 11 January 1833 (20th sitting); Thursday, 17 January 1833 (25th sitting); Lussier, Friday, 8 March 1833 (68th sitting).
26. La Fontaine, Saturday, 2nd March 1833 (63rd sitting).
27. Cherrier, Friday, 18 January 1833 (26th sitting)

28. Beaubien, Friday, 7 February 1834 (12th sitting); Monday, 10 February 1834 (13th sitting).

29. Rodier is probably confusing two different individuals. William Creed was the name of the man left prostrate on the ground outside the polling station shortly after 5 pm. The incident he is describing here took place ten minutes later. Was this second victim the Irishman that La Fontaine had dragged away from Henderson's store a few minutes earlier? Rodier must have tried to discover the victim's identity and confused the two incidents.

30. Rodier, Tuesday, 12 March 1833 (70th sitting).

31. Jobin, Wednesday, 2 January 1833 (13th sitting); Thursday, 3 January 1833 (14th sitting).

32. Kennedy (ed), *Statutes, treaties and documents of the Canadian Constitution*, 287.

33. Orders, resolutions and references, *JHALC* 42 (1832-33), Appendix M.

34. Affidavits, Ogden to governor, 4 June, 1832.

35. "Oh the twenty-first! Unforgettable day/Be imprinted in all our hearts./ A contemptible cohort came to conquer our defenders./The children of the soil assembled/To choose a candidate/The bureaucrats gathered /And committed their murderous attack on us." Carrier and Vachon (eds), *Chansons politiques du Québec* 1: 302.

36. "L'humble requête de Josephte Gagner, veuve de François Charpentier dit Languedoc, et de Scholastique Labranche, veuve de Jean-Baptiste Billet, de la cité de Montréal, expose humblement à Votre Excellence: Que le 21 mai 1832, leurs époux revenant de leurs travaux habituels, furent tous deux frappés à mort par les balles tirées par les troupes de Sa Majesté, pour disperser un attroupement tumultueux dans une élection. Les deux infortunés qui furent ainsi frappés étaient à plusieurs arpents du lieu où était le tumulte et n'avaient en aucun temps pris part à l'élection. Depuis lors, vos pétitionnaires ont reçu plusieurs encouragements à espérer que le Gouvernement viendrait à leur secours dans leur âge avancé, ayant perdu leurs seuls supports en perdant leurs époux; ce qui n'a pas eu lieu. Elles supplient Votre Excellence de prendre leur état et leurs malheurs, dans sa gracieuse considération, et quels que soient les secours qu'il plaira à Votre Excellence de leur accorder, Elle recevra les prières et les voeux des deux infortunées qui s'adressent à Elle." BAnQ-Q, Événements de 1837-1838, no. 3929. The document is dated 25 July 1838.

Bibliography

Manuscript Sources

Archives de la ville de Montréal
VM 35 - Fonds des juges de paix de Montréal

Bibliothèque et Archives nationales du Québec à Montéal (BAnQ-M)
TL.19 — Fonds Cour du banc du roi

Bibliothèque et Archives nationales du Québec à Québec (BAnQ-Q)
Événements de 1837-1838, no. 3929.

McCord Museum
Bagg Papers

Musée de la civilisation du Québec
Archives du Séminaire de de Québec, P32 - Fonds Viger-Verreau

National Archives (UK)
PRO WO76/317.

Stewart Museum Library, Montreal
RB 971.038 M18 1833 - Macintosh on Canada

Université de Montréal, Service des Archives
Collection Baby

Newspapers

Canadien Courant
Le Canadien
La Minerve

Montreal Gazette

Montreal Herald

Quebec Gazette

Quebec Mercury

Published sources

Abbot-Namphy, Elizabeth and MacKinnon, Margaret. 'Jean-Marie Mondelet.' *DCB*.

Alexander, James Edward. *Passages in the life of a soldier, or, Military service in the East and West*. London: Hurst & Blackett, 1857.

Appendix to the Journals of the House of Assembly of the province of Lower-Canada (Canadiana.org).

Aubin, Georges and Blanchet, Renée (eds). *Louis-Joseph Papineau. Lettres à divers correspondants*. Tome 1:1810-1845. Montréal: Les Éditions Varia (collection Documents et Biographies) 2006.

— *Louis-Joseph Papineau. Lettres à Julie* Sillery: Septentrion 2000.

Bensley, E.H. 'William Robertson.' *DCB*.

Bernard, Jean-Paul; Linteau, Paul-André; Robert, Jean-Claude. 'La croissance démographique et spatiale de Montréal dans le 1er quart du 19e siècle.' *Groupe de recherche sur la société montréalaise au 19e siècle*. Rapport et travaux, 1973-1975. Montréal: UQUAM 1975.

Bilson, Geoffrey. *A darkened house: cholera in nineteenth-century Canada*. Toronto, Buffalo, London: University of Toronto Press 1980.

Blackstone, William. *Commentaries on the Laws of England: in four books; with an analysis of the work*. 2 vols. New York, W.E. Dean, 1838

Boileau, Gilles (ed). *Le 21 mai 1832 sur la Rue du sang*. Montréal: Éditions du Méridien, 1999.

Boily, Raymond. *Les Irlandais et le canal de Lachine: La grève de 1843*. Montréal: Leméac 1980

Bosworth, Newton. *Hochelaga Depicta: The early history and present state of the city and island of Montreal*. Montreal: W. Grieg 1839.

Bradbury, Bettina. 'Women at the hustings: gender, citizenship and the Montreal by-elections of 1832.' In Gleason, Mona and Perry, Adele (eds). *Rethinking Canada: the promise of women's history*. 5th ed. Don Mills: Oxford University Press 2006: 72-94.

Bouchette, Joseph. *The British Dominions in North America*, 2 vols. London: Longman, Rees, etc 1832 (CIHM 48011).

Browde, Anatole. 'Settling the Canadian colonies: a comparison of two nineteenth-century land companies.' *Business History Review* 76, no. 2, (2002): 299-335.

Buckner, Phillip A. *The transition to responsible government: British policy in British North America, 1815-1850*. Westport, Conn: Greenwood Press 1985.

— 'Matthew Whitworth-Aylmer, 5th Baron Aylmer.' *DCB*.

Cannon, Richard. *Historical record of the Fifteenth, or the Yorkshire East Riding Regiment of Foot: containing an account of the formation of the regiment in 1685, and of its subsequent services to 1848*. London: Parker, Furnivall & Parker 1848.

Caple, Jeremy. *The Bristol Riots of 1831 and social reform in Britain*, Lewiston, NY: E. Mellen Press 1990.

Carrier, Maurice and Vachon, Monique (eds). *Chansons politiques du Québec*. 2 vols. Montréal: Leméac 1977.

Chitty, Joseph. *A practical treatise on the Criminal Law*. 4 vols. London: Brooke 1826.

Clark, C.D. *Movements of Political Protest in Canada 1640-1840*. Toronto: University of Toronto Press 1959

Crémazie, Jacques. *Les lois criminelles anglaises, traduites et compilées de Blackstone, Chitty, Russell et autres criminalistes anglais et telles que suivies en Canada, arrangées suivant les dispositions introduites dans le code criminel de cette province [...] la ci-devant province du Bas-Canada*. Québec: Fréchette 1842.

Dessureault, Christian. 'L'émeute de Lachine en 1812; la coordination d'une contestation populaire.' *RHAF* 62 no. 2 (2008): 215-251.

Dupont, Jean-Claude and Mathieu, Jacques, eds. *Les Métiers du cuir*. Sainte-Foy: Les Presses de l'Université Laval 1981.

Filteau, Gérard. *Histoire des Patriotes*, Sillery: Septentrion 2003.

Foster, Josephine. 'The Montreal riot of 1849.' *Canadian Historical Review*. 32 no.1 (1951) 61-65.

Fyson, Donald. 'Jurys, participation civique et représentation au Québec et au Bas-Canada: les grands jurys du district de Montréal (1764-1832).' *RHAF* 55 no.1 (2001): 85-120.

— *Magistrates, Police, and People: Everyday Criminal Justice in Quebec and Lower Canada, 1764-1837*. Toronto: Osgoode Society for Canadian Legal History / University of Toronto Press 2006.

Galarneau, France. 'Daniel Tracey.' DCB.

— 'L'Élection dans le quartier-ouest de Montéal en 1832; analyse politico-sociale,' Master's thesis, Université de Montréal 1978.

— 'L'Élection partielle du quartier-ouest de Montréal en 1832: analyse politico-sociale.'" RHAF 32 no. 4 (1979): 565-84.

Jackson, James. 'The radicalization of the Montreal Irish: the role of The Vindicator.' Canadian Journal of Irish Studies/Revue canadienne d'études irlandaises, 31 no. 1 (2005): 90-97.

Journals of the House of Assembly of Lower Canada (Canadiana.org).

Journals of the Legislative Council of the province of Lower-Canada (Canadiana.org).

Keele, W.C. The Provincial Justice, or Magistrates Manual: being a complete digest of the criminal law, and a compendious and general view of the provincial law: with practical forms, for the use of the magistracy of Upper Canada. Toronto: Upper Canada Gazette 1835.

Kennedy, W.P.M. (ed). Statutes, treaties and documents of the Canadian Constitution, 1713-1929. Constitutional documents of Canada. 2nd. ed., rev. and enl. Toronto: Oxford University Press 1930.

Lamonde, Yvan and Larin, Claude, eds. Louis-Joseph Papineau: un demi-siècle de combats: interventions publiques/choix de textes et présentation. Saint-Laurent, Québec: Fides 1998.

Langelier, J.-C. List of lands granted by the Cown in the province of Quebec from 1763 to 31st December 1890. Québec: C.-F. Langlois 1891.

Lessard, Renald. 'Louis Gugy.' DCB.

List of the proprietors of the British American Land Company incorporated and established by charter and act of Parliament 1834. (CIHM 43101). [London?: s.n., 1834?].

Manning, Helen Taft. The Revolt of French-Canada, 1800-1835. A Chapter in the History of the British Commonwealth. Toronto: Macmillan of Canada 1962.

Maurault, Olivier. La Paroisse. Histoire de l'Église Notre-Dame de Montréal. Montréal: Thérien Frères 1957.

Mills, Sean. 'French Canadians and the Beginning of the War of 1812. Revisiting the Lachine Riot.' Histoire social/Social History 75 (mai 2005): 37-58.

Monet, Jacques and Tulchinsky, Gerald J.J. 'Austin Cuvillier.' DCB.

Monière, Denis. *Ludger Duvernay et la révolution intellectuelle au Bas-Canada.* Montréal: Québec/Amérique 1987.

Morris, R.J. *Cholera 1832: the social response to an epidemic.* London: Croom Helm 1976.

Morton, Desmond. *A Military History of Canada.* Edmonton: Hurtig 1990.

Nish, Elizabeth. 'Charles-Elzéar Mondelet.' *DCB.*

Ouellet, Fernand. *Le Bas-Canada 1791-1840. Changements structuraux et crises.* Ottawa: Éditions de l'Université d'Ottawa 1976.

Ouellet, Fernand and Fort, André. 'Denis-Benjamin Viger.' *DCB.*

'Papiers Duvernay conservés aux archives de la province de Québec.' Archives de la Province du Québec *Rapport* (1926—27): 147-252.

Pariseau, Jean. 'Les mouvements sociaux, la violence et les interventions armées au Québec 1867-1967.' *RHAF* 37 no.1 (1983): 67-79.

Pentland, H.C. 'The Lachine Strike of 1843.' *Canadian Historical Review,* 29, no. 3 (1948): 255-77.

Pouliot, Léon. 'Antoine-Olivier Berthelet.' *DCB.*

— 'Clément-Charles Sabrevois de Bleury.' *DCB.*

Rumilly, Robert. *Histoire de Montreal,* 5 vols. Montréal: Fides 1970-74.

— *Papineau et son temps,* 2 vols. Montréal: Fides 1977.

See, Scott W. 'Variations on a borderlands theme: nativism and collective violence in northeastern North America in the mid-nineteenth century.' In Hornsby, Stephen and Reid, John G. (eds). *New England and the Maritime provinces: connections and comparisons.* Montreal and Kingston: McGill-Queen's University Press 2005:128-131.

Senior, Elinor Kyte. *British Regulars in Montreal: An Imperial Garrison 1832-1854.* Montreal and Kingston: McGill-Queens University Press 1981.

— *Redcoats and Patriotes: the rebellions in Lower Canada 1837-38.* Stittsville (Ont.): Canada's Wings, 1985.

— 'The influence of the British Garrison on the development of the Montreal Police.' *Military Affairs* 43 no.2 (1979): 63-68.

Senior, Hereward. 'George Perkins Bull.' *DCB.*

Ste-Croix, Lorne 'The first incorporation of the city of Montreal 1826-1836.' Master's thesis. McGill University, 1972.

— 'Charles Richard Ogden.' *DCB.*

Terrill, F.W. *A chronology of Montreal and of Canada from A.D. 1752 to 1893: including commercial statistics, historic sketches of commercial corporations and firms and advertisements, arranged to show in what year the several houses and corporate bodies originated: together with calendars of every year from A.D. 1752 to A.D, 1925.* Montreal: J. Lovell 1893.

The provincial statutes of Lower- Canada. Québec: P.E. Desbarats 1825.

Tulchinsky, Gerald J.J. 'George Moffatt.' *DCB.*

Vogler, Richard. *Reading the Riot Act: The Magistracy, the Police, and the Army in Civil Disorder* (New Directions in Criminology Series). Buckingham: Open University Press 1991.

Wallot, Jean-Pierre. 'Une émeute à Lachine contre la "conscription" (1812).' *RHAF* 18 no. 1 (1964): 112-137; 18 no. 2 (1964): 202-232.

Way, Peter. *Common labour: workers and the digging of North American canals, 1780-1860.* Cambridge: Cambridge University Press 1993.

Recycled
Supporting responsible use
of forest resources
www.fsc.org Cert no. SGS-COC-003153
© 1996 Forest Stewardship Council

FSC

Marquis Book Printing Inc.

Québec, Canada

2009

This book has been printed on 100% post consumer
waste paper, certified Eco-logo and processed chlorine free.